NONE OF THE ABOVE

NONE OF THE ABOVE

The Untold Story of the Atlanta Public Schools Cheating Scandal, Corporate Greed, and the Criminalization of Educators

SHANI ROBINSON
and ANNA SIMONTON

Beacon Press
BOSTON

BEACON PRESS
Boston, Massachusetts
www.beacon.org

Beacon Press books
are published under the auspices of
the Unitarian Universalist Association of Congregations.

22 21 20 19   8 7 6 5 4 3 2 1

This book is printed on acid-free paper that meets the uncoated paper
ANSI/NISO specifications for permanence as revised in 1992.

Text design and composition by Kim Arney

Library of Congress Cataloging-in-Publication Data

Names: Robinson, Shani, author. | Simonton, Anna, author.
Title: None of the above : the untold story of the Atlanta public schools
cheating scandal, corporate greed, and the criminalization of educators /
Shani Robinson and Anna Simonton.
Description: Boston, Massachusetts : Beacon Press, [2018] | Includes
bibliographical references and index.
Identifiers: LCCN 2018019565 (print) | LCCN 2018036166 (ebook) |
ISBN 9780807022214 (ebook) | ISBN 9780807022207 (hardcover : alk. paper)
Subjects: LCSH: Public schools—Corrupt practices—Georgia—Atlanta. |
Cheating (Education)—Georgia—Atlanta. | African American
teachers—Georgia—Atlanta. | African American school
administrators—Georgia—Atlanta. | Robinson, Shani, 1984-
Classification: LCC LC5133.A75 (ebook) | LCC LC5133.A75 R63 2018 (print) |
DDC 370.9758231—dc23
LC record available at https://lccn.loc.gov/2018019565

This book is dedicated to
my wonderful son, Amari

। । । । । । । । । । । ।

CONTENTS

PROLOGUE

ON APRIL FOOL'S DAY IN 2015, I found myself in an unthinkable position. I was a thirty-year-old Teach for America alum, former counselor, newlywed mom-to-be. And I was a convicted felon facing twenty-five years in prison for something I didn't do.

For two years I had lived under the shadow of RICO. Otherwise known as the Racketeer Influenced and Corrupt Organizations Act, RICO was designed in the 1970s to target the American Mafia. But in 2013, RICO was applied to an unlikely group: the educators of Atlanta Public Schools. Including me.

At issue were the district's scores on a Georgia standardized test called the Criterion-Referenced Competency Test, or CRCT. In 2008, the *Atlanta Journal-Constitution* investigated suspiciously high score increases on CRCT retests in several school districts, including Atlanta. This prompted a state agency to conduct an audit of CRCT scores in 2009, analyzing the number of wrong-to-right erasures on students' test booklets and finding a high likelihood that cheating had occurred in dozens of school districts across the state.

Governor Sonny Perdue eventually ordered a special investigation to probe Atlanta and one other school district. When the dust settled, thirty-five employees of Atlanta Public Schools were indicted on RICO charges. All but one were black. Some faced prison terms of up to forty years.

I never cheated. My first graders' test scores didn't even count toward "adequate yearly progress," a set of benchmarks that the federal government required schools to meet under the No Child Left Behind

Act. Nor did the scores count toward "targets," another set of benchmarks imposed by the Atlanta Public Schools administration and board.

But Perdue's investigation was conducted like a witch hunt, or, as one attorney would later characterize it, "Shoot first and whatever you hit, call it the target." Investigators used threats to get teachers to talk and offered immunity deals to those who told the "truth." That often meant dragging educators in for multiple rounds of questioning until their stories changed to reflect what investigators believed the truth to be. This approach produced false accusations against two of my colleagues, me, and probably many more people.

The trial that followed—the longest and most expensive in Georgia history—was a tragedy for Atlanta Public Schools, which had long served a majority-black student body under majority-black leadership in a city known as the Black Mecca, a place where black folks have thrived economically, politically, and culturally in spite of bitter oppression.

It was a personal tragedy too, as I came from a family of teachers and social justice activists whose legacy I made it my life's work to build upon.

Growing up, I was always known as a "good girl." It was what my mom, Beverly Robinson, expected of me because of the way she had been raised. Her mother, Dorothy, worked as a salad maker in the cafeteria at Peabody College—which later merged with Vanderbilt University—in Nashville, Tennessee. Dorothy raised my mother and her three sisters as a single parent with the income from her cafeteria job. They lived with Dorothy's sisters and their children—ten people in a two-bedroom apartment. Dorothy did the best she could with what she had, and she filled the household with a lot of love and laughter.

As a single parent, Dorothy was wary of the societal stigma surrounding her life. "I don't want any attention called to us," she often told her children. They had to act right, plus some. But she encouraged them too. She valued education and praised them for doing well in school. My mother raised me to care about education and respect, just like Dorothy taught her.

On my dad's side, I was instilled with a social and political consciousness. My dad, Jessie Robinson, was a big proponent of learning about African and African American history. He was mentored by a renowned black scholar, writer, and activist, Yosef Ben-Jochannan, who taught and inspired some of today's foremost black intellectuals. "You have to know where you come from to know where you're going," he often told me. That's the meaning of the Ghanian word *sankofa*, which is symbolized by a bird looking backward or by a swirling heart. I have a tattoo of the sankofa heart on my right ankle.

My parents met in college and married in the 1980s. They moved to Decatur, a small city on the eastern edge of Atlanta, buying a home in an area that was predominantly black. Ours was the "neighborhood house." On any given day, seven or so kids would come over to play games with my brother, Jamal, and me. My mom would cook huge meals to feed us all. Then she would sit us down to do our homework and tutor us in reading and math.

Like many of the women in my family, my mother was a teacher. Her first teaching job in Georgia was in a town that was mostly white, Stone Mountain. The town was named for a huge mound of granite that had a sordid past. It was on top of Stone Mountain that the Ku Klux Klan was revived in 1915. Throughout the twentieth century, the Klan held rallies and cross-burnings there.

Jamal and I attended Stone Mountain Elementary, where our mother taught. Getting in trouble was not an option, and we were expected to do our best to get straight A's. When I was in sixth grade, I became the first black girl at Stone Mountain Elementary to win a Daughters of the American Revolution award.

By the time I reached junior high, more black people were moving to Stone Mountain. My parents talked about moving there to be nearer our school. Our neighborhood in Decatur was having problems with drugs and crime. Sometimes we heard gunshots nearby. One time, a pregnant neighbor escaped a burglar and fled to our house. That was the last straw for my parents—their plan to move solidified.

When I first saw it, I couldn't believe the two-story white house with antebellum columns could become ours. At our old house, my brother and I shared a bedroom, but there we would have our own rooms, plus a family room and basement to play in. Down the road was a clubhouse with a pool. The neighborhood seemed so perfect that I couldn't understand why so many houses had "for sale" signs in their yards.

"It's called white flight," my mom explained. "That's when black people move into a white neighborhood, but the white people don't want to live with the black people, so they move out as fast as they can. It's like birds that flock together. When one takes off they all follow."

We moved into our dream house, and as high school approached I enrolled in the Majority-to-Minority program, or M-to-M. In an effort to desegregate schools, the program allowed kids to transfer from a school where they were a racial majority to one where they were the minority. During my freshman year, my friends and I attended high schools that weren't zoned for our neighborhood. We all caught the same school bus at six in the morning and rode it to a central location that we called "the shuttle." When all the buses arrived, everyone switched to the bus going to their respective school. There were hundreds of black kids going to the white schools—but where were the white kids going to the black schools? I didn't see many of them.

My bus took me to Druid Hills High School in an affluent neighborhood on the northeast side of Atlanta. One of the city's first suburbs, Druid Hills was full of lush, tree-lined streets and palatial homes built in the early twentieth century. The high school, also built during that time, looked like it was plucked from the pages of a fairy tale compared to some schools in my area that were known for not having any windows.

At first I experienced culture shock. There had been few white people or non-black people of color at my old school and fewer subcultures—definitely none of the kids with purple Mohawks and goth makeup. I grew to love the diversity at Druid Hills High, so it frustrated me to see how segregation persisted. I was one of few black students in the National Honor Society, and there were hardly any of us in the Advanced Placement classes.

In 1999, during my sophomore year, a lawsuit by a conservative legal group with an anti-affirmative-action agenda forced DeKalb County schools to end the M-to-M program. Those of us already in the program were allowed to continue, so I attended Druid Hills until I graduated in 2002.

When I became embroiled in the Atlanta Public Schools cheating case, I often thought about these experiences as I tried to make sense of the situation at hand. Some of the social and political shifts that shaped my life had also set the stage for what became known as the "cheating scandal." But the dominant narrative that developed about the scandal rarely acknowledged the bigger picture: federal policies that encouraged school systems to reward and punish educators based on student test scores; a growing movement, driven by corporate interests, to privatize education by demonizing public schools; and land speculation—correlated to new charter schools springing up—that was gentrifying black and brown neighborhoods across the country.

In fact, Atlanta's school board funded gentrification on the backs of students by handing millions of education dollars to private developers to build everything from luxury condos to office towers. Meanwhile, the state cut billions of dollars from its education budget, forcing schools to furlough teachers, increase class sizes, and eliminate enrichment programs. And at the same time that Perdue was persecuting educators, he used the questionable test scores to win a big federal grant. Yet no one involved in those real estate deals or policy decisions has been accused of "cheating the children," the way that my colleagues and I were.

Also missing from the public dialogue was a sense of historical perspective. How badly were children "cheated" by their teachers, relative to decades of racist policies and practices that had torn their families and communities apart? From urban renewal, to the drug war, to the dismantling of public housing—Atlanta might be the Black Mecca, but its black working class has been under attack for years. With the cheating scandal, some of the same people responsible for these attacks hypocritically declared cheating the worst thing to befall the children of Atlanta. Judge Jerry Baxter called it "the sickest thing that's ever happened to this town," apparently forgetting about things like slavery and Jim Crow.

Perhaps most obscured is what actually went on in the courtroom. Compared to the sensationalized coverage of certain moments, like when educators were jailed, news media paid little attention to the numerous times the case was nearly dismissed, repeated calls for a mistrial, clear examples of prosecutorial misconduct, witnesses who perjured themselves, and some who recanted during testimony. The evidence against us was flimsy at best, but this case wasn't tried on evidence. It was tried on emotion.

People had strong reactions to the Atlanta Public Schools cheating scandal because it's true that there are real problems facing our public education system. Education is integral to a healthy democracy, so our concerns about education often illicit deeper anxieties about societal well-being. But the only way toward a public education that benefits all students, and society as a whole, entails addressing the root causes of the inequities and shortcomings that now exist. The Atlanta Public Schools cheating scandal was a distraction that deferred the real reckoning that we need to have. This book is my story, and it's an attempt at that reckoning so that someday justice may truly be served.

NONE OF THE ABOVE

CHAPTER ONE

Hook, Line, and Sinker

■ I I I I I I I I I I I I I I I I I I I I I I I I ■

THE SCHOOL BUS LURCHED TO A STOP AT A RED LIGHT, the morning traffic still thick even after the peak of rush hour on the west side of Atlanta. I gazed at the throng of cars on Northside Drive, where exhaust wafting through summer heat created a shimmering effect, blurring the metallic sheen of idling vehicles with the garish hues of fast-food restaurants, billboards advertising personal injury attorneys, and storefront signs exclaiming "We Finance! Build Your Credit Now!" As I mentally recited my lesson plan for the day, groggy after only five hours of sleep, I overheard snippets of the conversation two white guys were carrying on in the seat behind me.

"I feel like I'm going to be part of the achievement gap. I don't feel prepared to go in a real classroom," one of them said. The bus's noisy acceleration drowned them out for a moment, but I listened harder, feeling incredulous. They couldn't be talking about the teacher-training program of Teach for America.

"They just put sappy music over these photographs of kids, and everyone gets wrapped up in it," the same young man scoffed.

My face grew hot as I realized that he was indeed talking about Teach for America (TFA) and criticizing corps members like me who got goose bumps and sometimes even cried during the screenings of emotional videos about disadvantaged kids succeeding in school. *What*

1

a cynic, I thought, and went back to drilling myself on the lesson plan I'd finished preparing in the wee hours of the morning. I believed wholeheartedly that every child can learn if given the opportunity, and I was passionate about training to be a teacher who would bring that opportunity to a struggling school in a poor neighborhood. It was the summer of 2007. With four weeks of training down and one to go, I was soon to become an educator in the ranks of TFA.

The previous month had been a whirlwind of workshops at the Georgia Institute of Technology, where former TFA teachers instructed incoming corps members on classroom management, lesson planning, and issues like overcoming cultural bias in the classroom. Every subject was steeped in TFA's philosophy, which contends that closing the "achievement gap" between impoverished children and their affluent peers will only happen by recruiting recent college graduates to teach in low-performing schools for two years, bringing high expectations and strong leadership to the classroom. I soaked up the buzzwords and didn't have time to pause in the fast-paced, high-energy training sessions to think about what they implied: that non-TFA teachers like my mom *didn't* have high expectations for their students.

When we weren't in workshops, corps members were busing back and forth between local schools where we taught math and reading to summer school students who had failed the state-mandated Criterion-Referenced Competency Test (CRCT) and needed to make it up to advance to the next grade. Or we were gathered, more than a hundred of us altogether, for motivational programs that sometimes took on the tenor of a pep rally. In fact, it was like a pep rally had been distilled to the kids with the most school spirit. Like me, my fellow corps members were in their early twenties and had recently graduated from college. A diverse group of mostly black and white and some Asian and Latino men and women, we were clean-cut overachievers who had spent our college careers getting good grades, participating in clubs, and volunteering. Like many strivers, we partied as hard as we worked, banding together after a long day of training to hit the bars, where conversations from the day's lessons continued. With a few exceptions, like the guys on the bus, we shared an eagerness to excel and a cultish enthusiasm for TFA that our leaders encouraged.

During the motivational programs, which were replete with the videos of smiling children that the guys on the bus had found ridiculous, current and former TFA corps members would give us talks like a coach or camp counselor might, sharing stories that all had a similar narrative arc: a child was failing in school, she lived on the wrong side of town, her mom was a drug addict, then a TFA teacher stepped in, and now the child was reading ahead of her grade level. Despite the obvious conformity of these tales, there were details that grabbed me, like when one corps member shared with the group that her father had died during the school year. Rather than swallow her grief, she had told her elementary school students what she was going through. These children had seen more than their share of struggle and were eager to help her through the tragedy. The bond they formed motivated her to work as hard as she could for her students.

I knew what that was like. After graduating from Tennessee State University one year earlier, I had worked as a substitute teacher in Nashville's public schools. At first, subbing was just a way to pay the rent while I worked part-time at a local television station. During my junior year, I had set my sights on a career in journalism. After all, Oprah Winfrey went to TSU during the same time that my parents were students there. One of my mom's friends told me that she went on a double date with Oprah back in the 1970s. By the time I graduated, I had interned at two local television stations, including the one where Oprah got her start, and had the opportunity to assist reporters in the field and even produce some segments of my own.

After graduation, the last news station where I had interned hired me as an assistant producer. I helped to write news stories and teasers and ran the teleprompter during live newscasts. I enjoyed learning those skills, but I missed being out in the field. I wanted to be a reporter.

I started looking for other opportunities, and as my interest in the station noticeably waned, management cut my hours. To make up for the lost income, I applied for a substitute teaching position with Metropolitan Nashville Public Schools that I saw advertised on a jobs website. I didn't have teaching experience, but I knew how to handle kids from years of babysitting. And with advice from my mom, a long-time teacher, I figured I could make it work.

One of my first jobs was a two-week assignment taking over for a teacher who was healing from an injury inflicted by one of her first-grade students. *What am I getting myself into?* I wondered as I pulled into the parking lot of the old brick school building on my first day.

I checked in with a receptionist in the office, and then an administrative assistant with a friendly but matter-of-fact attitude guided me to a classroom on the first floor. She showed me where the teacher had left a schedule for each day with detailed instructions, information about activities, and worksheets to complete. She told me to let her know if I needed anything, and, with that, she left me on my own with a roomful of energetic six-year-olds.

The teacher's instructions included plenty of interactive lessons, like teaching math using toy blocks. I found that by being fun but firm, I could keep the students' attention focused and de-escalate the outbursts that inevitably happened. By my second week in the classroom, the children had developed respect and even affection for me. One boy playfully asked, "Ms. Robinson, will you be my mama?"

Over the following months, I subbed for many different classes and continually found that even in a short time I could connect with kids in ways that felt incredibly gratifying. When students struggled to understand a concept, then suddenly got it after I explained it a different way, we shared an epiphany. Their relief and pride at conquering even seemingly small obstacles made me feel that these victories could accumulate and eventually set a new direction for struggling students.

So when I got a phone call from Danielle, one of my oldest friends and an engineering student at Georgia Tech, I was intrigued by the teaching program she described having recently applied to.

"You never heard of Teach for America? You should check it out," she encouraged me. "It's extremely competitive. But if you get in, they train you and help you find a teaching job. Like, you could be in the classroom next semester and getting your teaching certificate at the same time."

Fast-forward a few months, and there I was at Georgia Tech, a placement I requested so I could be back in my hometown, barreling through five weeks of teacher training (sustained by copious amounts of coffee), which culminated with a lightning round of interviews for full-time teaching positions.

About a dozen principals were gathered in one of the larger classrooms at Tech. Each was at a different table, and we were to cycle through interviewing with them like it was speed dating. Just like with my teacher training—a mere twenty-five days of intensive instruction and practice—interviewing was a whirlwind. Only two conversations made an impression on me. One was with a male principal whose eyes darted over me as he read my resume.

"Shani Robinson," he said in a slow, syrupy voice. "Beautiful." He paused and grinned at me. "The resume, I mean."

I prayed that TFA wouldn't place me at his school and moved on to the next interview.

The other came toward the end of the session, when I sat down at a table with a middle-aged woman who immediately made me feel comfortable. Unlike some of the other principals, she wasn't slickly dressed, though she wasn't shabby, and her manner wasn't imposing. She was calm and inquisitive. She wanted to know about my experiences in Nashville, and we had a pleasant, relaxed conversation. Her name was Betty Greene, and she was the principal at Dunbar Elementary in Atlanta's Mechanicsville neighborhood. I knew right away that I wanted to work there.

On the last day of the TFA summer program, all the corps members attended a huge assembly featuring guest speakers who had come up through TFA and were now in high places, running charter schools, holding elected office, and helming corporations. With lapel mics clipped to their sharp outfits, they stood in a wash of bright stage lights, under a huge screen that offered photos of me and my fellow corps members with our summer school students, smiling as they filled in bubbles on answer sheets. Now we were the characters in the narrative arc of the TFA success story.

The speakers told us about the achievement gap (our number-one enemy by that point), and we heard that if we had the right mind-set (one that accepts nothing less than success) and worked hard (never stopping until reaching one's goals), our impoverished students would make astronomical progress. They would soar beyond anybody's expectations simply because they would now have teachers who believed in them. The achievement gap would narrow, and we would be one step closer to racial justice, just like Martin Luther King Jr. envisioned, right here in Atlanta, home of the civil rights movement. Cue the thunderous applause.

I clapped right along with everyone else. I had found my path, and it was a righteous one. I still had no idea how problematic TFA really was.

IIIIIIIIIIIII

In 1988, a Princeton University senior named Wendy Kopp admittedly did not know what to do with her life. As an Ivy League student, she had inroads with financial firms and big corporations that recruited from her school, so she half-heartedly applied for jobs at Morgan Stanley and a few other companies. None offered her a position.

Kopp, though, had become interested in education by observing the disparity between her Princeton classmates who came from under-resourced public schools and struggled to keep up and students like herself who had attended wealthy public or elite private high schools and were better prepared. This didn't seem fair to Kopp, so at the same time she was seeking corporate positions she was also thinking about teaching. She wanted to address educational inequities.

It was too late for her to enter Princeton's teacher licensure program, a fact that she found frustrating. Kopp seemed to think that graduating from Princeton should be qualification enough to teach children in public schools. She had learned from a speaker at a conference that many urban and rural schools were facing teacher shortages. This gave her an idea. What if there were a teacher corps, modeled on the Peace Corps, that recruited altruistic graduates from high-ranking universities to teach in impoverished schools and streamlined the process of teacher training and job placement? Teach for America was conceived.

From its inception, TFA had a remarkable trajectory. Kopp secured a $26,000 grant from Mobil and free office space from the chemical company Union Carbide before she graduated in the spring of 1989. Within a year, she had raised enough money to hire staff and recruit nearly five hundred corps members to teach in six regions. Like the initial seed grant, much of that funding came from big corporations, and corporate executives filled TFA's board. During its first decade, TFA was widely hailed as a success.

But there were early detractors. In her book *One Day, All Children . . .*, Kopp acknowledges that some school district superintendents and philanthropists she approached were offended by the thought of "do-gooders" with no teaching experience parachuting into a classroom for two years to "find themselves" and then leave. Though Kopp said she hoped the program would produce some career teachers, TFA was designed as a pathway to higher-paying professions and positions in which its alumni would influence politics and society. Kopp believed that if judges, elected officials, and corporate leaders had the experience of teaching disadvantaged students, they would be more likely to make decisions that positively impacted educational opportunities for such children. But that meant that TFA, for all its talk of helping poor kids, was designed with the needs of privileged college graduates in mind. "The teacher corps would make teaching in low-income communities an attractive choice for top grads by surrounding it with an aura of status and selectivity," Kopp wrote.[1]

That aura was also attractive to influential people who already held power. Kopp's approach to catalyzing change in the education system aligned with ideas that had grown increasingly popular among policymakers and corporate leaders in the years leading up to TFA's founding. There had been a fundamental shift in the public discourse around education beginning in 1966 when a massive government study—called the Coleman Report, after the sociologist commissioned by the Lyndon Johnson administration to produce it—concluded that adding resources to a school, without making structural changes to address systemic inequities, did not by itself produce greater academic achievement. Decontextualized from the rest of the report's extensive findings, this conclusion fueled outcries from conservatives who opposed what they viewed as excessive government spending on public schools.[2] The year prior, President Johnson had signed the Elementary and Secondary Education Act of 1965, which dramatically increased federal funding for public schools as part of his War on Poverty initiative. But the deeper issue for many conservatives was school desegregation, which had seen varying levels of tumultuous enforcement across the nation since the 1954 *Brown v. Board of Education* Supreme Court ruling found public school segregation to be unconstitutional. Many of the people who were up in arms over increased education funding were rancorous not because they were opposed to federal funding for schools but because that funding was going toward busing and other measures to improve education for students of color.

Nothing illustrated this better than widespread conservative support for vouchers. In 1955, free-market economist Milton Friedman first proposed vouchers as a means of subsidizing education while enabling parents to choose where their children attended school.[3] Implicit in his proposal was the possibility of white parents using public funds to pull their children from desegregated public schools and enroll them in whites-only private schools. From that point on, "choice" was invoked to thinly shroud racist backlash to school desegregation while advocating for a free-enterprise approach to education, in which privately managed but publicly funded schools competed for students and parents, with limited government intervention.

The Coleman Report gave critics of public education fodder to challenge the prevailing idea that more funding and better resources begat better schools. They flipped the script on what constituted educational success, arguing that measuring "outcomes" (student performance) rather than "inputs" (funding and resources) was key to determining whether the education system was doing what it should. Thus, they laid the groundwork for a turn toward standardized testing as a means to assess school quality and hold teachers and administrators "accountable."

These two concepts—choice and accountability—remained a part of the national discourse around education as major political changes were taking place. The 1970s ushered in a backlash to the social movements that had challenged unjust power structures and social norms over the previous decade. Powerful people from both liberal and conservative camps grappled with how to tamp down the democratizing force of social movements. From the conservative side came the Powell Memo, a document produced in 1971 for the US Chamber of Commerce by Lewis F. Powell Jr., a corporate lawyer and later a Supreme Court justice. Powell laid out a blueprint for how corporations could exert political control by wielding influence over the media, the courts, elected officials, and education. This sparked the founding of conservative think tanks like the Heritage Foundation and the American

Legislative Exchange Council, as well as corporate coalitions like the Business Roundtable, that would eventually stage a strong intervention in education.

Liberals also felt that they were losing control as disenfranchised and exploited members of society gained power. In 1975, the Trilateral Commission, a group founded by business tycoon David Rockefeller and chaired by Zbigniew Brzezinski, who would go on to serve as Jimmy Carter's national security advisor, published a report warning that an "excess of democracy" posed a threat to their idea of economic order. According to the report, this excess of democracy resulted in part from the failure of schools and other institutions to fulfill their role in the "indoctrination of the young."[4]

The formation of the Trilateral Commission marked a turn toward "neoliberalism," an approach to governance, shared by conservatives and liberals, characterized by deregulation in favor of corporate interests coupled with cuts to social spending that hurt the middle and lower classes.[5] This model of replacing social welfare with corporate welfare accelerated under the administration of President Ronald Reagan in the 1980s, and that's when the push for private-sector involvement in education policymaking, with a focus on "choice" and "accountability," intensified. There was yet another government-commissioned report, and this one produced shockwaves across the country.

A Nation at Risk: The Imperative for Educational Reform, published in 1983 by Reagan's National Commission on Excellence in Education, was a short, alarmist tract that declared public education to be in such a deep state of crisis that the ability of the United States to compete in the global economy was imperiled.[6] The report had a profound impact on commonly held ideas about education. It emphasized education's economic purpose over all others and placed the onus for fixing education directly on schools rather than the whole of society.[7]

Critics took issue not only with the crisis-oriented narrative that *A Nation at Risk* constructed but also with the evidence the authors used to back it up. The report cited the low performance of US schools in international comparisons, as well as a decline in SAT scores. But some analysts countered that the report didn't account for important variables, like the fact that other countries were more selective about which

students took standardized tests, that higher numbers of poor and minority students in the United States had begun taking the SAT in recent years, and that SAT scores had actually increased over the previous
three years. Such details were no match for the overpowering message
of *A Nation at Risk*—that the downturn in scores signaled a crisis of epic
proportions. Task forces formed in all fifty states to develop plans of
action in response to the report. Corporations followed suit, with the
Business Roundtable launching a committee on education in 1987.[8]

The Business Roundtable had formed fifteen years earlier in response to the Powell Memo, bringing together the heads of about seventy of the largest US corporations. The group spent its first decade
working to bust labor unions, lower the corporate income tax, cut social security pensions, and weaken environmental regulations.[9] Members of the Business Roundtable clearly heard a clarion call in *A Nation
at Risk*, publishing in 1990 their own 117-page education primer that
began with the none-too-original sentence, "We are a nation at risk."[10]
Rather than considering how their own corporate practices may have
negatively impacted public education by diverting wealth away from
poor and middle-class families while weakening the social safety net,
the Business Roundtable laid out a platform that fused the burgeoning
ideas about choice and accountability into a corporate model of education reform.

Schools, the group argued, should be run like businesses in order
to expand the nation's "market share" of well-educated students.[11] To
Business Roundtable members, this meant implementing rigorous testing and systems of reward and punishment to hold educators accountable for the performance of their students. It also meant enabling school
choice, possibly with vouchers, in order to "subject schools to the disci-
plines of the marketplace."[12] And they asserted that teaching should not
be limited to traditionally trained educators, whom the group characterized as reluctant to innovate (though the relative strength of teachers'
unions surely informed their opinion as well). Rather, there should be
opportunities for people from other professions to become educators.[13]

This was the climate that Wendy Kopp stepped into, espousing the
idea that without any extra government "inputs," inexperienced young
people who were in the pipeline from the Ivy League to the echelons of

the business elite could be temporarily rerouted into schools where, by sheer force of leadership and management acumen, they would ramp up production of high-achieving students.

It's little wonder then that Robert D. Kennedy, CEO of Union Carbide and a member of the Business Roundtable, was an early proponent of TFA and connected Kopp to a slew of corporate heads who would fork over sizeable grants. Kopp quickly raised $2.5 million, from the foundations of petroleum, pharmaceutical, and auto companies, among others. Her staff recruited corps members throughout the spring of 1990, and when fall rolled around, the first cohort of Teach for America teachers was stationed in schools in New York, New Orleans, Baton Rouge, Los Angeles, and rural districts in North Carolina and Georgia.[14]

In Georgia, the burgeoning corporate education reform movement manifested in an organization that formed in 1991, the Georgia Public Policy Foundation. It was part of the State Policy Network, which the American Legislative Exchange Council (ALEC) launched to link state-level and national conservative think tanks and legal groups. Like the Business Roundtable, ALEC had formed in response to the Powell Memo, and since then it had become singularly effective at translating corporate interests into public policy. In 1991, ALEC's membership included nearly a third of the nation's state legislators, who convened at the group's annual meetings with corporate sponsors. Corporate members were enticed to join by ALEC's promise that "winning the public policy debate will continue to have a tremendous positive effect on the 'bottom line' of your company."[15] At ALEC meetings, corporate executives could present lawmakers with legislation they crafted, and there was a good chance it would become law.

With the State Policy Network, ALEC could advance its agenda through local groups that gave the impression that ALEC legislation had grassroots support. These groups would lobby for ALEC bills and shape public opinion by publishing reports and op-eds, hosting speakers, and waging campaigns. The Georgia Public Policy Foundation quickly took up education reform, launching a pilot voucher program that proved to be a blunder and lasted less than a year.[16]

But the Georgia Public Policy Foundation barreled ahead, led by Matthew Glavin, a spotlight-loving gadfly who also headed the Southeastern

Legal Foundation, an organization that billed itself as the "'conservative alternative' to the American Civil Liberties Union."[17] It was the Southeastern Legal Foundation that brought about the demise of the busing program that had enabled me to attend Druid Hills High School. The group attacked other affirmative action programs in the state too, and it even had a moment on the national stage when Glavin attempted to have President Bill Clinton disbarred. Though he fancied himself a rising star in the conservative milieu, he would suddenly disappear in 2000 after being arrested for masturbating in a public park.

The corporate education reform movement in Georgia got off to a rocky start, but it would soon hit its stride.

|||||||||||||

Beverly Hall was pleased with her four TFA teachers. In December 1990, at the tail of TFA's inaugural semester, the Brooklyn middle school principal told a *New York Times* reporter that one TFA recruit had taught the best math lesson she'd ever seen, and another had "a great presence" in the classroom.[18] And she should know. After teaching for six years beginning in 1970, Hall had been steadily rising through the administrative ranks of New York City's public schools for more than a decade.

Her approach to school management conformed to, and sometimes preceded, the trends of the time. She was an early advocate of private-public partnerships; in the wake of *A Nation at Risk*, she wooed Chemical Bank to "adopt" her elementary school by supplying it with mini-grants. The school made good use of the resources and saw improvements. If the grants had come from the government they would have been ignored as more "inputs" being thrown into the void of the supposedly disastrous public school system. But coming from a private company, the grants were hailed as innovative, and Hall began to build a reputation as a change-maker.[19]

From the Brooklyn middle school, Hall moved on to become superintendent of a Queens school board in 1992 and from there was tapped to be deputy chancellor of New York City public schools. In the summer of 1995, a legal ruling enabled New Jersey to take over Newark's public schools, and the state government asked Hall to turn the troubled district around. That's when she really began to flex her muscle as a reformer.[20]

In one fell swoop, Hall laid off five hundred employees—an act that some Newark residents called the "Beverly Hall massacre."[21] She replaced half of the district's principals and tied their raises to student test scores. She privatized part of the food service system. The reforms sparked outrage, evident in protests that sometimes drew hundreds of school district employees, parents, and their supporters.

But Hall's proponents applauded her success reigning in the budget and overhauling facilities badly in need of repair. The state extended her initial six-month contract for another three years. At the end of her tenure, she still hadn't won broad public support. The mayor at the time told a reporter that Hall might have slapped paint on some buildings, but Newark's test scores hadn't improved. Hall's response was unwavering: "If I could walk on water they'd say, 'Look, she can't swim.'"[22]

In the fall of 1998, Hall was approached by a recruitment firm seeking a new superintendent for Atlanta Public Schools (APS). The job description promised an opportunity for Hall to continue her hard-line managerial approach, this time with a community that seemed to want it. The job description didn't call for a superintendent but a "Chief Executive Officer" whose "customers" were the parents and children of APS.[23]

The recruitment firm reported back to a search committee made up of APS officials and several prominent business executives. The Metro Atlanta Chamber of Commerce, known simply as the chamber, had proclaimed a stake in school board matters, and it was not for the first time. Decades earlier, when a court order forced the desegregation of Atlanta Public Schools, the chamber had worked closely with elected officials to orchestrate a massive public relations campaign to ensure that there were no news reports of white mobs descending upon black students like in other Southern cities. It's not that members of the chamber weren't segregationists—many were. But they were also terrified that widely broadcast images of violence would damage the local economy. One summed up the chamber's position by saying that members weren't "do-gooders" but rather "hard-headed businessmen who realized you can't sell peanuts at a funeral."[24]

This time around, the chamber was afraid that low-performing schools were holding back the city's economic growth. Good schools, they reasoned, attracted wealthier residents and companies looking for a place to headquarter, both of which would grease the city's economic gears. There was also a racial element that went unspoken. Atlanta had long been home to a flourishing black middle and upper class; attracting them was not a problem. The wealthy people whom the chamber wanted to entice were the white suburbanites who'd remained outside the city long after school desegregation prompted an exodus of white families. That said, some of the city's black corporate executives were leading the charge on school-focused economic development, such as James Bostic, an executive at Georgia Pacific. He chaired the chamber's education committee and was a cheerleader for Hall, singing her praises in news reports.[25]

For nearly everyone invested in bringing big changes to Atlanta Public Schools, the expectations were clear: good test scores make good schools. The new superintendent's foremost goal should be to improve the district's test scores. From the moment Hall was selected to lead APS in the spring of 1999, she was under a microscope. "Everyone is watching her," wrote the *Atlanta Journal-Constitution*. "From Gov. Roy Barnes—who is hammering out his statewide school reform effort—to corporate leaders, college presidents, and parents considering whether to entrust their children to the urban public schools."[26]

Hall made it clear that she wasn't a miracle worker, and she cautioned the public not to expect overnight results. Still, the school board agreed to pay Hall a $49,500 bonus on top of her $165,000 annual salary if she met certain performance goals (commonly referred to as "targets") in her first year, which included raising test scores, improving attendance, and increasing the number of students in advanced classes. Bonus money was also allocated to school employees who met specific targets, which were determined by education consultants working for the APS Research, Planning, and Accountability Office and approved by the school board annually. Those employees in turn created a rewards system for students; one school treated children with perfect attendance to lunch at a restaurant, which they traveled to in limousines. From the outset, the fervor for metrics translated to activities that didn't bear much relationship to any pedagogy.

When the end of the year came, Hall had met only twelve of the twenty-six target and hadn't met any that concerned test scores. The school board president said he was disappointed the scores didn't "skyrocket."[27] Nonetheless, Hall remained in the good graces of her supporters. She was proving instrumental in ushering along projects that were popular among corporate education reformers.

Shortly before Hall began her tenure, the school board had approved the first charter school in the district. The charter was granted to a subsidiary of the East Lake Foundation, a nonprofit organization created by real estate mogul Tom Cousins to redevelop East Lake Meadows, a public housing project, into a mixed-income apartment complex that was half market rate and half subsidized. The redevelopment created a net loss of more than three hundred subsidized units, pushing out poor people and actively seeking to attract middle-class residents. Like the Metro Atlanta Chamber of Commerce, the East Lake Foundation saw the local school as a key ingredient for bringing in well-to-do families.[28]

With the charter school approved, the foundation made plans to hire a for-profit company, Edison Schools (which has since changed its name to Edison Learning), to operate it. The company, whose vice president was a former TFA teacher and the husband of TFA founder Wendy Kopp, had launched in 1995 and was operating more than one hundred schools by the year 2000. In that short time, Edison had come under fire for allegedly using harsh disciplinary tactics as a cure-all for the challenges facing impoverished students, excluding special needs students in order to raise schools' test scores, overworking and underpaying teachers, and encouraging cheating on standardized tests.[29]

Numerous groups in Atlanta, including the Concerned Black Clergy and the NAACP, vocally opposed the Edison contract. But when the school board approved the charter, it gave up control over such decisions. Now that decision rested with a private foundation that did not have to answer to the community. Edison secured a five-year contract with the East Lake Foundation and reported to its shareholders that it expected revenues over that time to exceed $17 million.[30]

With Drew and Edison, Atlanta entered a realm of the corporate education reform movement that had been growing elsewhere in leaps and bounds for a decade. Charter schools were originally conceived in the late 1980s by Albert Shanker, president of the American Federation of Teachers, as a model for giving teachers more creative control in the classroom. But following the establishment of the first charter school, in St. Paul, Minnesota, in 1992, that vision was quickly co-opted by corporate education reformers who saw in charter schools the potential for privatization and began throwing their weight into getting more states to pass laws allowing charters.

Charter schools did not have to abide by the same regulations as traditional schools so long as they met the goals set forth in their contracts with local school boards or state education departments. This enabled charter school administrators to spend their budgets with far less oversight than traditional schools. Education management organizations (EMOs) like Edison Schools sprang up to vie for contracts, and many charter schools readily outsourced everything from food preparation to classroom instruction to these profit-driven companies. Many of them racked up allegations of mismanagement, cutting corners, and plain wrongdoing nearly as fast as they raked in the money. By the 1999–2000 school year, there were 1,692 charter schools in thirty states, Washington, DC, and Puerto Rico, and 10 percent of them were operated by EMOs.[31]

The wheels of corporate education reform were already in motion in Atlanta when Hall was tapped for superintendent. With her arrival in 1999, Atlanta's power players got what they wanted: someone who would drive that train full steam ahead.

    I I I I I I I I I I I I I

"There are ways to fight terror other than wearing a uniform. A teacher fights terror every day by walking into a classroom and teaching children how to read and write and add and subtract."[32] President George W. Bush stood under a giant Teach for America banner as he addressed a crowded auditorium at Booker T. Washington High School, two miles west of downtown Atlanta, on an unseasonably warm winter afternoon.

It wasn't clear whether the president was implying that the majority-black students of Washington High were potential terrorists, but if members of the audience took issue with his metaphor, they kept it to themselves.

It was January 31, 2002, and Bush was on a roll. Two days prior, he had delivered the first State of the Union Address since the terrorist attacks of September 11, 2001, and he was riding high on an approval rating of around 80 percent. Now he was on a speaking tour, drumming up support for his newly conceived volunteer program, USA Freedom Corps, along with his budget proposal for a $38 billion homeland security initiative. For this audience of high school students, state legislators, and education policymakers, the president had one recent accomplishment in particular to talk up: earlier in the month he had signed a historic education bill, No Child Left Behind (NCLB).

Joining Bush on stage was Wendy Kopp, who had been chummy with the president since a private breakfast he held with select TFA people during his 2000 presidential campaign. Teach for America had launched in Atlanta shortly after Hall took the reins at APS; fifty-seven TFA teachers were placed in Atlanta schools during her second year on the job.[33]

Next to Kopp was Rod Paige, Bush's education secretary, whose reform efforts in his previous position as superintendent of the Houston Independent School District, coupled with statewide education reforms in Texas, served as the model for NCLB.

In 1990, the Texas Education Agency began rating schools and school districts based, in part, on standardized test scores. Schools that scored well received cash awards, and those that didn't were subject to serious sanctions, including closure.[34]

Paige took leadership over Houston's schools in 1994 and raised the stakes. The school board had agreed to pay him a $25,000 cash bonus if enough schools scored high. Paige plied principals with school-specific goals for increasing test scores and reducing dropout rates, handing out bonuses to those who met the targets. Principals replicated the tactic, rewarding—with money, candy, and flowers—teachers whose students performed well. The trickle-down even reached the kids, who were incentivized with movie tickets and trips to the AstroWorld theme park.

By 1998, Houston's test scores had taken a sharp upturn, and dropout rates had plummeted. Across the state, other districts experienced similar gains. Governor George W. Bush proclaimed it a "Texas Miracle," and many members of the press ate it up—hook, line, and sinker. But some journalists in Houston reported evidence of widespread cheating by district employees. Education researchers and scholars also called the Texas Miracle into question, pointing out that the students making vast improvements on the Texas tests weren't seeing the same gains on national standardized tests.[35]

Tying incentives to test scores wasn't only going on in Texas. In 1994, Congress had reauthorized the 1965 Elementary and Secondary Education Act (which it must do every five years), adding provisions that required states to establish curriculum standards and assessments to ensure that schools made "adequate yearly progress" toward improving student performance. The law was vague about what constituted adequate yearly progress, and it didn't include any way to enforce the new rules, so the impact varied from state to state.[36] Numerous states went down the same road as Texas, establishing high-stakes testing. Several of those states, including Kentucky and North Carolina, were similarly receiving both fawning praise for heightened test scores and serious skepticism over their validity.[37]

Georgia was also among the early adopters of high-stakes testing. In 1992, long before Beverly Hall arrived, the Georgia legislature introduced a "pay for performance" program that awarded bonuses to schools that improved their scores on the Iowa Test of Basic Skills (ITBS), a standardized test used nationwide. The bonuses amounted to $2,000 per faculty member, and over several years, the program doled out millions of dollars to schools that scored well. As schools vied for cash, numerous allegations of cheating surfaced. Between 1996 and 1999, twenty-five cases of cheating were reported in school districts across the state. Jean Dodd, a member of the Atlanta school board, publicly expressed her skepticism of one school's precipitous score jumps shortly before Hall arrived in 1999. "We know it is totally impossible for scores to go up like that," Dodd said. "Somebody possibly changed a few scores. When I say changed a few scores, I say they cheated."

In 2001, an *Atlanta Journal-Constitution* reporter dug into suspiciously high scores in Atlanta schools, but it didn't spark much of an outcry.[38]

Bush disregarded the holes that were getting punched in the myth of the Texas Miracle and confidently touted it on the presidential campaign trail. One of his first priorities as president, he said, would be to enact on a national level the same reforms Texas had undertaken. After Bush narrowly won the election—its validity too was hotly contested before being decided by the US Supreme Court—he quickly assembled a team to craft a legislative blueprint for education reform, which he released three days after his inauguration. A bipartisan conference committee then worked for nearly a year to hammer out the bill and succeeded in getting it passed through the House and Senate in December 2001.

The bill, dubbed No Child Left Behind, was the latest reauthorization of the 1965 Elementary and Secondary Education Act. Over one thousand pages long, NCLB was extremely complex, but its focal point was clear: every school had to test its way to "accountability." The road map it set forth was a mash-up of nearly every corporate education reform measure that had been gestating, and in some places birthed, over the past three decades. The notable exception was that it didn't legalize vouchers, to the chagrin of many Republicans.

The law set what some education experts said was an unlikely goal: 100 percent of public school students needed to be "proficient" in reading and math by the 2013–14 school year. To get there, states had to create standardized tests to annually assess students in grades three through eight, and once in high school. States were also required to develop criteria for adequate yearly progress (or, as most educators called it, AYP) and submit them to the federal government for approval. At that point, schools had to meet their AYP benchmarks or face consequences that increased in severity each year that they fell behind, from an initial warning to "choice" measures enabling students to transfer schools and state intervention in school operations. By year five of failing to exhibit AYP, schools could be forcibly converted to charters or taken over by the state.[39] The stakes had never been higher.

For all the detail concerning testing and accountability, NCLB offered no guidelines for how to actually make learning happen. Diane

Ravitch, who served as the assistant education secretary under George H. W. Bush, later summed up the law as "a measurement strategy with no underlying educational vision at all," a measure that "had everything to do with structural changes and accountability and nothing at all to do with the substance of learning."[40] Codifying such a strict system of rewards and punishments, she warned, created "fear and obedience among educators."

That was evidently the case when, barely a year after NCLB was enshrined into law, damning reports finally sounded the death knell for the Texas Miracle. A Houston assistant principal exposed to reporters how schools had artificially inflated test scores by preventing low-scoring students from testing. In some cases, they held students back in ninth grade and then passed them on to the eleventh, effectively keeping them out of tenth grade—the year that students had to take the state standardized test. The "miraculous" decline in dropout rates was manufactured too. School officials underreported dropouts by saying they had transferred or left school for other acceptable reasons.[41]

The disintegration of the Texas Miracle unfortunately didn't lead to a rollback of NCLB, though Rod Paige did resign as education secretary in 2004. Instead, as 2014—the year all students had to be proficient—drew near, allegations of cheating to boost test scores grew rampant in districts across the country. These were met with inaction, internal investigations that led to some educators being fired, or, in a few cases, law enforcement investigations that resulted in fines and other low-level consequences.

As teachers and administrators in Atlanta found themselves between the same rock and the same hard place as so many others across the country, there was no reason to think that following the trend would lead to the longest, most expensive, most sensationalized investigation and trial to ever take place in the state of Georgia.

I I I I I I I I I I I I I

"RRRRAAAAAAAWWWWW!"

"See you tomorrow, Darnell. Have a good evening, Ms. Ford."

I waved as Darnell, pretending to be a dragon, was tugged down the hall by his mom, who turned her head and flashed me a tired smile in response. With my last first-grader headed home for the day, I shuffled back into my classroom at Dunbar Elementary, fairly exhausted myself. I opened my laptop to dive into lesson planning for the next day and groaned. Another Teach for America blast in my inbox.

I clicked open the email and scanned the announcements before landing on the "Atlanta Corps Member Highlight." As usual, there was a photo of one of my fellow corps members in her classroom, surrounded by grinning kids, followed by a list-style profile. Number one, her name. Number two, the year she joined TFA. Number three, the school where she was placed. I scrolled down to number six: biggest success this year. As usual, there were a couple of glowing sentences about how great her students were doing.

Was I the only one who was struggling?

I never could have anticipated the challenges of my first year as a full-time teacher. Looking back, my days as a substitute had been such a breeze because I didn't have to create lesson plans on tight deadlines, maintain meticulous portfolios for each student, or contact parents every week to update them on their child's progress. Not to mention the veritable flood of paperwork from the district that seemed to never end. All of which I juggled on top of actually teaching seventeen rambunctious six-year-olds for seven hours every day.

TFA's summer training hadn't come anywhere close to approximating what I was dealing with. I had taught a small group of fifth graders one lesson a day, accompanied by three other TFA corps members and an experienced teacher.

Some of my first-graders had serious behavior problems. Fistfights broke out during reading lessons. A few students hurled curse words as deftly as any foul-mouthed adult. Others would just clam up and refuse to follow any direction I gave them, no matter how many different approaches I tried. Every now and then, just when I thought I had everybody calmed down and on task, a squirrel would stick its fat head out of a hole in the ceiling, and the kids would lose it all over again.

I tried implementing classroom management strategies my mom suggested. One of her activities was a huge success. When I told her how the kids were often mean to each other, she told me to tape a piece of paper to each of their backs. Then they had to go to each classmate and write nice words about them on their paper. When everyone was done, they could take their papers off and read aloud the nice things people wrote about them. Everyone seemed deeply proud of the compliments they received, and it hit me just how much they suffered from low self-esteem. The rest of that day went more smoothly than usual.

I also had support and advice from my TFA advisor, who conducted classroom observations and held biweekly work sessions for all the TFA first-grade teachers. We would get together and make posters for our classrooms or write up behavior plans and get feedback. But when we talked about how things were going, my fellow corps members mostly shared positive stories. Our training had taught us that if we cared enough and worked hard enough, our students would excel. When that didn't happen, we figured it must be our fault. No one wanted to shed the ecstatic optimism TFA had instilled in us or let on that we had doubts. I grew increasingly uncomfortable in those biweekly meetings as I struggled to keep up a veneer of positivity.

My favorite colleagues at Dunbar were another story. I struck up friendships with other teachers my age, and we would go out for drinks after work and commiserate. A couple of the veteran teachers had taken to affectionately calling me "the young girl," and they were always ready to vent, share a joke, and get back to work. They were my real support.

Diane Buckner-Webb was the other first-grade teacher, and we worked closely together. She had an artistic streak and was always dreaming up craft projects that made our drab classroom walls come to life. She had a tough exterior and could be reserved, unless she was around Pamela Cleveland, a third-grade teacher who was warm and chatty and could get a laugh out of anybody. Cleveland, who had taught at Dunbar since the mid-1980s, liked to look out for me, and she was the one who reassured me during a tense staff meeting about preparing for standardized testing at the end of the year.

"Don't worry," she said, leaning over to me during a break in the conversation. "First- and second-grade scores don't count toward AYP or the district targets. They're just for practice." I was beyond relieved.

It was never clear to me when I was a teacher what the specific targets for Dunbar were. Later I would learn that the year before I started teaching, 29 percent of fifth graders at Dunbar (about 8.7 students in a class of 30) had exceeded expectations on the reading portion of the CRCT. Based on that, the target the next year was for 31 percent of fifth graders to exceed expectations in reading. To meet the target, 9.3 fifth grade students in a class of 30 would have to exceed expectations. It was the difference of about one student, which didn't seem so tough, except that the teachers would have an entirely different batch of students who were being compared to those from the previous year. If the new students weren't as advanced, meeting the target could be difficult.

As I sat at my desk, feeling deflated by the cheery email from TFA, I reminded myself that things could be even harder. I gathered my resolve and opened a new lesson plan template. My cell phone began to buzz, and I saw a parent's name flash on the screen. I had given all the parents my personal phone number at the beginning of the year.

Sheila Houston was an active mom, even though I could tell she was sometimes under duress. She and her husband were separated, and she worked long hours for a trucking company while raising Tiffany, who was in my class, and her three-year-old brother. I loved teaching Tiffany. She was a shy, quiet child, but when I could get her to come out of her shell she shined. For a science lesson about shadows, I had the class make popsicle-stick shadow puppets for a production of *The Three Little Pigs*. Tiffany hung back initially, but I encouraged her, and she finally went all in, giving a lively performance with her popsicle-stick pig.

My lesson plan could wait another ten minutes while I talked with Sheila.

"Hey, Ms. Houston," I said.

"Ms. Robinson," she said, her voice strained. "I need to ask you a favor."

CHAPTER TWO

Finding My Way

■ | | | | | | | | | | | | | | | | | | | | | | | | |

MY FOOTSTEPS ECHOED as I climbed the wrought iron staircase up to a second-story landing and the front door of Sheila Houston's apartment. She lived in a squat, brick building a ten-minute walk from Dunbar Elementary through the Mechanicsville neighborhood. I waved to an elderly woman, who was slowly making her way out of the apartment next door, bundled in a heavy coat against the February chill. A preteen boy dribbling a basketball around the parking lot was the only other sign of life, but I knew that in the warmer months this complex, like others in the neighborhood, would be a hive of activity, with residents posted up in plastic chairs on the small stoops and landings, little charcoal kettle grills puffing fragrant smoke at their feet, and kids running all over the place.

I knocked on the iron burglar door of Sheila's apartment and waited, not sure what to expect. On the phone, she had beaten around the bush, reluctant to let me know that she needed help with money. Not a lot, she assured me, maybe just ten or twenty dollars. She was calling all her family and friends so she wouldn't overburden one person. If enough people could spare a little bit, she could piece together the two hundred dollars she needed to fix her "situation," something to do with a bad landlord, a hasty move, and furniture in storage.

"Ms. Robinson, you didn't have to come up here," Sheila said in greeting as she swung the door open.

"It's no problem at all! How're you doing?" I stepped into the apartment and glanced around, slowly registering what was going on as Tiffany bounded up to hug me. Her little brother toddled behind, dragging a loud corn-popper push toy behind him. Aside from a couple of other toys strewn around the room and a large garbage bag stuffed with clothes, the apartment was completely bare. It wasn't the emptiness of a new home still being moved into. There were no moving boxes, no flat packs of ready-to-assemble furniture, no paint cans or tools. Just emptiness.

I followed Sheila toward the kitchen as she offered me a bottle of water. Passing the single bedroom, I could see a pallet of pillows and blankets on the floor. There were no beds.

"It's been over a month," she said, handing me the water. "We had to move out of our last place when the lease was up or else sign on for another year. Well, I just couldn't do it anymore—we had a dope dealer next door, people coming and going all hours of the day and night, trash everywhere, electrical outlets looking like a fire hazard. I mean it was bad."

She went on, explaining that her work schedule made it difficult to apartment-hunt, so when the lease ended, and she still hadn't found a new place, she had put most of their belongings in storage and stayed with a cousin. Her landlord never returned her deposit, so when she finally found an apartment she skipped her storage payment to afford the move-in costs. Late fees piled up, and now she would have to fork over more than two hundred dollars, or the storage company would auction her things.

As Sheila's frustrations spilled out, mine grew. We shouldn't even be having this conversation, I thought. We should be talking about regular parent-teacher things, like the upcoming Black History Month program or how Tiffany had stayed impressively focused during the reading portion of the CRCT practice test last week. Tiffany struggled with reading more than any other subject, and Sheila monitored her progress and setbacks closely. She was a very spiritual person and often told me that, in addition to working with Tiffany on her reading assignments, she was praying to God to help her daughter.

Instead of discussing school matters, we were caught trying to solve a problem that shouldn't exist. No one, I thought, should lack a bed to sleep on and a table to eat at. No wonder Tiffany had seemed so tired all the time. She probably wasn't getting good rest at night. I could give Sheila the twenty dollars she asked me for, but she would still have to find more people to do the same. How much more time and energy would this take? No, I decided, we are going to take care of this here and now.

"Ms. Houston, I'm going to pay the storage bill," I said. Before she could protest, I told her, "Let me do this. It won't be any trouble for me at all, and I know you won't take it for granted. We just need to get this thing out of the way, okay? And then you'll be back on track. It's no problem."

Her eyes welled with tears as she thanked me.

It was hardly the first time I had helped my students and their families outside of the classroom. And I wasn't alone. It was pretty much a given at Dunbar and plenty of other schools in the district that teachers stepped up to fill in the gaps where the economy and social services fell short in meeting families' needs. Dunbar was just south of downtown Atlanta, wedged into the southwest corner of the two interstates that divided the city into quadrants. The school was within a few blocks of the giant concrete barrier walls of the interstates, an industrial shipping center, a junkyard, and a shabby commercial strip featuring a coin laundry and the only place to buy groceries in the area, a mini-mart that sold packaged goods.

There were few houses in the neighborhood; most people lived in apartment complexes that ranged from decent to decrepit, punctuated by vacant lots with patchy brown grass and piles of trash. Adjacent to Dunbar was a vast expanse of land where McDaniel-Glenn, a public housing project built in the late 1960s, had stood. It was demolished in 2006, the year before I started teaching at Dunbar and would be replaced with a shiny new complex that stood out from its surroundings like a sore thumb a few years later. Mechanicsville was among several neglected neighborhoods that were becoming targets for redevelopment.

Dunbar opened in 1969 and had seen few updates since then. It was a squat, two-story brick building surrounded by a chain-link fence. About 99 percent of the students qualified for free or reduced lunch.[1]

My students, who were all black, clearly came from struggling families; there was only one child who I knew was middle class based on my conversations with her parents. She was such a rarity that I remember her distinctly. The other students came to school with so many problems stemming from poverty that I soon was acting not only as a teacher but as a social worker too.

One Monday morning, a student of mine showed up to school with a bloody nose and told me he'd gotten into a fight with his brother over the last Pop-Tart, claiming it was the only food they had in the house. After that, I bought snacks to send home with some of my kids on Friday afternoons. I also bought them school supplies and collected gently used clothing from my family and friends to give to some of the parents. Every teacher did these things.

Our efforts helped, of course, but nothing we did could pull students and parents out of the constant state of crisis that gripped the neighborhood. At first, I assumed that this was just how things were. There have always been poor people in the world, I thought, and here they happen to be, in Mechanicsville. But the more I got to know the teachers and families who had been in the community for years, I came to learn that things had not always been this way. On the contrary, the once stable, proud, black community of Mechanicsville had come under attack decades ago and had been torn to shreds.

| | | | | | | | | | | | | |

Atlanta's beginnings were not exactly fortuitous. In 1837, when the chief engineer of the Western and Atlantic Railroad oversaw a surveying party that drove a zero-mile marker into the ground where downtown Atlanta now exists, he declared that the settlement would amount to little more than "a tavern, a blacksmith's shop, a general store, and nothing else."[2] Thus the area was called Terminus—the end of the line—for several years. But the railroad industry attracted workers, and businesses to serve those workers, and Terminus grew into a sizeable town, which was renamed Marthasville before it was incorporated, in 1847, as Atlanta.

An area southwest of downtown housed rail yards and locomotive repair shops, and it came to be known as Mechanicsville for the workers who settled there. At first, the neighborhood was a mix of lower-income, white railroad workers and wealthier whites who worked in offices downtown. After the Civil War, black people from rural Georgia migrated to Atlanta en masse, and many found work and homes in and around Mechanicsville. Summerhill, one of the neighborhoods bordering Mechanicsville, was founded by newly emancipated black folks. The area attracted Eastern European Jewish immigrants as well, and for a long time the neighborhoods directly south of downtown were unusually diverse and thrived economically.[3]

By the mid-twentieth century, many of the white residents had moved to neighborhoods north of downtown, and Mechanicsville was majority-black. The Great Depression had taken a toll on the area, compounding the struggles of working-class black people who were shut out of most well-paying jobs. But the state of affairs for black people in Atlanta was far better than many places in the South. In the Sweet Auburn business district, just east of downtown, the country's first black millionaires started and grew their businesses, contributing to a black economic hub that became relatively autonomous from the city's white power structure.

This independence was reflected in the black neighborhoods on the outskirts of downtown. Mechanicsville, Summerhill, and Peoplestown—all south of the city center—had grocery stores, pharmacies, libraries, a school, a movie theater, dry cleaners, a hospital, and many more businesses and services operated by and for the black community.[4] Vine City, directly west of downtown, was even more vibrant, with the Atlanta University Center (a consortium of black colleges), a popular entertainment venue called the Magnolia Ballroom, and the only amusement park for black people in the area.[5]

People who grew up in Mechanicsville during the 1940s and '50s remember a neighborhood where residents rarely locked their doors, and children played freely outside until a giant lightbulb on a tower at the General Electric factory lit up at dusk, signaling their dinnertime. The community was tight-knit, and adults looked out for all the children in the neighborhood.[6]

But thriving communities are not what Atlanta's white business elite saw in Sweet Auburn, Vine City, Summerhill, Peoplestown, and Mechanicsville. In their eyes, the black neighborhoods surrounding downtown were a "ring of slums around the neck of the core" that ought to be eliminated.[7]

Throughout the twentieth century, Atlanta's white business leaders functioned as a sort of shadow government, guiding city planning and policymaking as much as, and sometimes more than, elected officials. Executives from prominent, Atlanta-based companies like Coca-Cola and Rich's held forth over city politics informally in private meetings, letters, and phone calls, and formally through institutions like the Metro Atlanta Chamber of Commerce.[8]

As a new era of economic growth sparked by World War II yanked the country out of the final throes of the Depression, these powerful men became concerned that growing suburban economic development threatened to compete with downtown Atlanta as a business hub for the metro area. More white people were moving to the suburbs and taking their spending with them. At the same time, black prosperity and a growing black population was translating into greater black political power, something that also concerned Atlanta's white elite.

"Our negro population is growing by leaps and bounds," Mayor William Hartsfield wrote in a letter to his white constituents in 1942. "The time is not far distant when they will become a political force in Atlanta if our white citizens are going to move out and give it to them . . . do you want to hand them political control of Atlanta?"[9]

Around this time, the city's leading bankers, realtors, lawyers, and other businessmen founded the Central Atlanta Improvement Association—it later merged with a similar organization to become Central Atlanta Progress—to revitalize downtown, where they owned property and headquartered their businesses, in order to make the area more appealing to the whites who were flocking to the suburbs. One of their first undertakings was to urge local and state officials to commission a traffic study with the stated aim of improving access to downtown. City planners initially proposed constructing an expressway that would be elevated over railroad tracks with minimal residential destruction. But the Central Atlanta Improvement Association intervened, bringing in private consultants and guiding the plans. The consultants produced the Lochner Plan, published in 1946, which proposed an expressway that would cut through black neighborhoods instead. The unstated goal was to displace as many black people as possible from the neighborhoods surrounding downtown.[10]

Over the next twenty years, highway construction ripped through Sweet Auburn, eliminating black businesses and geographically disjointing the community with a north-south expressway. Hundreds of homes in Mechanicsville and Summerhill were taken through eminent domain and destroyed for construction of an east-west expressway, which created a physical buffer between downtown and the black neighborhoods to the south. The devastation of highway construction was extensive, but the dismantling of these communities had only just begun.

In the early 1960s, Mayor Ivan Allen Jr., the millionaire president of an office supply company founded by his father and former head of the Metro Atlanta Chamber of Commerce, used millions of dollars in federal urban renewal funds to raze an entire neighborhood adjacent to Mechanicsville to make way for Fulton County Stadium, home of baseball's new Atlanta Braves following the franchise's move from Milwaukee in 1966. Allen would follow this development with more large-scale civic projects that ran roughshod over black communities.[11] Though the federal urban renewal program required new housing to be constructed for displaced residents, Allen and other city leaders largely flaunted the rule, leaving thousands of families to relocate on their own. Over the course of twenty-two years of highway construction and urban renewal, an estimated fourteen thousand to seventeen thousand households were forced to move without receiving replacement housing. Nineteen out of twenty people displaced were black.[12]

Many more black people were displaced due to the conditions created by the upheaval. As the population dwindled, businesses lost customers, churches lost congregants, schools lost students. Many of these institutions eventually shuttered, leaving a ghost town in their wake. Without amenities, residents who could move chose to do so, and fewer newcomers put down roots in the neighborhoods south of downtown. In the census tracts comprising Mechanicsville and a sliver of Summerhill, the population shrank from 24,384 in 1940 to 10,898 in 1970.[13] By the time I visited Sheila Houston at her apartment in the heart of Mechanicsville, the area was home to fewer than 5,000 people, who struggled to live in a broken neighborhood devoid of some of the most basic amenities and civic institutions.[14]

On the west side of downtown, the city's attack on black communities mirrored the assault on the south side. In 1970, Allen's last year as Atlanta mayor, the local chamber of commerce commissioned a feasibility study for a new convention center. That eventually led to the construction of the Georgia World Congress Center, financed with $35 million in state-issued bonds and built on the site of a black neighborhood called Lightning. Real estate tycoon Tom Cousins, who would create Atlanta's first charter school decades later, played a leading role in pushing elected officials to locate the convention center there. As a board member of Central Atlanta Progress, successor of the business association that orchestrated the construction of the freeways through black neighborhoods back in 1946, he held sway over city politics. And he had a vested interest in the site, as he was building a massive hotel-coliseum complex on an adjacent parcel and saw the potential for a guaranteed clientele of conventioneers. [15]

Altogether the convention center and hotel complex, surrounded by car-centric viaducts, formed a morass that cut off the west-side neighborhoods from downtown in much the same way that the interstate isolated south-side neighborhoods. In 1992, the state added a massive football stadium, the Georgia Dome, to the complex at a cost of $214 million. This public investment served to enrich the private owners of the Falcons football team. It was never matched with community investments, and the closest west-side neighborhoods came undone just like Mechanicsville and the other south-side neighborhoods. Between 1970 and 2000, Vine City lost nearly two-thirds of its population and became a nexus of Atlanta's drug trade.[16]

The concerted efforts by Atlanta's political and business leaders to diminish the stability of black neighborhoods for their own gain undoubtedly had a lasting impact on the schools. Both the children who were uprooted and those who remained were increasingly deprived of the things a healthy community offers—accessible goods and services, economic opportunities, vibrant public spaces, and a supportive social fabric. Teachers and school employees were left to fill in the void, which would only expand in the years following urban renewal.

I I I I I I I I I I I I

Beverly Hall was a speck on the mobile stage inside the cavernous Georgia Dome. Instead of football players, school employees sat in folding chairs before her on the turf, creating a bright checkerboard of matching T-shirts that proudly displayed each school's colors. Some even waved pompoms and pennants. I was light years away with my coworkers in the riser seats, which we called "the bleachers." Dunbar hadn't met 70 percent of its targets—which included reaching certain test score goals—the requirement to "make the floor" at the Atlanta Public Schools convocation in 2008.

Hall conceived of the convocation, held each fall, as a celebration honoring the thousands of educators in APS. It was also as an incentive to achieve the highest test scores. The convocation was a grand event, with performances by the high school marching bands and school choirs, inspirational videos (not unlike the ones TFA screened in their boot camp) blaring from the JumboTron, and prestigious keynote speakers.

The schools that topped the list got special recognition with VIP seating on the field, while the rest of us were relegated to the bleachers. Buckner-Webb and Cleveland, the veteran teachers who took a liking to me, were busy chatting with former coworkers who had moved on to other schools. They had been part of APS for so long, and had so many friends in the system, that to them the event was like a big teacher reunion no matter where we sat. But not everyone felt that way. I would later learn that some educators felt humiliated by having to sit in the bleachers.

I could not have cared less about the seating arrangement. I was just proud to have survived my first year of teaching and to have seen my students come such a long way. About 70 percent had passed the CRCT, which was what I had expected. I was overjoyed when I saw that Tiffany had passed reading. I had worked so hard with her, and it was obvious that she was making strides, but I wasn't certain if her abilities would translate to the test. The testing environment was extremely taxing for six-year-olds who weren't used to sitting silently for hours on end. Of course, we had practiced, but on the real testing days my students were restless. By the end, their test booklets were covered with doodles, and the testing coordinator instructed me to go to the media center and erase them. First-graders didn't use separate answer sheets: they filled in multiple-choice bubbles directly on the test booklet. We had to erase any stray marks so that the booklets would be graded correctly by a machine.

When I had met with Principal Greene for my end-of-year evaluation, she said that I had done well for a new teacher. I would stay in first grade and work with Cleveland, who was switching from third grade, while Buckner-Webb moved to second. As we chatted at the APS convocation, Cleveland said she was happy with the change, exclaiming, "I'm glad not to stress about these tests anymore!" I agreed wholeheartedly. It was enough to be concerned about my students doing well for their own benefit. I didn't want to worry about meeting district targets and AYP. Again, I was thankful that first-grade scores weren't included in the metrics.

That fall, Dunbar was abuzz with a new energy that felt alternately exciting and tense, like walking a tightrope. Change was palpable. The old building, a relic of the 1970s, was undergoing renovations (no more squirrels in the ceiling, I hoped), so we were temporarily housed in another school building nearby. Outside of our little school world, Barack Obama was campaigning to become the first black president of the United States, and his name was constantly on everybody's lips. In class, Obama was the ultimate role model we impressed upon our students, a shining example of what they could become with hard work and belief in themselves. In the faculty lounge, we eagerly discussed the latest news from the campaign trail, laughing over Sarah Palin's gaffes and parsing the presidential debates. When Obama won, nearly everyone was overcome with what felt like a collective catharsis.

But there were other tumultuous changes. On September 29, 2008, the biggest single-day crash in stock market history rocked the US economy to its core. The first thing on everybody's mind at Dunbar was budget cuts. In 2002, Georgians had elected Republican Sonny Perdue governor, based largely on his promise to make the Confederate battle flag the state's official flag again, which his incumbent opponent, Democrat Roy Barnes, had done away with. Once he was in office, Perdue followed through on that pledge and set to work on other regressions.

He began defunding education by millions of dollars every year. By 2008, he had cut a total of $1.5 billion from the state's K–12 education budget. Many counties furloughed their teachers and docked their pay. APS stopped giving teachers a cost-of-living raise. Under Perdue, the schools were already in a recession. How could we withstand the collapse of the US economy?[17]

I channeled the tension by going into overdrive. As a second-year first-grade teacher, I was more confident in my teaching abilities and became more involved in the school. I was the assistant Girl Scout troop leader, I served on the Health and Wellness Committee, and I was chosen to be a part of a new district-wide behavioral management program. My mother and I were even the keynote speakers at the school's first mother-daughter tea. And Principal Greene appointed me grade-level chair for first grade.

I felt like I was finding my way as a role model and leader, despite the upheavals in the world around me, so it hardly registered when a report in a December issue of the *Atlanta Journal-Constitution* questioned the validity of CRCT test scores at a number of schools throughout the state. It was the first year that students who failed the CRCT could retest during the summer, and the federal government would use the new scores to determine whether their school met AYP. Schools in DeKalb, Fulton, Glynn, and Gwinnett Counties, as well as one elementary school in APS, had seen astronomical gains in their summer retest scores. At one school, kids who had failed only a few months before increased their scores by an average of forty-eight points—three times higher than the statewide average. Reporters interviewed a testing expert who said that increases that high were as "extraordinary as a snowstorm in July. In Atlanta."[18]

I read the article with curiosity but soon forgot about it. With Christmas approaching, there was so much to do. My family always had a big Christmas dinner with cousins, my godsisters Arlissa and Patrice, and their dad, Uncle Rudy. It was my job to help my mother prepare the food and decorate the house. On top of that, each year I would create a trivia game from scratch, based on popular TV sitcoms. We would split up into two teams to compete, and it was always a big hit. At Dunbar, there were class parties, holiday programs, and toy drives underway.

"You know, the parents used to do all of this," an older teacher told me one day as we were hanging tinsel in the hallway. "The parents in this community used to really participate; you wouldn't believe it. PTA meetings were always packed. They would even argue over who got to chaperone the field trips and who got to help with the holiday parties. We had to put them on a waiting list, make them take turns. You don't see that anymore. Not since crack came to the neighborhood."

ı ı ı ı ı ı ı ı ı ı ı ı

As Atlanta's black neighborhoods were still reeling from urban renewal—or as James Baldwin aptly called it, "Negro removal"—in the late 1960s, a new threat was forming. Civil rights victories had shaken the apartheid social order of the United States, and, in response, conservative politicians sought to leverage the rage and fear of whites who thought their world was falling apart. Richard Nixon exemplified this tactic in his 1968 presidential campaign, which he built around the claim that the nation faced a crisis of law and order.

In his speech accepting the Republican presidential nomination in 1968, Nixon linked the supposed lack of law and order to the revolutionary fervor of the moment. He referenced the civil rights and antiwar movements, painting both as lawless, practically in the same breath that he vowed to "open a new front against the filth peddlers and the narcotics peddlers."[19] Years later, a top Nixon aide (who was by that time working at an engineering firm in Atlanta) told a journalist that Nixon's subsequent crackdown on drugs was aimed at quashing political dissent. In stunningly blunt terms, he explained: "We knew we couldn't make it illegal to be either against the war or black, but by getting the public to associate the hippies with marijuana and blacks with heroin, and then criminalizing both heavily, we could disrupt those communities. We could arrest their leaders, raid their homes, break up their meetings, and vilify them night after night on the evening news. Did we know we were lying about the drugs? Of course we did."[20]

During his presidency, Nixon declared a "War on Drugs" and poured federal funds into ramping up a law enforcement offensive against drug crime. He created the Drug Enforcement Agency (DEA), pushed a bill through Congress allowing "no-knock warrants" so that police could raid homes without announcing themselves, and rejected the recommendation of a congressional commission to decriminalize marijuana.[21] In so doing, Nixon laid the groundwork for a racialized blitzkrieg on drugs during the Reagan era.

Under President Ronald Reagan, who announced his continuation of the war on drugs in 1982, federal budgets for antidrug law enforcement swelled. Between 1980 and 1991, the annual FBI antidrug budget went from $8 million to $181 million, and both the Department of Defense and the Drug Enforcement Administration saw increases from tens of millions of dollars to over one billion each. Meanwhile, federal funding for drug treatment programs shriveled up, as did funding for a slew of social welfare programs that the Reagan administration cut.[22]

Reagan justified his "war on drugs" with alarmist rhetoric that often focused on the boom in crack, a solid, smokable form of powdered cocaine. It was so potent that small doses could be sold for extremely low prices, opening a market for a robust street trade in poor areas.

Crack hit the streets at a time when black communities in Atlanta and throughout the country were in turmoil. Their social fabric had been shredded by urban renewal projects, and corporations were boosting profits by sending manufacturing jobs overseas, where they could exploit cheaper labor. Black men were hit hardest by this economic shift, as nearly half of black men in the workforce in 1980 held blue-collar jobs. Income inequality between black people and white people, which had narrowed during the 1960s, expanded again. In 1980, the median income for white people was more than three times greater than that of black people; by 1990, it was more than five times higher.[23]

It was in this context of displacement and economic insecurity that crack entered black communities like Mechanicsville, with disastrous results. There were a few teachers who had worked at Dunbar for decades, and they told me that the advent of crack demarcated two completely different eras for the school and the Mechanicsville neighborhood. Before crack, parental involvement was high, students were more or less studious, and the school had a "gifted" program for kids who excelled. Once crack took hold, that all began to change. Parents became estranged, and there were more single moms who didn't have time to be involved in their kids' education. Children started coming to school unprepared, falling asleep in class, and were generally losing interest in learning, seemingly because their lives at home were increasingly volatile. The world between their homes and school was changing too. One teacher told me she used to walk through the neighborhood with kids and visit their families until the drug trade became so heavy that walking around Mechanicsville was no longer safe. Some of the elementary school students were drawn into the drug scene, recruited as lookouts or as couriers carrying drugs from one person to another.

As waves of despairing, destabilized people became addicted to crack, Reagan turned a public health crisis into a purported crisis of "law and order" designed to put black people in cages. With the 1986 Anti-Drug Abuse Act, the Reagan administration established mandatory minimum sentences for drug crimes involving crack and cocaine that created a huge disparity in how the two were punished. Crimes involving just five grams of crack, which was associated with black people, carried the same minimum sentence—five years—as crimes involving five hundred grams of cocaine, which was associated with white people, even though the two drugs are virtually the same. Follow-up legislation two years later would deepen the disparity, establishing a maximum sentence of twenty years in prison for simple possession of more than five grams of crack, while the maximum sentence for simple possession of any amount of cocaine was only one year in prison.[24] The 1986 law also channeled $2 billion into antidrug policing, permitted the death penalty for some drug crimes, and militarized narcotics control.[25]

The effects were swift in coming. By 1991, the United States incarcerated more people than any country ever before in history, and most of the people behind bars were black. That year, one in four young black men were under the control of the criminal justice system.[26]

The disparity was due not only to disproportionate sentencing laws but also to a focus on urban centers as the supposed locus of drug use. Though government reports showed that 80 percent of cocaine users were white suburbanites, heightened antidrug policing focused on poor, minority neighborhoods in cities. In the mid-1980s, many urban police forces created special units to focus on drug crimes in these areas, with the goal of making as many arrests as possible.[27] In 1987, Atlanta's police chief launched a drug squad called Run Every

Drug Dealer Out of Georgia—RED DOG.[28] Red Dog officers, known for their militarized getup, became ubiquitous in Atlanta's struggling black neighborhoods, and drug indictments more than tripled in Fulton County during the unit's first four years of existence. Complaints of police brutality and excessive force also skyrocketed as the Red Dogs treated their beat as a battlefield.[29]

These trends played out similarly on the state level; between 1980 and 1995 Georgia's prison population nearly tripled, while its jail population quadrupled.[30] In 1995, Georgia had the sixth-highest incarceration rate in the nation, and spent a larger percentage of its budget on corrections than any state except for Texas.[31] These dramatic shifts happened under the tenure of state attorney general Mike Bowers, who would later lead the investigation that dragged me into the APS cheating scandal. Bowers had a tough-on-crime stance that mirrored, and often exceeded, federal trends.

In 1981, when Governor George Busbee appointed Bowers attorney general, Bowers's track record already boded ill for black people. After graduating from law school in 1974, Bowers joined the staff of Georgia's then attorney general, Arthur Bolton, who had worked closely with the state's segregationist governor in the 1960s to fight the implementation of the Voting Rights Act of 1965. Bowers carried on this legacy when he succeeded Bolton and immediately sued the US attorney general, William French Smith, for denying Georgia preclearance under Section 5 of the Voting Rights Act.

White state legislators had tried to redraw electoral maps and create majority-white voting districts to stop black legislators from creating majority-black districts. But without federal preclearance, the state couldn't legally finalize the new maps. The US attorney general had denied preclearance because he believed the creation of the white districts was racially motivated. Nobody doubted this, as the chair of the House committee tasked with redistricting plainly stated, "I'm not going to draw a nigger district if I can help it." Bowers tried to overturn the preclearance denial anyway, but he lost in court.[32]

When it came to the war on drugs, Bowers was a foot soldier. He called drug abuse "the biggest single legal problem in this country today," and he set out to make Georgia's drug laws more punitive.[33]

During his first few years in office, Bowers unsuccessfully pushed to make possession of less than one ounce of marijuana a felony offense and proposed a bill that would have enabled the criminal prosecution of teachers who didn't report suspected drug use by students.[34]

Bowers's vision of a more punitive state code was carried out in the 1990s, after President Bill Clinton signed an unprecedented $30 billion crime bill. The bill made many changes, but perhaps most notorious was the "three strikes law," which mandated life sentences for people who committed felonies after two prior convictions. Stories like that of Leandro Andrade, who was sent to prison for life for stealing Disney videotapes to give to his nieces for Christmas because he had two prior burglary convictions, became commonplace.[35]

Georgia legislators, not to be outdone, followed up by passing a *two-strikes* bill in 1995 that applied to a list of violent crimes they called the "seven deadly sins"—murder, kidnapping, armed robbery, rape, aggravated sodomy, aggravated sexual battery, and aggravated child molestation. Anyone convicted of one of these crimes who had only one prior conviction for any of the seven crimes would spend the rest of his or her life in prison, and parole was abolished for most first-time offenders.

Bowers applauded these measures but warned that they were not enough. More prisons, he said, were needed to house the rapidly growing incarcerated population.[36] In answer to his call, Georgia officials took advantage of the funding afforded by the federal crime bill.[37] The state received more than $82 million for prison construction between 1996 and 2001.[38] At the same time, Georgia prisons were gaining a reputation as hellish places devoid of rehabilitation. In 1996, a contraband sweep at Hays State Prison turned into a "blood bath," with corrections officers beating inmates to a pulp. Afterword they went out for a chicken dinner to celebrate their brutal rampage, accompanied by the state corrections commissioner, who was known for saying that many Georgia inmates "ain't fit to kill." Cases like this made headlines but didn't reverse the tide of public support for mass incarceration.[39]

Georgia's prison boom posed an opportunity for the burgeoning private prison industry, which got its start in the mid-1980s. Suddenly there was a profit motive in putting people behind bars, and the business was increasingly lucrative. In 1996, the private prison industry was valued at around $650 million; within a year that figure had grown to over $1 billion.[40]

Georgia contracted with its first three privately operated state prisons in 1997. The state would eventually become home to four state prisons, three federal prisons, and three immigration detention facilities, all operated by private corporations.[41] These corporations are paid per inmate, so they are incentivized to do everything they can to keep prisons full. In amendments to Georgia's contracts with the Corrections Corporation of America (CCA) and GEO Group—the two largest private prison companies in the country—both companies imposed "bed guarantee clauses" stipulating that their prisons had to be 90 percent full or else the state would be fined. Such quotas, which have become typical, encourage states to maintain and expand the war on drugs and harsh sentencing laws or else lose money on unused prison beds.[42] CCA, now known as CoreCivic, and GEO Group have also poured millions of dollars into lobbying for laws that keep the "mass" in mass incarceration. They haven't done it alone; they've been helped along by groups like ALEC, which in 1995 successfully pushed model bills in twenty-five states that created harsher sentencing laws like the ones Georgia adopted that year.[43] The Georgia Public Policy Foundation, an ALEC-affiliated think tank, advocated to expand private prisons in step with its calls to privatize education.[44]

As the war on drugs and prison privatization drove up incarceration rates—with the highest proportion of prisoners being black—the number of children of incarcerated parents ballooned. Between 1991 and 2007, the year I began teaching, the number of children who had a parent in prison grew by 80 percent to a total of more than 1.7 million nationwide.[45] Numerous studies have shown that children experience extremely negative effects as the result of parental incarceration—from emotional, behavioral, and cognitive problems to low academic performance and higher suspension and dropout rates.[46]

Juvenile incarceration also spiked during the 1980s and early 1990s, as many states, including Georgia, enacted severe juvenile sentencing laws. As with adults, black children in confinement far outnumbered their white peers.[47] In Georgia, harsher juvenile sentencing enacted in 1994 led to immense overcrowding in juvenile jails and prompted a slew of lawsuits responding to the inhumane conditions that resulted. One 1996 lawsuit against the state cited allegations of physical abuse and sexual molestation at a juvenile detention facility in Dalton, Georgia, that imprisoned children as young as nine years old. The facility was so run-down and overcrowded that children were forced to sleep in the bathrooms, and multiple children had attempted suicide. One girl tried to drown herself in a toilet. A boy who attempted to kill himself was discovered by a staff member who threw him against a wall, sending him to a hospital.[48]

Revelations of abuse in juvenile detention did nothing to sway officials like Mike Bowers, who continued to defend harsh sentencing, clamor for more prisons, and vilify black youth. In November 1996, speaking at a Georgia Public Policy Foundation forum, Bowers stirred up fear of child criminals, telling his audience, "Do not be deceived by these slightly dropping crime rates. It's the lull before the storm. Most crimes are committed by young people. We've got a helluva lot more five-year-olds today than ten years ago. You better watch your goodies, Hawkeye. They're coming. They're superpredators."[49]

With this outrageous claim, Bowers parroted an idea that had gained significant traction over the previous year, thanks to a right-wing professor and commentator, John Dilulio, who penned an article for the conservative *Weekly Standard*, "The Coming of the Super-Predators." In this and other writings, Dilulio combined centuries-old racist stereotypes of black men and boys as violent savages with pseudo-sociological theories blaming poverty on the moral failings of black people, ultimately to stoke white hysteria and justify policies that fueled mass incarceration. The racism in Dilulio's ideology was not sneakily coded in suggestive undertones but prominently on display. "We are terrified," he and two coauthors wrote in a 1996 book, "by the prospect of innocent people being gunned down at random, without warning and almost without a motive, by youngsters who afterwards show us the black, unremorseful face of a feral, pre-social being."[50]

This dehumanized view of black youth shaped public policies, like Georgia's juvenile sentencing law of 1994, as Dilulio and his colleagues channeled their ideas through think tanks and media outlets to politicians who found political favor in taking a "tough" stance on crime.

That was certainly the theme of the 1996 Fulton County district attorney election. That year, residents of Fulton County elected Georgia's first black district attorney, Paul Howard, who ran on a promise to try more youth as adults.[51] Since the 1994 law, Georgia children as young as thirteen who committed the so-called "seven deadly sins" crimes could be charged as adults and incarcerated in adult prisons.

Howard got his chance in the first few weeks of his new job, when Darrell Woods was fatally shot while waiting for his wife with their two children in a car outside a convenience store in the Bluff. This neighborhood on Atlanta's west side had become the epicenter of the city's drug trade as displacement and disinvestment gripped the area in the years following construction of the Georgia World Congress Center and the Georgia Dome.

Police initially arrested a local drug dealer who was on the scene, but the dealer blamed the killing on thirteen-year-old Michael Lewis, known to everyone in the neighborhood as Little B. Little B maintained his innocence, insisting that the dealer had framed him. In juvenile court, the maximum sentence Little B could have received was five years of incarceration. But Paul Howard moved quickly to indict the child as an adult and send him to prison for life.

In a sensationalized trial that played off the growing fear of so-called superpredator children, Howard's prosecution team landed the conviction, affording Howard a "career-making" victory that cemented his place in the Atlanta power structure. Never one to miss a chance to pursue a headline-grabbing case, Howard would bask in the spotlight again years later when he charged me and dozens of other educators with conspiracy and racketeering.[52]

After condemning Little B to a lifetime behind bars, Howard continued his tough-on-crime approach, calling for the construction of a second jail to keep the county jail from bursting at the seams as Atlanta's Red Dog unit made more and more drug arrests.[53]

Nine blocks southwest of the convenience store where Woods was killed and Little B was pinned as the culprit, the wrath of the Red Dogs would come to a head in an incident that exemplified the horrific nature of the war on drugs. On November 21, 2006, at around seven in the evening, ninety-two-year-old Kathryn Johnston heard the unmistakable sound of her front door being broken down. She grabbed an old pistol and headed toward the door, where she saw a group of men breaking in. She fired a warning shot above their heads, and they returned fire with thirty-nine bullets, striking Johnston at least five times and killing her.

Some of the men then planted drugs in the house. They were Red Dog officers who had just botched a drug raid—lying to obtain a no-knock warrant to search a house that had no connection to drug dealers, then killing the elderly owner—and they were determined to cover it up. Their plan was exposed, though, and several of the officers involved were eventually convicted. But that wasn't the end of the Red Dogs. It would take another violent, illegal raid three years later before the unit was finally disbanded.[54]

This was the world my students inhabited. A world of decent-paying jobs outsourced to countries where companies could more easily exploit workers, close-knit black communities unraveled by city planners and their corporate influencers, black homes lost to expressways, black parents in despair succumbing to addiction and locked in cages for profit, black children left to fend for themselves and treated like hardened criminals, black grandmas shot down in their own homes by police, a court system with a penchant for theatrics and an acquiescent media industry to feed it spectators, white politicians suppressing black votes and gunning for the criminal justice system to swallow black families whole, and an education system telling black students to forget all that, just bubble in the right answer.

I I I I I I I I I I I I I

"Middlebrooks sent me to watch your class while you erase stray marks," a kindergarten paraprofessional said, popping her head into my classroom. "They're in the computer lab."

It was April 2009, my second year facing the CRCT, and my first-graders had just completed the last round of testing. Again, it had been excruciating as the children struggled to sit still and focus. One boy fell out of his chair on purpose just to get attention. And again, their test booklets were covered with doodles of airplanes, flowers, cartoon characters, you name it.

Just like the preceding year, the school testing coordinator instructed teachers to erase these doodles, which we called "stray marks." In 2008, Principal Greene assigned one of her deputy administrators to be the testing coordinator, but in 2009 it was Lera Middlebrooks, who was Dunbar's literary specialist.

I liked Middlebrooks; most of us did. She occupied a gray area between teacher and administrator. In some ways she was Principal Greene's right-hand woman, an unofficial position she relished. She dressed like an administrator, always in heels and carefully coordinated outfits, but at the end of the day her responsibility rested with getting kids to read on grade-level through personalized instruction she gave in her office. She had a loud, snarky attitude that could be hilarious, withering, or both. She liked to invite coworkers out for drinks once in a while and cut loose at the end-of-the-year party. She brought a jolt of energy to every room she entered.

I didn't know it at the time, but as Middlebrooks administered the CRCT at Dunbar—the first time she'd worked as a testing coordinator—she was under investigation by the Georgia Department of Education for allegedly sharing a state writing-test prompt with a former colleague who worked at a school in another county several hours away.

When I arrived at the computer lab, Rose Neal, the second-grade teacher, was already there. Neal was pretty much the opposite of Middlebrooks in terms of likeability. She was usually irritable and abrasive in her complaining, not funny like Middlebrooks. She seemed calculating to me. I noticed her say and do contradictory things depending on who was around. They were always minor things, but regardless, I didn't place much trust in her. And I didn't like the way she treated students. The previous year, Neal had been on probation from regular teaching and worked as an Early Intervention Program (EIP) teacher. Her job was to pull from class kids who needed extra help and work with them one-on-one. One of the first times I dealt with her, she lumbered into my classroom to retrieve a boy who was acting up and hollered the worst things I'd ever heard an adult say to a child.

A few minutes after I began erasing stray marks from my students' test booklets, Webb and Cleveland showed up and got to work on theirs. While Middlebrooks waited, the four of us mostly worked in silence, erasing stray marks and fixing illegible handwriting on the part of the booklets where students wrote their names and other information. After about twenty minutes, I had gone through my whole stack. I got up, handed the pile of booklets to Middlebrooks, and headed back to my classroom.

If I had known I would have to relive those twenty minutes again and again—first for an investigator working under Attorney General Bowers and Governor Perdue, followed by a grand jury convened by District Attorney Howard, and then in a trial where every detail was picked apart by prosecutors—maybe I would have committed more details to memory. Maybe I would have noticed something, anything, that would have helped me prove how ordinary and uneventful those twenty minutes were. But, of course, that's the catch. There was nothing to notice, nothing to remember. It was just another boring afternoon during testing season.

CHAPTER THREE

The Pot Calling
the Kettle Black

▮ | | | | | | | | | | | | | | | | | | | | | | | |

"I DON'T KNOW HOW THIS BOY PASSED THE TEST," Lisa said, swirling the straw in her margarita mocktail. The start of summer break was two weeks away, and I was ringing it in with Lisa Prescott, a second-year teacher at Dunbar. We had become fast friends in our trial-by-fire first semester back in 2007. We would go out for drinks after work every so often (hers were always nonalcoholic, mine not so much), and we sometimes hung out on the weekends.

Sitting on the patio of No Mas! Cantina, a Mexican restaurant close to Dunbar, we dissected the happenings at the school since our last get-together. After cracking jokes about the teacher sack race on Field Day and chatting excitedly about the engagement of one of our co-workers, we arrived at a more serious matter: the end-of-year faculty meeting. Once again, Principal Greene had delivered bad news. We hadn't met the district targets. We had met the federal standards for adequate yearly progress, though, which was no small feat. Greene didn't seem upset when she reported our CRCT scores. "I'm proud of our children anyway," she told us. "We have some really bright students."

She passed around reports to each teacher, and I was thrilled to see that more than 80 percent of my students were in the "meets the standard" and "exceeds the standard" categories. That was significantly

46

higher than the 70 percent who had passed the previous year. Because I was a first-grade teacher, my students' scores didn't factor in to the calculations for AYP or the district targets, but it was still gratifying to see that my kids were doing well. Surprisingly well, I thought. A couple of names caught my eye in the "exceeds" column in the math section. They were students who needed extra help with almost every lesson—patterns, measurements, arithmetic—and still never quite grasped the material. The reading section was similar; a few students who could sound out words but were at a loss when it came to comprehension had apparently exceeded the standard. Had I underestimated them? Their classwork told me otherwise, but maybe I was falling into the "culture of low expectations" that TFA had warned me about. Greene proceeded to the next topic of discussion, and I didn't give it further thought.

But now Lisa was telling me she'd been surprised by her students' test results too. There was one boy, she said, who simply could not have exceeded the standard based on his academic ability. He had transferred to Dunbar in the middle of the year after being out of school for two months while his family was homeless. He was a smart enough kid but just too far behind. "He must have done some good guessing," Lisa concluded. We moved on to talking about our end-of-year meetings with Greene.

"I wanted to loop with my class," I told Lisa, meaning I wanted to move up to second grade and have the same students. I knew what I'd taught them, and I knew their needs. They felt like *my* kids. Plus, test scores didn't count toward AYP and targets until third grade, so I would still be in the safe zone as far as that was concerned. But Greene had other plans for me.

She told me I had done well as new teacher, and she wanted to move me to fifth grade, since that is what I had taught during my TFA training. I felt proud, but I also dreaded teaching a grade where the CRCT scores counted. Fortunately, I had a whole summer ahead of me before I would have to face that reality.

"Tell me about your summer plans!" Lisa demanded. With that, our conversation turned to family reunions, beach trips, and a fun project I had cooked up with some of my TFA friends. We were going to shoot a pilot for a talk show about dating and relationships and see if we could get a network to pick it up. I still felt drawn to working in television

news, and our ambitious plan seemed like an exciting summer adven-
ture. A childhood friend who I had run into a few times since moving
back to Atlanta offered to loan us some seed money to get the project
off the ground. Moses and I had grown up in the same neighborhood
in Stone Mountain and met at the pool when I was twelve years old. He
had a crush on me then, and I got the feeling that the crush might have
lingered, but I wasn't sure.

As I spent the following months running all over the city, surveying
people about their love lives, holding auditions for a talk show host,
assembling a production team, and engaging in a million other tasks,
CRCT scores were far from my mind. But they were receiving increasing attention elsewhere.

In June, the Governor's Office of Student Achievement (GOSA),
an agency independent of the Georgia Department of Education, announced that an audit confirmed what the *Atlanta Journal-Constitution*
had reported the previous December: several schools, including Deerwood Academy in APS, had scored high on the 2008 CRCT retests
due to cheating. Someone at each school, the report stated, had erased
wrong answers from student score sheets and bubbled in the right ones.
GOSA hadn't found concrete evidence of tampering, but the statistical
evidence spoke volumes. The Georgia Center for Assessment at the
University of Georgia had conducted an erasure analysis at the request
of the state. It showed that the number of wrong-to-right erasures on
the score sheets of four schools was far higher than that of a control
group. The four school districts that were implicated quickly launched
investigations, and in DeKalb County the fallout was severe. A principal resigned and was soon arrested, along with his former assistant
principal, on charges of falsifying a state document, an unprecedented
occurrence in Georgia at that point.[1]

In July, the Georgia Board of Education voted to discount the retest
scores and revoke the AYP status of all four schools. Board members
said they would consider other sanctions and that the schools might
have to pay back federal reward money they had received. At the board
meeting, GOSA executive director Kathleen Mathers singled out Atlanta Public Schools, implying that the district had taken an obstinate
stance and did not accept the state's findings.[2]

The board soon heard from Beverly Hall herself. She promptly wrote a letter stating that APS would appeal the board's decision, saying that the district "strongly disagrees with the allegations, the proposed sanctions, and the merits of the state's case against Atlanta Public Schools and Deerwood Academy." It was the same sort of hard-nosed approach that had won Hall acclaim when applied to the task of reforming schools. In the first five years of her tenure, she had unapologetically replaced 85 percent of the district's principals, one move among many that led some educators and parents to label her "autocratic."[3] But graduation rates and test scores had improved, and chronic student absences and teacher vacancies had drastically decreased.

While some of the 2008 CRCT retest scores certainly looked suspicious, students were making significant academic improvements on another standardized test, the National Assessment of Educational Progress. The NAEP was given to a random sample of APS students in fourth, eighth, and twelfth grades in various subject areas and administered by a contractor for the federal government without any involvement from APS employees. Without any potential for tampering, APS's NAEP scores had been steadily rising since 2002.[4]

In February 2009, Hall was named National Superintendent of the Year, based in part on the fact that every APS elementary school had made AYP in 2008. With Deerwood's retests nullified, that was no longer the case, but Hall was as determined as usual to defend her work. This time, though, she miscalculated. A former APS superintendent who was a close friend and mentor to Hall would later tell me that the "Atlanta culture" had certain rules that Hall, coming from the North, sometimes didn't understand. Black people in public office, he explained, were never to cross the white governor. I wasn't sure what had caused the rift between Hall and Governor Perdue, but challenging the state audit only seemed to exacerbate it.

"GOVERNOR CALLS OUT CITY'S SCHOOL CHIEF," blared a front-page headline in the *Atlanta Journal-Constitution* three days after the Georgia Board of Education meeting. Perdue had issued a press release stating, "It is outrageous that . . . Dr. Beverly Hall has simply ignored all of the evidence."[5] A month later, when the 2009–2010 school year was underway, Middlebrooks sounded off about the public sparring between

Hall and Perdue while we were on break in the teacher's lounge. She complained that Perdue wouldn't treat Hall that way if she weren't a black woman. "Uh-huh," the rest of us in the staff room agreed.

Despite the tension, Hall was resolute. Penn Payne, a lawyer APS hired to examine the state audit and investigate further, completed a report in August finding that there wasn't conclusive evidence of test tampering. She determined that it would have been time-intensive and logistically difficult to change answers on the score sheets and that, after interviewing numerous people involved in administering the tests, she didn't see indicators that anyone had done such a thing. Payne also noted that while GOSA backed its allegations by comparing students' 2008 retest scores with their 2009 CRCT scores, which were much lower, this approach ran counter to the state's own CRCT Interpretation Guide, which warned against comparing scores across grade level and content area. Because state agencies were continuing to investigate the matter, Payne didn't obtain access to the score sheets, so she couldn't verify the results of GOSA's erasure analysis.[6] Altogether it seemed that while the scores certainly looked suspicious, there just wasn't hard proof of cheating.

On the heels of Payne's report came a *Journal-Constitution* article comparing APS' handling of cheating complaints with school systems in five other metro area school districts. Heather Vogell, one of the reporters who had broken the story about the 2008 CRCT retests, found that APS had received significantly more complaints from employees and parents and was more likely to have ruled them unsubstantiated or to have disciplined implicated teachers rather than to have asked for their resignation. Then, in October, Vogell and her colleague John Perry published a damning article analyzing the 2009 CRCT scores in comparison to those from 2008. They found nineteen schools, a dozen in APS, that made "statistically unlikely" gains.[7] Dunbar was on the list.

At that point, I was two months into teaching fifth grade. The talk show hadn't found a buyer, so that project was on hold, and I was back in the swing of things at Dunbar. I found that, despite my misgivings, I enjoyed working with older children. I could incorporate more sophisticated lessons on subjects I was passionate about, like African American history and culture. I worked with Gloria Ivey, the other fifth-grade teacher, who had taught at Dunbar since 1973.

Throughout her long teaching career, Ivey had witnessed the upheavals that brought Mechanicsville down from a flourishing black neighborhood to a community barely surviving, changes that took an exacting toll on Dunbar and its students. She saw the fallout of urban renewal displacement, the rise of the drug epidemic, mass incarceration, and police brutality, all things that plagued black people nationwide. But she also lived through a horrifying time in Atlanta's history that was unlike anything that happened anywhere else. Ivey had been teaching for six years when a reign of terror befell the children in the city's poorest neighborhoods. Atlanta's public housing projects were ground zero for a gruesome series of crimes that coincided with a political shift that would have deep ramifications on both housing policy and education for decades to come.

I I I I I I I I I I I I I

On a warm October day in 1979, Gloria Ivey was headed home for the weekend when she saw Yusuf Bell, a charismatic nine-year-old, leaving Dunbar Elementary out of a back door. Yusuf often took a shortcut home to the McDaniel-Glenn public housing complex, which was near the school. Ivey called goodbye to Yusuf, who waved back. She was the last Dunbar employee to see the boy alive.

On Monday, children who lived in the area came to school with the news: Yusuf was missing. He'd gone on an errand to a nearby store for an elderly neighbor and never came home. Eighteen days later his body was found in the crawlspace of a nearby abandoned school. He had been strangled to death.[8] A local pastor, Timothy McDonald, gave remarks at Yusef's funeral and said the boy's potential to liberate his people had been "blighted out." McDonald went on to form a group called Concerned Black Clergy, which championed social justice causes for years to come. It would be one of few groups to rally in defense of teachers accused in the APS cheating scandal.[9]

Three other black children had similarly gone missing and were found murdered in the months preceding Yusuf's death, and over the next year and a half, many more, at least twenty-nine altogether, would follow. The sinister series of killings became known as the Atlanta Child Murders, a reign of terror that shook Atlanta's poor and working-class black communities to their core. "I still get chills when I think about it," Ivey told me. "The whole community was in an uproar."

The children were snatched from Atlanta's struggling black neighborhoods, the same ones that were impoverished by urban renewal and development projects that tore communities apart. Some victims lived in the same housing project or just a few blocks from one another; some were even friends. It seemed that children were being sadistically picked off. Terrified parents cloistered their youngsters indoors, and kids whose friends went missing anguished that they could be next.

Adults organized neighborhood patrols, and the mothers of murdered children banded together to challenge the city's initially lax handling of the crisis. My father worked with a communications committee that formed when the children first started disappearing. He had a CB radio that he used to relay messages between search parties. He was on duty when the body of a young girl named Angel Lenair was found tied to a tree, though her death was later determined to be unrelated to the others. Angel was a student at Venetian Hills Elementary, one of the first schools that state investigators would probe for evidence of cheating years later. Whole communities mobilized to address the crisis, including kids. Eleven-year-old Kasim Reed, who would go on to become mayor of Atlanta, participated in search parties supervised by adults.[10]

The racial tension underlying the tumult was missed by no one. Atlanta's first black mayor, Maynard Jackson, was elected in 1973, and though he was supported by a coalition of white and black city leaders, his affirmative action policies and hiring of a black public safety commissioner (ending an era of sanctioned KKK affiliation within the ranks of the Atlanta police) enraged many whites.[11] Many black people suspected that the child murders were the result of a violent backlash perpetrated by whites in response to the shifts in political power, even though in many ways black elected officials remained beholden to the white business class. Both verified and rumored reports of white men seen with or near the victims shortly before they disappeared fueled that theory, and the first law enforcement profile of the suspected killer presumed that he was a white man. So when Wayne Williams, a young black man aspiring to be a music promoter, was arrested in July 1981 for the murders of two black men, ages twenty-one and twenty-seven, that appeared to be connected to the child murders, many black folks were skeptical that he was the culprit.[12]

In February 1982, Williams was convicted based on "trace evidence." Forensic experts testified that fibers found on the two adult victims matched fibers from Williams's bedroom carpet, bath mat, and other items, and that hairs found on the bodies belonged to Williams's German shepherd. There were many limitations in the field of forensic science at that time, and it was highly unusual for such circumstantial evidence to land a conviction without other evidence to support it.[13]

Among the public, doubt remained as to Williams's guilt. Yusuf Bell's mother, Camille Bell, gave the most scathing response. Wayne Williams, she said, was "the 30th victim of the Atlanta slayings."[14]

Atlanta's elite, on the other hand, were ready to put the matter to rest. Business leaders were worried that the city was now perceived as dangerous, a reputation that could hurt the convention industry, which had grown into a booming business thanks to the recently completed Georgia World Congress Center.[15] Furthermore, the longer the case stayed open, the greater the potential for racial tensions to bubble over, tarnishing Atlanta's image as "the city too busy to hate." (This odd motto had been coined by former mayor William Hartsfield in his attempt to gloss over white dissent against school desegregation two decades earlier.) Members of the local chamber of commerce applauded Williams's conviction, and local newspapers followed suit. When Williams's lawyer, Alvin Binder, told national television reporters that two murders fitting the same pattern as the other child killings had taken place since his client's arrest, the local evening newspaper lashed back with an editorial headlined "Trial Is Over, Mr. Binder."[16]

Decades later, four of the cases were reopened, and *Atlanta Magazine* featured the news on its cover alongside a headline about Beverly Hall "fighting to fix Atlanta's public schools." But nothing much came of the revived investigation. The murders lived on as a dark specter, a haunting symbol of the accelerating degradation of Atlanta's working-class black communities in the post–civil rights movement era. While black families in Atlanta's hard-pressed neighborhoods and public housing projects dealt with the harrowing murders, the federal government launched an attack on housing policy that would further destabilize their communities.

More than forty years before Yusuf Bell went missing, in November 1935, President Franklin D. Roosevelt stood on the football field at the Georgia Institute of Technology, just west of downtown Atlanta, and presided over the grand opening of the nation's first public housing project, Techwood Homes. Nine city blocks adjacent to the university had been cleared of dilapidated housing, eliminating a mixed-race, impoverished neighborhood called Tanyard Bottom. It was replaced with a whites-only complex of six hundred low-rent apartments in attractive, sturdy, brick buildings.[17] The federal government had footed the bill, an experiment that would lead Congress to pass the 1937 Housing Act, expanding public housing across the country and enabling the formation of local housing authorities that governed and managed the projects. The Atlanta Housing Authority formed, took charge of Techwood, and set out to build more housing at a rapid pace. By the 1970s, Atlanta had more public housing units per capita than any other large US city.[18]

Though the federal government committed significant funding to public housing over the years, lawmakers who didn't want to create competition for the private housing market made sure the money was never really enough to consistently develop decent housing for poor families. Instead, housing authorities had to cut corners, use cheap materials, and implement cost-saving "innovations" recommended by the federal government, like elevators that stopped on every other floor. Aside from being underfunded, many local housing authorities were mismanaged, run by political appointees who lacked expertise. Housing authorities also frequently faced local opposition to public housing development and responded by locating the projects on the margins of civic life, near industrial zones, landfills, and prisons.[19]

Throughout the 1940s and '50s, the federal government offered, exclusively to white families, insured mortgages that required little or no down payment. As white people transitioned from subsidized apartments in cities to subsidized houses in suburbs, black and brown people took their place. When the demographics of public housing began to shift from predominantly white to predominantly people of color, these conditions became fodder for derision. And it was the residents who were stigmatized, not the lawmakers and agencies that neglected public housing.[20]

In the 1960s, a new narrative emerged in the mainstream media, one that negatively linked public housing with race, welfare dependency, and crime. In this narrative, public housing residents were either criminals or helpless victims, a portrayal that totally ignored a long and rich legacy of tenants developing meaningful community ties and organizing for better living conditions.[21] In a 1976 presidential campaign rally, Ronald Reagan capitalized on this stereotype when he introduced the character of the "welfare queen," a black, single mother who he claimed lived in public housing and used false names to cheat the government out of thousands of dollars in welfare checks. The person Reagan described did not actually exist, and Reagan did not make it to the White House that year, but the welfare queen became a powerful symbol, one that Reagan continued to exploit with increasing success as an economic downturn prompted people to seek an explanation for their troubles and settle on Reagan's simplistic, fabricated scapegoat.[22]

When Reagan became president in 1981, he had already laid the ideological groundwork for massive budget cuts to the Department of Housing and Urban Development (HUD), the federal agency responsible for public housing. In his first budget, Reagan raised the rents of public housing tenants, drastically scaled back new public housing construction, and cut funding for upkeep of existing units. The Atlanta Housing Authority (AHA) was already struggling when Reagan was elected. In 1980, the Techwood and Clark Howell Homes projects alone had about ten thousand code violations. By 1987, AHA found itself with six hundred unlivable units in need of major repair and no rehabilitation funds.[23]

Reagan's professed alternative to public housing was Section 8 vouchers, a program created under Richard Nixon that offered low-income families a subsidy they could use to obtain market-rate housing from private landlords. In Atlanta, as in many cities, that essentially translated to subsidizing slumlords. In 1987, a full one-third of Atlanta's rental housing stock was woefully substandard. Even this program

Reagan cut, so that by the end of the 1980s, seven thousand people were on the waiting list for section 8 vouchers in Atlanta, and ten thousand more were homeless.[24] The homeless, Reagan claimed, were in dire straits due to their own personal failings. "They make it their own choice for staying out there . . . on the grates or the lawn," he told an *ABC News* reporter in 1988.[25]

While the fate of public housing in Atlanta rested largely with the federal government, the city's elected officials did not make much effort to improve the lives of impoverished residents. In 1982, Andrew Young, a close collaborator of Martin Luther King Jr. and a former congressman, replaced Maynard Jackson as mayor. Young's politics had transformed since the days of the civil rights movement. As mayor of Atlanta, one *Washington Post* reporter observed, Young "made rich white people feel good again 15 years after transition to black government."[26] Young was decidedly more pro-business than his predecessor and focused on development projects that were popular among his corporate supporters. A city councilman who headed a "slumlord commission" formed in response to a deadly 1985 apartment fire declared, "I don't think housing is a real priority of the city. Not compared with the sexy projects." Those included a multimillion-dollar effort to revitalize a downtown entertainment district at the behest of the business group Central Atlanta Progress, the same group that had orchestrated the construction of the interstate through black neighborhoods decades earlier. CAP also influenced Young to subsidize developers to build middle- and upper-income housing in downtown Atlanta, in the midst of an affordable-housing crisis.

Meanwhile, the housing authority director Young appointed had to return $3.5 million in construction funds to the federal government in 1987 (at the same time that the housing authority sorely lacked for rehab money) after failing to obtain a site for a new public housing development. "Everything we've tried in Atlanta has turned to gold except housing," Young lamented. City councilman Bill Campbell suggested that perhaps that was because the administration hadn't tried very hard, describing the city's approach to affordable housing as "a hodgepodge of volunteer efforts and a few city-sponsored projects that are marked with incompetence and mismanagement and outright fraud."[27]

Campbell would successfully run for mayor in 1992 and usher in a dramatically different era for public housing, before eventually facing federal corruption charges himself. During Campbell's reign, the Atlanta Housing Authority wouldn't solve the problems plaguing public housing by rebuilding the social safety net that Young had largely ignored. Instead, it would place that responsibility squarely in the realm of the private sector. This was in keeping with national trends. Just as *A Nation at Risk* had shrilly declared a crisis in public education, a growing chorus of policymakers and pundits were deeming public housing an absolute failure rather than a vital resource in need of better stewardship. Privatization was increasingly the policy position of both liberals and conservatives in response to these dual alarms. As cities and states across the nation embarked down the twin paths of education and housing reform, in Atlanta, the wholesale remaking of the two would collide into one big opportunity for private companies to profit from the longtime suffering of black communities.

| | | | | | | | | | | | | |

"Can you believe this?" Lisa asked. "Sixty-nine percent of classes at Dunbar were flagged for high erasures."

"So they're saying that someone changed the answers?" I responded.

It was February 2010, my second semester as a fifth-grade teacher, and Lisa and I were poring over the latest *Journal-Constitution* article about suspicious CRCT scores. This one was a bombshell. Reporters Heather Vogell and John Perry had reported the results of an erasure analysis of the state's 2009 CRCT scores. The Governor's Office of Student Achievement had requested the analysis from CTB/McGraw-Hill, creator of the CRCT and one of the largest providers of textbooks and standardized testing materials in the world (and one of ALEC's major funders). The company used a statistical method called "standard deviation" to plot the average number of wrong-to-right erasures for each class on a graph and measure how far the outliers were from the norm. In a typical distribution, more than 99 percent of results are expected to fall within three standard deviations of the norm.[28]

CTB/McGraw-Hill's findings were momentous. One in five Georgia schools had classes flagged for an abnormally high number of wrong-to-right erasures. That included fifty-eight schools in APS, about 69 percent of elementary and middle schools in the district. That was higher than any other district, though Dougherty County, in southwestern Georgia, wasn't far behind.[29]

Governor Perdue ordered every district where schools had 11 percent or more classrooms flagged—191 schools statewide—to conduct investigations. Another 178 schools would face extra monitoring when testing time rolled around in the spring. Though Dunbar was high on the list, there was surprisingly little conversation about it at school, nor was there much talk about meeting AYP and district targets that year. When testing time rolled around, everything was closely scrutinized. A state monitor, instead of a coordinator appointed by Principal Greene, oversaw the process. No one was summoned to erase stray marks, and no Dunbar staff or administrators were alone with the tests.

The same week that article was published, another *Journal-Constitution* reporter followed up on the state's probe into the 2008 CRCT retests—the one that had led to the arrest of two DeKalb County school administrators, James Berry and Doretha Alexander, the previous summer. The Georgia Professional Standards Commission, which licenses teachers, ended up banning thirteen educators from schools in four counties for at least ninety days. Berry and Alexander were banned for two years and one year, respectively. They also faced criminal charges for falsifying a state document. Berry pleaded guilty and received two years of probation and a $1,000 fine, while Alexander was required to complete forty hours of community service. They were the first Georgia educators to ever face criminal charges that stemmed from cheating on a test, as the state had no law explicitly prohibiting it. The DeKalb district attorney who indicted Berry and Alexander was hailed as "creative" for applying the charges that he did.[30]

To make it easier for prosecutors to bring charges, Perdue and his right-hand woman, GOSA director Kathleen Mathers, introduced a bill during the 2010 Georgia legislative session that would make cheating on a test a misdemeanor punishable by thirty days in jail and a $1,000 fine. The law, they said, was necessary to deter the rampant cheating that in their view had obviously plagued the 2009 CRCT. Stunningly, as the bill was pending and school district investigations were kicking off, Mathers and Perdue headed to Washington to promote their application for a $400 million federal education grant, touting the 2009 test scores as proof that the state was making improvements. For all the tough talk they were doing at home, they made little mention to the grant committee in DC that they believed the test scores to be illegitimate. It was like the pot calling the kettle black, but no one seemed to notice their hypocrisy.

The grant they applied for was from Race to the Top, President Obama's $4 billion education initiative overseen by Secretary of Education Arne Duncan. The program offered states huge grants to advance education reforms, including data-driven teaching, charter schools, and tying teacher evaluations and pay to student test scores. Even though Obama had promised to overhaul No Child Left Behind during his presidential campaign, his administration was doubling down on the most problematic aspect of Bush's education regime: high-stakes testing.[31]

Duncan, for his part, was already well versed in the world of corporate education reform when he began shaping Obama's education agenda. When he was appointed superintendent of Chicago Public Schools in 2001, Duncan likened education to a business, and he then presided over sweeping layoffs, closing and reopening dozens of schools under new management, and shutting down public schools and replacing them with charter schools. Like Rob Paige, Houston's school superintendent turned Bush-era education secretary, and Beverly Hall in Atlanta, Duncan created a bonus system to reward teachers for improved student test scores. In the end, test scores in Chicago's schools were stagnant, while graduation rates increased incrementally. Regardless, Duncan sang the praises of such reforms, often with an obvious tone-deafness to racial issues. Several years after the federal government left black communities to perish in the wake of Hurricane Katrina, Duncan said that the storm was "the best thing that ever happened to the education system in New Orleans" because it enabled the state to take over the city's public schools and convert almost all of them to charters.[32] After the storm, more than seven thousand school employees, most of them black, were fired without due process, and many teachers were replaced with white TFA recruits.[33]

Now Duncan was dangling billions of dollars in front of states that could prove they had started down a similar path. And the money was badly needed. The country was in the depths of a recession, and schools everywhere were slashing programs and laying off staff to contend with severe budget shortfalls. In Georgia, the problem of plummeting tax revenues was compounded by years of Perdue's austerity cuts. In the spring of 2010, Beverly Hall announced that the upcoming Atlanta Public Schools budget would be 11 percent below what it was before the Perdue cuts began. Even Georgia's education superintendent, Kathy Cox, a Perdue ally, acknowledged that the state's education system was facing "a category 5 crisis."[34]

The application that Perdue, Mathers, and Cox put together noted many things underway in Georgia that aligned with the goals of Race to the Top—a new teacher evaluation system in the making, pro-charter laws on the books, and a "rapid rise" in CRCT scores in just a few years' time. The latter, they said, was due to "higher standards" and "harder assessments," accompanied by "effective professional development for teachers." The application didn't mention that 20 percent of the schools in Georgia were flagged for high numbers of wrong-to-right erasures on the CRCT.[35]

While Perdue, Mathers and their colleagues were lying their way toward a multimillion-dollar payout, I was considering a career change. That semester, one of my students had been assigned a counselor who sometimes visited my class to see how he interacted with his peers. We would talk after class, and she told me how she helped the boy and his siblings by advocating for them in the juvenile court system. She made sure they were being provided for at home and that they had the resources they needed to be successful. I told her, "I would love to find out more about your job." She gave me her card and told me to call her when I was ready to apply at the counseling agency where she worked. I decided to apply to several counseling agencies. I thought it would give me a chance to gain experience related to my bachelor's degree in psychology and to address some of the problems my students came to school with that I just wasn't in a position to change as a teacher.

In May, I got a call from one of the counseling agencies where I had applied. They wanted me to come in for an interview. I had to decide whether to continue teaching or embark on a new journey in the mental health field. If I stuck with teaching, I would have second graders next year; Principal Greene was moving me again. I was glad to have the option of teaching younger children, and I would be able to avoid the CRCT altogether, as the state was phasing out testing first and second graders, whose scores never counted toward the metrics anyway. But I ultimately went with my gut feeling and decided to go to the interview. I got the job on the spot and resigned from teaching shortly after.

I started working with teenagers in a therapeutic camp that summer and loved it. I also reconnected with Moses, who had lent my TFA friends and me the money to create our talk-show pilot a year earlier. He sent me a message on Facebook asking if we were going to give the show another try. Later he told me that was a pretense to eventually ask me on a date. Moses had tried to date me before, once when we were just kids and again the summer after our freshman year in college. But his timing was always off. This time I was ready for him, so I accepted his invitation for a night on the town with dancing to live music.

We went to a popular restaurant in Atlanta's upscale Buckhead neighborhood. He tried to warn me in the car that he wasn't much of a dancer. That was an understatement. When he took me out on the dance floor, it was clear that dancing was not his best attribute, but I thought it was cute that he was willing to step out of his comfort zone and embarrass himself. We enjoyed each other's company so much that we went out on a few more dates and realized that we had a lot in common. We found out that our fathers knew each other when they were in college back in the 1970s. One day I drove him through the first neighborhood where I lived as a kid, in Decatur, before my family moved to Stone Mountain. He told me he had lived in the same neighborhood and showed me where his house was. We had lived in the same neighborhood twice and didn't even know it. I couldn't believe he had been right under my nose this whole time.

As our romance flourished, I was cutting my teeth at my new job, and it was challenging. A lot of the teens I worked with were in foster care, and many had experienced the horrors of verbal and sexual abuse, suicidal thoughts, abandonment, and homelessness. Their families were living in poverty, and though they once might have at least had the assurance of a roof over their head in a public housing apartment, that era was over. By the summer of 2010, all of Atlanta's public housing complexes had been demolished.

⸻

Fireworks woke the city on the morning of September 18, 1990 as cheering throngs packed the pavement around Underground Atlanta in the heart of downtown. The president of the International Olympic Committee (IOC) had made the announcement from Tokyo, just shy of 8 a.m. Atlanta time, that the city to host the bicentennial Olympic Games in 1996 would not be Athens, as expected. It would be Atlanta.

An unlikely contender, Atlanta had been thrust into the bidding process by Billy Payne, a real estate lawyer and inveterate city booster, whose overpowering enthusiasm seemed to have carried the underdog across the finish line. Later would come revelations that the IOC was bought off with gifts of antiques, fine china, and a trip to Disney World.[36]

On that September morning, though, the celebration was unsullied by scandal and the sense of possibility was limitless, especially for those who saw what urban policy professor Harvey Newman would describe as "an opportunity for redevelopment on a scale not seen in Atlanta since General Sherman's departure in 1864."[37] Among the opportunists were Coca-Cola executives who had long desired to get rid of Techwood and Clark Howell Homes, public housing projects located blocks away from the international corporation's downtown Atlanta headquarters. When Techwood and Clark Howell desegregated in 1968, Coke's CEO lamented that with black people moving in "the felony rate would triple," and he teamed up with Central Atlanta Progress to pressure Mayor Maynard Jackson to demolish the apartments. But the mayor had held the powerful businessmen at bay.[38]

Now Jackson was mayor again, having run for a noncontiguous third term after Andrew Young's two-term tenure during the 1980s. This time, Atlanta's status in the global limelight was at stake. Olympic Village, housing for athletes, was slated for construction on the Georgia Tech campus, right next door to the housing projects, which had suffered years of neglect. Jackson agreed that improvements to Techwood and Clark Howell were necessary, and he assembled a committee to plan a massive rehab. The planning process was still underway in 1992 when Congress passed legislation creating HOPE VI, a program that made grants available to local housing authorities to remove and replace their most distressed properties. Jackson's committee submitted a proposal for a $40 million rehab of Techwood and Clark Howell, which HUD approved shortly before the mayoral election of 1993.[39]

Bill Campbell, the former city councilman who criticized Young's handling of the affordable-housing crisis, won the election, and one of his campaign aides, Renee Glover, took over the Atlanta Housing Authority. She immediately began to retool the Techwood proposal with a new vision that went far beyond rehabbing a few properties. Glover wanted a widespread transformation that would simultaneously downsize and privatize public housing.

Glover was among a group of advisors to President Bill Clinton's new HUD secretary, Henry Cisneros, who were enthralled with the burgeoning New Urbanism movement.[40] This school of thought rejected suburban sprawl in favor of traditional neighborhood design and "mixed use" development. Many New Urbanists believed that certain structural elements could encourage positive social behaviors. Some even argued that the built environment of public housing projects discouraged positive behaviors, a theory that reduced complicated social issues into an improbably simple matter of design.[41] At the same time, some sociologists were denouncing public housing for "concentrating poverty" into isolated areas where poor people were cut off from "the mainstream."[42]

Glover and Cisneros married these ideas with the neoliberal notion that the free market is more efficient than government. The result was a goal to "deconcentrate poverty" by hiring developers to raze public housing projects and replace them with privately managed, mixed-income housing in the New Urbanist style. They believed that this approach would go beyond providing housing for poor people and propel them into the middle class. Underlying their vision was the assumption that poverty is the result of personal failings, as Reagan asserted, and that many people with these imagined personal failings living in a community together create a self-perpetuating "culture of poverty."

Ignored were the systemic barriers to building wealth that poor people, especially poor black people, faced. In 1988, an *Atlanta Journal-Constitution* investigation found that lending institutions discriminated heavily against black would-be-homeowners, making five times more loans to whites throughout the 1980s. Unable to purchase homes, black Atlantans faced discrimination in the rental market as well; in 1990, 60 percent of black people in the city paid excessive rent, compared to 40 percent of their white counterparts.[43] These challenges piled onto existing crises in black communities that fell outside of anyone's personal control.

To accomplish their mission, Cisneros lobbied Congress to lift a rule requiring public housing authorities to replace all demolished units with an equal number of new ones. Congress suspended the requirement in 1995, and Glover was ready with a proposal to tear down the 1,195 stately brick apartments and row houses of Techwood and Clark Howell and build 900 new units called Centennial Place, of which only 360 would be reserved for public housing residents.[44]

Glover contracted with two development firms: Integral, based in Atlanta, and McCormick Baron Salazar, a St. Louis company whose co-founder worked with Glover and Cisneros to shape the HUD reforms. These firms would manage Centennial Place, exacting hefty fees from AHA, when it was completed.[45]

Glover also worked closely with Norman Johnson, a Georgia Tech administrator and APS board member whose mission was to reconstitute Fowler Elementary, the school that served Techwood and Clark Howell. Johnson's view of the struggling school mirrored Glover's view of public housing. He argued that the entire staff should be fired and the school rebuilt and renamed so that teachers couldn't return with a "culture of low expectations." He maintained that poor students needed to be around middle-class students for the same reason their parents supposedly needed middle-class neighbors.[46]

However, low-income students were not ultimately the intended beneficiaries of the school remodeling, which, according to Integral founder and CEO Egbert Perry, served as an "anchor for the long-term financial strategy [of the housing redevelopment]."[47] The new school was meant to attract middle-class families to Centennial Place and the surrounding neighborhood. This was critical for the developers. They were banking on the redevelopment of public housing setting off a chain reaction of gentrification that they could mine for greater profits in the future.[48]

This quickly became a template that was replicated in other parts of Atlanta. Legendary developer Tom Cousins, who had contributed to the displacement of black communities during the urban renewal era with his Omni Hotel project, and who had wielded an outsized influence on Atlanta's government as a leading member of Central Atlanta Progress, began courting Glover's favor in 1993 when he bought a struggling golf club near a public housing project in Atlanta's East Lake neighborhood. Cousins hoped to restore the club to its former glory. It had been a resort for wealthy white people until AHA built a complex of brick garden apartments and duplexes called East Lake Meadows next door, prompting club members to decamp to the suburbs.

Cousins created a nonprofit called the East Lake Foundation to turn East Lake Meadows into mixed-income housing.[49] Glover cosigned and handed the property over to the foundation to redevelop with a $32.5 million HOPE VI grant. Cousins raised additional funding from the golf club's steep membership fees ($250,000 a head), reaping big tax breaks for his real estate company and club patrons in the process.[50] Glover announced the plan in 1995 and met pushback from the residents, with good reason. The plan called for a reduction of units, from 650 to 542, only half of which would be subsidized.[51]

In response to the outcry, Cousins hired Shirley Franklin to try to quell the unrest among tenants. Franklin was a political insider who, after working for both the Young and Jackson administrations, had started a private consulting firm. The tenants fought the plan in court but lost, and by 1999 East Lake Meadows had become the Villages of East Lake.[52]

At the Villages of East Lake, paternalistic theories about poverty were manifested in heightened levels of social control. There were strict rules for subsidized tenants that limited visitors (including romantic partners and family members), discouraged "hanging out" with neighbors, imposed a dusk curfew on children and teens, and required adults to be employed, regardless of their ability to pay rent. Still, Cousins complained that public housing residents had "inherent problems" and lamented that there was an even mix of subsidized and market-rate tenants. He told a congressional commission in 2001 that 70 percent market-rate would be ideal, since developers need to make higher profits.[53]

Like the Techwood and Clark Howell redevelopment, the East Lake plan included taking over the local elementary school to pave the way for gentrification. Greg Giornelli, founding director of the East Lake Foundation and son-in-law of Tom Cousins, said the school plan was "consistent with the effort to lure middle-class residents back to the city."[54] Drew Charter School, which opened in 2000, became the city's first charter school. Cousins acclaimed it as "a way to ensure the [East Lake] apartment community's market rate units are in demand."[55]

By the turn of the millennium, the redevelopment of Techwood and Clark Howell, East Lake Meadows, and both schools was complete, and few of the original residents remained. At Centennial Place only 78 families returned out of the 1,128 that had resided at Techwood and Clark Howell in 1990.[56] At the Villages of East Lake, between 70 and 80 out of 400 families came back.[57] Displacement wasn't only a problem for public housing residents. The East Lake redevelopment sparked a steep uptick in property values throughout the neighborhood—20 percent each year in the first five years following the project's completion—gradually pushing out lower-income black people and resulting in an influx of wealthier whites. Between 1995 and 2006, the average household income in the East Lake Neighborhood spiked 477 percent.[58]

Proponents of the East Lake model cited falling crime rates, climbing employment numbers, and improving student test scores, claiming that these outcomes amounted to neighborhood revitalization. In reality, what took place was a neighborhood replacement. The statistics didn't reflect improvements in the lives of low-income black people; they represented the wealthier, mostly white people who supplanted them.

This new model for privatizing public housing and public schools in one neat package created a boon for the real estate and education industries, which were becoming increasingly entwined. In 2000, Mark Riley, a former vice president at Cousins Properties, launched his own development firm, Urban Realty Partners, and then ran for the board of APS in 2001, telling voters that schools are "an extension of business interests working on revitalization of intown areas."[59] Backed by the Metro Atlanta Chamber of Commerce, Riley won a seat on the board, where he would oversee an era of charter school expansion fueled not only by his votes but also by the pro-charter philanthropy of a foundation he directed and the political lobbying of the Georgia Charter Schools Association, where he later held a board position. In 2002, Riley's Urban Realty Partners was selected by AHA to redevelop two public housing projects, Grady Homes and Capitol Homes, into mixed-income complexes.[60]

Riley exemplified a trend: real estate developers, bankers, and corporate executives began filling the boards of charter schools and nonprofits that funded charter schools, sometimes cycling between corporations, philanthropic foundations, and elected office, where they pushed pro-charter policies amenable to their business pursuits.

After the East Lake Meadows redevelopment was complete, Cousins focused on making sure Atlanta's administration remained friendly to developers by cochairing Shirley Franklin's campaign for mayor. Franklin won, enabling Glover, the AHA director, to continue transforming public housing into a private, profit-driven enterprise.

Glover went on to garner HOPE VI funding from the federal government to tear down Atlanta's public housing at a rapid pace. By 2004, AHA had knocked down seventeen thousand units of public housing. Only 17 percent of residents were able to return and live in the mixed-income developments that replaced them.[61] At that point, many cities had followed in Atlanta's footsteps and were using the HOPE VI program to do away with public housing, even though it had originally been intended to replace a small portion, 6 percent, of the nation's public housing that was truly dilapidated.[62]

In 2007, the year I started teaching, Glover announced that the remainder of Atlanta's public housing, ten projects, would be demolished and replaced with mixed-income developments by 2010. Atlanta would come full circle, from being the first city in the nation to build public housing to being the first city to destroy all of it.

In the spring of 2010, as the school year ended and I began my new job as a counselor, excavators clawed down the sturdy brick walls of Thomasville Heights, home to three victims of the Atlanta child murders, and the last public housing project in Atlanta to be razed. That year, there were five thousand people on AHA's waiting list for housing vouchers; many of them had been on the list for nine years.[63]

As property values skyrocketed in areas where public housing dwindled and charter schools proliferated, it became clear that whatever varied purposes public education had served over time, in Atlanta it increasingly had a singularly powerful function: to drive the real estate market.

||||||||||||||

I spent the summer of 2010 settling into my new job and whiling away humid evenings with my new boyfriend, Moses. Sonny Perdue and Kathleen Mathers were still gunning for the Race to the Top grant using the faulty test scores. And APS was trying to dispel cheating allegations once and for all.

The school board had assembled a "blue-ribbon commission," largely made up of corporate executives, to conduct an independent investigation into the 2009 test scores. But the probe was hardly impartial. Shortly after GOSA publicized its audit of the 2009 test scores the previous February, the head of the Metro Atlanta Chamber of Commerce, Sam Williams, had distributed a memo pledging support for Beverly Hall and dictating what the APS response would be, including who should compose the commission. He chose executives from companies that had received millions of dollars in contracts from APS over the years as well as individuals who had been active in the chamber's political action committee, created to back school board candidates, and a foundation established by chamber members to channel philanthropic dollars to the school district.[64]

On August 2, the commission released its findings: cheating had only been pervasive at twelve schools, where 109 employees were implicated, and there was no evidence of district-wide coordination. Perdue deemed the investigation "woefully inadequate," and on August 19 he stunned the city by commencing a state investigation into cheating within APS. Investigators would additionally look into cheating in Dougherty County, the district with the second highest percentage of schools implicated, which had also handed in an internal probe the governor deemed insufficient. Within days, Perdue appointed former

DeKalb County district attorney Bob Wilson and former attorney general Mike Bowers to lead the investigation. They would have the Georgia Bureau of Investigation agents at their disposal, and Perdue would shell out $2.2 million for their work. The pair appointed Richard Hyde, an investigator who worked for Bowers's law firm, to take a lead role. Hyde had been an Atlanta beat cop during the era of the child murders—he told *Atlanta Magazine* that he patrolled an area of Southwest Atlanta where residents thought the killer was a cop. Hyde chose to start the cheating investigation at Venetian Hills elementary in Southwest Atlanta, where Angel Lenair, one of the murder victims, had been a student. [65]

Less than a week after the investigation launched, Perdue called another press conference, this time to announce that the state had won $400 million in Race to the Top funding. "We are going to use this $400 million to literally show what we can do in transforming education," he said, explaining that local school districts would use the money to improve test scores. Perdue made no mention of having used the inflated 2009 test scores to win the grant.[66]

At this point I wasn't following the news about the cheating scandal, but it would catch up to me soon. On an afternoon in October, I was at home, typing behavioral-health notes for clients I had seen the previous day, when the phone rang. I answered and was greeted by an unfamiliar male voice.

"This is agent Rocky Bigham with the Georgia Bureau of Investigations. I'd like to talk with you about CRCT testing at Dunbar Elementary. Are you available to meet today? I'm in your area. We could just have a quick conversation at South DeKalb Mall if that's convenient for you."

In my area? That seemed strange. I had never been approached by a law enforcement officer before, and while I perhaps should have had my hackles up, I was too curious. Besides, I thought, I didn't have anything to hide. What could it hurt? Maybe I would find out what all the fuss was about this cheating scandal.

"Sure," I said, "I can meet you there in half an hour."

CHAPTER FOUR

Pushing the Envelope

■│││││││││││││││││││││■

I FIDGETED WITH MY CAR STEREO as I sat parked near the mall entrance, watching people trickle in and out beneath the trio of awnings crowned by blocky yellow letters that read "Gallery at South DeKalb." The spot was both iconic and mundane—an Atlanta landmark where on any given day you could catch rapper Gucci Mane signing CDs or renew your driver's license. I usually went to the mall for the cute clothes on sale at Macy's. Now instead of rummaging through a rack of blouses, I was living out what felt like a spy movie. Growing slightly nervous, I scanned the parking lot. Agent Bigham had called again shortly after I arrived to find out where exactly I was in the massive parking lot. I expected a sleek, dark Crown Vic with Georgia Bureau Investigation (GBI) insignia to pull up any minute.

A group of teenagers ambled past in a tight cluster, jostling each other and laughing as one of them danced for a quick second on the way inside. The last boy in the group held the heavy glass door open for a stooped, elderly woman exiting with shopping bags hanging on the handles of her walker. As I watched her inch toward the blue benches by the curb, a plain white sedan cruised slowly past her and turned into the aisle where I was parked, pulling into the empty spot on my left. Inside the vehicle were a man and a woman, both young and white, dressed in nondescript business casual outfits.

The woman got out of the passenger side and, without looking at me, switched to the backseat. The man had emerged from the driver side and motioned me to come toward him, saying, "Shani?" "Yes," I replied, stepping out of my Nissan SUV and making my way around the hood of his car. We shook hands and he showed me his badge, the only thing indicating that he was a GBI agent.

"Would you mind sitting in the car while I ask you some questions?"

"Not at all," I responded.

Once I was sitting in front where the woman had been and he was back in the driver's seat, Agent Bigham explained straightforwardly that there had been an erasure analysis of the 2009 CRCT for the entire state of Georgia. He said that in my class there was a statistically improbable number of answers changed from wrong to right on each section of the test.

"Can you explain this?" he asked, his eyes locked on mine.

"No," I said. "I can't explain that."

He paused for a beat and cracked a half smile. "Why did you quit teaching?" he ventured.

I explained to him that as a Teach for America teacher I had only committed to two years at Dunbar but had decided to stay a third year before I was offered a job at a counseling agency. He asked me if I still talked to the teachers at Dunbar, and I told him that Lisa had been the only person I'd been in contact with lately.

Narrowing his eyes, Bingham continued, "When your students were done testing, you took your tests to the computer lab, right? And some other teachers were there, is that correct? What was going on in that computer lab?"

"We erased stray marks because the children wrote all over the test booklets," I told him.

"Did you know you didn't have to erase stray marks on those tests?" he asked. I was taken aback. Was that true?

"No," I said. "I was told the marks would cause errors when a machine graded the tests."

Bigham continued to pepper me with questions, and all the while the woman sat silently behind me, apparently taking notes. Who else was in the computer lab? First- and second-grade teachers and the testing coordinator, Lera Middlebrooks. Did you ever receive bonus money for high test scores? No. Have you ever reported any testing problems to your superiors? No. Did Principal Greene or Middlebrooks pressure you to change answers on the test? No. Did you witness anyone changing answers on the test? No. Did you change answers on the test? No!

Then Bigham's tone softened slightly as he explained that investigators didn't plan on sending teachers to jail. As I recall, he said that children were cheated out of educational opportunities and he was just trying to get to the bottom of what happened. With that, he looked at me expectantly and implored me to tell the truth, assuring me that I wouldn't get in trouble. But I had already told him the truth.

I tried to mask my exasperation with a heightened politeness, repeating all the details I could remember from those twenty minutes, over a year ago, in the Dunbar computer lab. Bigham's exasperation was not as guarded. In a huff, he procured a form and tersely asked me to sign it, a statement that I had no knowledge about cheating on the 2009 CRCT. Then he gave me his card and asked me to call him if I remembered anything else.

As I drove home, I felt unsettled. I had assumed that Bigham wanted to talk with me to glean information on other suspects, not to interrogate me as if I had done something wrong. As I replayed our conversation in my mind, I realized I was approaching a street that I recognized. It was the street where Pamela Cleveland lived. She was one of the older Dunbar teachers who I liked, who erased stray marks with Diane Buckner-Webb, Rose Neal, and me in the computer lab. I had been to Cleveland's house once before, to pick up some classroom supplies from her garage. I hadn't seen her since the end-of-year staff celebration at a restaurant last May. On an impulse, I turned onto her street and slowed down, looking at each house to see if I could pick hers out. Halfway down the block I saw her car in a driveway and pulled in.

"Robinson!" she exclaimed when she answered the door. She was startled to see me on her porch, but she gave me a big hug and invited me in.

"I was just interrogated by a GBI agent about the CRCT," I told her as we sat down in her living room. "I thought I would stop by on my way home and see if you've heard anything about this. What is going on?"

Cleveland told me that the investigators had come to Dunbar earlier that day to interview some of the teachers. And, prior to that, she had been interviewed by some investigators from the APS blue-ribbon commission, whose report Perdue had called "woefully inadequate." From her description, it sounded like she had been asked similar questions, but she didn't know any more than I did about how the test scores got so high or where this whole ordeal was going. Like me, she was disconcerted. "But I guess there's no point in worrying too much about it," she said. We chatted for a little while, catching up on our families and the latest happenings at Dunbar before I got up to leave. I asked Cleveland to keep me informed if she heard anything else about the GBI investigation, and I told her I would do the same.

I didn't hear anything for a while, and, as fall turned to winter, a different story was making the news. The gubernatorial election was in full swing, Sonny Perdue had reached his term limit, and Republican US representative Nathan Deal was running to replace him. Deal, who had held a congressional seat for eighteen years, resigned in the spring of 2010, just as the Office of Congressional Ethics was launching an investigation into his finances. He claimed that his bid for governor was his reason for stepping down. While that thwarted the congressional investigation, the FBI was not deterred from opening its own probe into Deal's business operations.

For years, Deal had apparently been reaping hundreds of thousands of taxpayer dollars through a company he owned that had a monopoly on mandatory, state-funded title inspections of salvaged cars. When a commissioner attempted to eliminate title inspection funding from the state budget, Deal allegedly strong-armed state officials into keeping it. As the scheme came to light, Deal appeared to siphon off campaign funds to pay for his legal defense. By October 2010, as I encountered the GBI for the first time, the State Ethics Commission was launching a probe into Deal's campaign finances and sharing information with federal prosecutors and the FBI.[1] Regardless of his hypocrisy in railing against government spending while fighting tooth and nail to keep his own publicly funded racket going, and despite being the subject of both a federal and state investigation, Deal won the election.

Aside from Deal's campaign, the midterm election season served as something of a referendum on President Obama's education agenda and the corporate education reform movement writ large. Candidates facing midterm elections in numerous states squared off against opponents of Race to the Top and other Obama policies. And in Washington, DC, Mayor Adrian Fenty lost his bid for reelection in part because of the backlash to drastic reforms carried out by the school chancellor he appointed, Michelle Rhee. A Teach for America alum, Rhee founded a TFA spinoff called the New Teacher Project before she was tapped to run DC's schools. Over three years, she drew heavily on the corporate education reform handbook, shuttering traditional schools, approving charters, tying teacher evaluations to student test scores, and so forth, all with a flair that made her a media darling. Time magazine featured her on its cover, defiantly holding a broom as if to sweep out the "bad teachers" a subhead alluded to. But Rhee's reforms drew the ire of teachers and parents alike, and, when Fenty lost the election, she resigned. But she did not retreat. Instead Rhee founded an organization called StudentsFirst and said she would raise $1 billion to advocate for her brand of education reforms nationwide. She would soon make her mark on Georgia, where Deal was picking up where his predecessor had left off.[2]

As soon as Deal was inaugurated in January 2011, he followed through on a promise to cut state spending, starting with the State Ethics Commission, where he eliminated the jobs of the officials who were investigating him. Then he turned his attention to education, where he followed in Perdue's footsteps and even outpaced him. In his first few years in office, Deal would underfund K–12 education by an average of $1 billion per year, forcing local school districts to raise taxes, increase class sizes, decrease the number of school days in the year, lay off teachers, and cut arts programs, electives, and Advanced Placement classes.[3] Meanwhile he continued the investigations into the CRCT cheating, a probe that Perdue had started.

In April 2011, I got another call from the GBI. It was a different agent, a man who sounded more upbeat than Agent Bigham. This time the investigator wanted me to meet him at the headquarters of the law firm where Mike Bowers was a senior partner. Unsure whether it would be wise to refuse, I agreed to the follow-up interview.

The office of the Balch & Bingham law firm was downtown, near Centennial Olympic Park, in a building mostly taken up by the headquarters of energy giant Southern Company. I took the elevator to the seventh floor and emerged into a corridor of marble-tiled floors and polished, wood-paneled walls. I followed it to a receptionist's desk and was ushered into a spacious conference room filled with a huge table and soft, leather swivel chairs.

The friendly agent I spoke with on the phone wasn't there. Instead it was Agent Bigham again, accompanied this time by a different silent woman. Bigham's measured tone from our first encounter was gone. Now, sitting across from me and staring unyieldingly into my eyes, he attempted a bad-cop persona.

"You know, another teacher says she saw you change answers on the test," he challenged. I almost laughed, it was so preposterous. Bigham clearly was fishing for information he didn't have. I sat up straighter, cocked my head slightly, and raised my eyebrows.

"I didn't change any answers on those tests," I said, and proceeded to recount the same things that I had before.

"Who are you trying to protect?" he interjected.

"I'm not trying to protect anyone." I told him calmly.

He took a deep breath and pursed his lips together like he was disappointed in my response. "Do you know how much trouble you can get in for lying to me?" he asked.

"I guess I could go to prison if I wasn't telling the truth," I speculated.

"And you're still sticking with your same story?" he asked.

"Yes, I'm sticking to the truth," I said.

With that, Agent Bigham angrily dismissed me. The interview barely lasted fifteen minutes.

I called Cleveland as soon as I got home and told her that GBI agents had come up with a bogus story about someone claiming that they saw me change answers on the CRCT. She told me that she had decided to get a criminal defense attorney and suggested that I do the same.

"Has it really come to that?" I said in disbelief. "I've told the GBI everything that I know. It's like he was trying to force me to say I cheated."

I asked Cleveland if she could get her attorney to recommend a lawyer for me. The next day, she called me back with the office number for attorney Annette Greene. On the way to Greene's office in downtown Decatur, I kept thinking to myself, "I can't believe I have to get a *criminal* defense attorney. This is insane."

A month later, I received an unexpected call that I actually welcomed. It was from Lera Middlebrooks, the testing coordinator in 2009, inviting me to the end-of-year Dunbar staff party at her apartment. Cleveland and Lisa were the only Dunbar people I had been in touch with since leaving for my counselor job a year earlier, so I was excited for the chance to reconnect with my former coworkers. I had a great time at the party. People were dancing, drinking, and talking about their plans for the summer. Middlebrooks was her usual high-energy self, cutting up and making everyone laugh as she played hostess. At one point, she pulled me aside in the kitchen and asked me if anyone from the GBI had contacted me. I told her I had met with GBI agents twice.

"I didn't think it was that serious since they told me to meet them in a parking lot, of all places, at South DeKalb Mall," I told her. "But then the agent started interrogating me like I had done something wrong. I had to track Cleveland down to find out what was going on. I didn't know they had come to Dunbar that day too."

Middlebrooks wanted to know more about what the agents had asked.

"They asked me if you and Principal Greene put pressure on me to cheat! I told them not at all. I just think it's crazy how far this thing has gone," I said. Middlebrooks laughed and shook her head, saying that the entire ordeal would probably blow over.

I took Middlebrooks's confidence to heart. She had always seemed indomitable, someone who had been through a lot of tribulations but never lost her fire. I carried that confidence with me into the summer. Until one day it came crashing down.

It was early July. I was working from home. Again it was a phone call, this time from Cleveland.

"Have you seen the report?" Her voice sounded like she was ready to punch something.

"No, what report?" I asked.

"The GBI report about the erasures on the CRCT. Neal told them that we changed the answers." My stomach did a flip. So Bigham hadn't been lying when he told me that another teacher had accused me. But why would Neal make up a story like that?

I rushed to my computer and looked up the report. It was a staggering 828 pages long (about half was a seemingly random assortment of appendix materials), with a table of contents that listed a section for each school. I scrolled directly to the section on Dunbar and read that thirty-three teachers had been interviewed. One confessed to cheating and "described a schoolwide effort to systematically change students' answers." In a section that detailed Neal's testimony, the report read:

> Lera Middlebrooks approached Neal in 2009 and told her that she could "clean up" the tests if she wanted. Neal believed that Middlebrooks meant that she could erase and change answers. Neal erased her students' answers in the computer lab with fellow first and second grade teachers Pamela Cleveland, Shani Robinson, and Diane Webb Buckner [sic]. They all changed answers for approximately thirty minutes. Middlebrooks did not change answers but she was in the room.[4]

A wave of anger and embarrassment came over me, and I yelled every horrible name I could think to call Neal. What a fool she was to assume that "clean up the tests" meant "change the answers" and to assume that we all thought like her. Did she really believe that, or had she been stupidly frightened by Bigham's good-cop, bad-cop routine and lied to get him off her back? Later I would find out that some teachers throughout the district did use this coded language to refer to cheating. I would also learn that Neal had initially denied allegations of cheating but after multiple interrogations agreed to confess in exchange for immunity. Had she been pressured to name others to receive immunity?

I continued reading. There were summarized testimonies of six more Dunbar staff members who suspected their coworkers of cheating.

Several people implicated Gloria Ivey, the fifth-grade teacher I worked with in 2010.

Middlebrooks, Principal Greene, and a former principal were also suspected of cheating based on vague, overheard conversations and a claim that the former principal was seen pointing out correct answers to students years ago. Their testimonies and Ivey's were also included as short summaries. They all denied wrongdoing. Greene even went so far as to say that she didn't know Middlebrooks had instructed us to erase stray marks. But what about Cleveland, Buckner-Webb, and me? Our testimonies weren't there. Neither were the testimonies of the rest of the thirty-three teachers interviewed. What had they told investigators?[5]

I glanced over a chart showing the "standard deviation" for each test (reading, math, and language arts) in each flagged classroom. Standard deviation was a calculation that the original GOSA erasure analysis had used to determine how much a class's wrong-to-right erasures diverged from the norm. A standard deviation of 3 had only a 1 in 370 chance of happening by coincidence. All classes with a standard deviation higher than 3 were flagged as suspicious. In my class, the standard deviation for each test ranged from 11.79 to 13.48. The highest standard deviation at Dunbar was more than 25; that was on the special education teacher's fifth-grade reading tests. There were several other teachers on that chart with high standard deviations who weren't ultimately implicated by the GBI because investigators didn't find evidence of cheating beyond the dubious standard deviation. It seemed that Rose Neal's testimony had tipped the scale in my case.[6]

How, I wondered, did Neal purport that we had changed the answers? Didn't investigators find it improbable that we could each read all three tests, determine the correct answers, and change the wrong answers of at least fifteen students in a short amount of time? Not to mention the fact that it took time to write in our students' demographic information.

As I moved on from the Dunbar section and attempted to digest the rest of the report, I read allegations about other schools that were much worse. There were stories of principals who threatened teachers' jobs if they didn't raise test scores, and one principal who allegedly ordered a teacher to crawl under a desk during a staff meeting as a humiliating punishment. Nothing like that ever happened at Dunbar as far as I knew. At Parks Middle School, which had the highest percentage of flagged classrooms in both the district and the state, staff apparently took dramatic measures to cheat. One teacher confessed to slicing open shrink-wrapped test booklets with a razor and later resealing the plastic with a lighter. The district administration, investigators said, likely knew cheating was happening and may have tried to cover it up. There were numerous stories of people who tried to report cheating only to face retaliation from their higher-ups. An informant accused a top administrative official, Millicent Few, of ordering the destruction of early versions of the report produced by Penn Payne, the lawyer APS hired during the summer of 2009 to investigate suspected cheating on the 2008 CRCT retests at Deerwood Elementary. Officials allegedly rejected Payne's original findings and crafted their own version of the report while Few had the incriminating documents destroyed.[7]

I was growing more alarmed the more I read. There was clearly serious misconduct going on, and my name was now wrongfully tied up in it.

Altogether investigators found that cheating had occurred in forty-four schools. One hundred seventy-eight educators were allegedly involved in cheating, and eighty-two had confessed.[8] Investigators concluded that the root of the cheating outbreak, which they dated back to 2001, was Hall. According to the report, "A culture of fear and a conspiracy of silence infected this school system" because of the high pressure to meet targets, which Hall articulated as "no exceptions, no excuses." But I had heard that saying before I ever worked for APS. "No excuses" was the mantra of Teach for America and so many other school districts that had come under the influence of the education reform movement that advocated for running schools like corporations. And, of course, cheating on standardized tests in APS predated Hall becoming superintendent and the district introducing targets; there had been allegations of cheating in many of Georgia's school districts all through the 1990s when the state's "pay for performance" program rewarded teachers for high scores. But that bit of context was missing from the report.

The report blasted Hall for other practices that were the hallmarks of the corporate education reform movement as if they were her own cruel inventions. I kept waiting for the report to lambast No Child Left Behind, but according to investigators, only Hall and the targets were at fault. The report seemed to imply that Hall had come up with the targets herself, never mentioning the staff and consultants who crunched the numbers or the fact that the school board had the ultimate authority to approve them.[9]

After almost an hour of reading, I turned my attention from the report itself to the news. Nathan Deal had announced the findings in a press conference in which he bemoaned how students were harmed and "taxpayers were cheated."[10] *He should know!* I thought. Mayor Kasim Reed released a statement saying that it was "a dark day for the Atlanta Public School System."[11] Their somber reactions set the tone for much of the news coverage in the days that followed, which depicted those of us indicted in the report as criminals who were "cheating our children."

There were a few skeptical voices in the crowd. In an interview with the *Journal-Constitution*, former DeKalb County district attorney J. Tom Morgan said that he had never known an agency to publicly accuse individuals of crimes without approval from a grand jury. Sections of the report read like criminal indictments, he said, even though the investigative team hadn't taken the steps to secure real indictments. Now local district attorneys were under pressure to seek indictments while honoring immunity agreements, even though they had not overseen the investigation.[12]

Secretary of Education Arne Duncan soon echoed Deal's and Reed's dismay in an interview with 11Alive News, saying, "You really cheat the children; that's the part that's most disappointing about this whole situation." But he tried to distance the scandal from his department, calling the incident "isolated." It was a strange statement, given that only a few months earlier *USA Today* had published an investigative series that found more than sixteen hundred cases of standardized test manipulation in six states and Washington, DC, between 2009 and 2010, and that was using conservative measures.[13]

In fact, DC schools were embroiled in a cheating scandal on par with Atlanta's in which 103 were flagged for suspiciously high test scores, and a former principal had recently brought a whistleblower lawsuit against the district. She alleged that administrators provided illegitimate test scores to the Department of Education while applying for federal grants, including $75 million in Race to the Top funding.

Like other adherents of corporate education reform, Michelle Rhee had laid off teachers en masse, closed schools, and raised the stakes for standardized testing with a system of incentives. But before Rhee could be held to account, she stepped down.

The day after Duncan ignored cases like DC's and claimed that cheating in Atlanta was an anomaly, news broke that dozens of Pennsylvania schools, including twenty-two district schools and seven charter schools in Philadelphia, had likely cheated on standardized tests.[14]

The prevalence of similar cheating scandals barely registered in Atlanta, where the local media were quickly turning the APS case into a ridiculous spectacle. Channel Two Action News sent local celebrity reporter Monica Pearson to Hawaii, where Beverly Hall was reportedly vacationing. Hall had stepped down from her position as superintendent a month prior to the GBI report's publication. Reveling in the trappings of investigative reporting, Pearson stood on a tropical beach and exclaimed, "Once we knew she was here, we hopped a plane and flew ten hours!" Her camera crew staked Hall out, discreetly filming her eating at a seafood restaurant before confronting her outside of a hotel, where Hall quietly declined to be interviewed and Pearson sheepishly apologized for invading her privacy. Such theatrics would become a mainstay of the cheating scandal coverage. While the media attempted to track Hall's every move, many members of the Atlanta business community who had once championed Hall began distancing themselves from her.[15]

July 2011 was a hard month for me. I tried to keep my cool as I came to terms with the fact that some very bad things had happened in my school district, worked to remain self-assured that my name would be cleared, and attempted to quell my outrage at the naked hypocrisy of some of the public figures who scrambled to condemn educators for "cheating the children." There were so many ways that children, particularly black children, were being cheated out of a decent life. During the decade that some APS staff members were tampering with tests, most teachers were doing the best they could with few resources for contending with kids who suffered generational trauma stemming from urban renewal, racialized violence, the drug epidemic, mass incarceration, and the obliteration of public housing. Meanwhile, real estate moguls and financiers were finagling ways to line their pockets with the education dollars that should have been going to the classroom.

⁞ ⁞ ⁞ ⁞ ⁞ ⁞ ⁞ ⁞ ⁞ ⁞ ⁞ ⁞

Once developer Tom Cousins had transformed East Lake Meadows public housing into the privately managed, strictly surveilled, mixed-income Villages of East Lake, displacing hundreds of black families in the process, and converted the local elementary school into a charter school managed by a for-profit company, he turned his attention to the 2001 mayoral election. Cousins cochaired the campaign of Shirley Franklin, the political consultant he'd hired to face off with unhappy public housing residents. Franklin won and made her chief policy officer Cousins's son-in-law Greg Giornelli the director of the East Lake Foundation. Giornelli had admitted that creating Drew Charter School was part of an effort to "lure middle-class residents back to the city." From there, Giornelli took charge of the Atlanta Development Authority in 2003.[16] The ADA was the city's economic development arm, responsible for spurring economic activity. Giornelli took helm as the agency was increasingly doling out public money to private developers like his father-in-law through a financing strategy called "tax allocation districts."

In Georgia, a tax allocation district (TAD) designates a "blighted or distressed" area as a place where private developers can qualify for funding from local legislative bodies (including city councils, county commissions, and school boards) for projects that "revitalize" the area. In a TAD contract, the participating governments generally agree to sell municipal bonds and give the proceeds to the developer, based on the assumption that the new project—usually an upscale, mixed-use development or luxury condos—will cause property taxes in the area to increase, bringing them greater tax revenue in the future. But the government can't use that new revenue right away. TAD contracts freeze the amount of tax revenue that the government can collect each year over the life of the TAD, usually twenty-five years. As property taxes rise over time, the new revenue goes into a special fund, where it is used to pay back the bond debt, including interest, and is given away to developers to finance additional projects. Once the TAD expires, the government, in theory, has a higher revenue stream from the redeveloped area. Meanwhile, the developer rakes in profits from the new retail units or condos they build, which residents in the TAD area are paying for with higher property taxes.[17]

Atlanta Public Schools joined the City of Atlanta and Fulton County in the state's first TAD agreement to come to fruition, which they established in 1999 to channel $76.5 million in public funding, half of which came from APS, toward the infrastructure for a private mixed-use development near Georgia Tech called Atlantic Station. Built on a reconstituted brownfield where a steel mill once operated adjacent to a neighborhood called Home Park, Atlantic Station would eventually feature chain stores, restaurants, a movie theater, office towers, condos, an IKEA, and a sliver of green space with a Romanesque arch called the Millennium Gate. The assessed value of the 138 acres under Atlantic Station rose astronomically, by more than $126 million in five years, but APS couldn't use the increasing tax revenue for school operations. Instead it had to use all but the base rate (the tax value before the TAD was established) to pay back the bond debt. The school district, in effect, was using education funds to pay for the IKEA, the condos, and everything else packed into the old steel mill site.[18]

The school board, along with the county and city, quickly sought to hash out more TAD deals, hailing them as a tool for community betterment. Their consensus said that TADs were a way to attract development to underserved neighborhoods. No one seemed to acknowledge the serious shortcomings of the TAD model.

For one, it relied on unending growth, never accounting for a downturn in the real estate market, which would soon happen in a major way. Also, Georgia's TAD laws were lax, making it easy to designate a neighborhood as "blighted" even if it really wasn't, and setting the bar low for elected officials to argue that developers wouldn't pursue a project unless enticed with a subsidy. Thus, APS and the others threw millions of dollars at projects that likely could have happened without their involvement, impacting neighborhoods that were hardly the deserted wastelands that the term "blight" implies. Most problematic of all was that TADs were designed to boost property taxes as high as possible, meaning that the vision of a "revitalized" city that elected officials were promoting was one in which few if any poor people remained in Atlanta, not because they would magically be made wealthy by the presence of an IKEA in their neighborhood, but because they would be gradually forced out by the rising cost of living. Not only was APS throwing away needed school funds, the district was also contributing to pushing out its poorest students.[19]

By the time Giornelli took the helm at ADA, the agency had entered into four TAD agreements, three of which included both Fulton County and APS, that anticipated allocating up to $280 million in bond proceeds to developers. (This pales in comparison to what the TADs would eventually cost taxpayers; over the next fourteen years the subsidies would balloon to well over a billion dollars as new TADs were created and additional payouts were made from the original TADs.) Within a month of Giornelli's arrival, ADA inked a fifth TAD deal that included all three parties and was expected to provide between $29 million and $91 million in bond funding for a slew of projects, mostly luxury condos and high-end office space, in the area comprising the East Side TAD over the next thirteen years.[20]

More than $11 million of the East Side TAD funding went to projects involving Urban Realty Group, the development firm founded by former Cousins Properties vice president and Atlanta school board member Mark Riley. In a particularly egregious twist, Riley's firm used $5.3 million in TAD funding (about half of which came from school property taxes) to turn Capitol Homes public housing into mixed-income housing, displacing the very students whose education the money was intended for. Riley had abstained from the school board vote approving the East Side TAD, ostensibly because he recognized the conflict of interest between his board position and his development ventures, though it's hard to imagine that he didn't have some influence over the board's decision.[21]

Giornelli, on the other hand, seemed to have little regard for conflicts of interest as he doled out TAD funding to Riley and other developers with ties to his family's business. Barry Real Estate, a close partner of Cousins Properties, got $2.3 million for a new office building that would later house Mike Bowers's law firm, where GBI agents interrogated me.[22]

The proliferation of these sweetheart deals that diverted education funds to a select group of connected developers initially happened with little public awareness. But that began to change in 2003, as City Council member Cathy Woolard hyped a $2 billion transit project that called for the creation of the largest (geographically and financially) TAD yet. The idea came from a Georgia Tech graduate student, Ryan Gravel, who proposed replacing twenty-two miles of unused railroad tracks ringing the city with a combination of light rail transit, linear parks, and paths for walking and biking, which he called the BeltLine.[23]

The plan held the promise of sparking new development in the forty-plus neighborhoods it touched, including Mechanicsville and others on the west and south sides of the city that were struggling with the problems that decades of anti-black, anti-poor policies had wrought. Proponents acclaimed the BeltLine as a potential "emerald necklace," echoing the language of an earlier generation of Atlanta's business elite who sought to get rid of the "ring of slums around the neck of [downtown]." Giornelli quickly became a BeltLine advocate, placing the power of the ADA behind the plan.[24]

Others in the Cousins network also clambered aboard the BeltLine bandwagon. In 2004, Woolard left her city council post to run for a seat in the US House of Representatives. Tom Cousins backed Lisa Borders, a Cousins Properties vice president and lobbyist to replace her. That August, Borders was elected Atlanta City Council president, despite having no prior political experience, and she was instrumental in pushing the BeltLine plan forward. In 2005, Cousins Properties bought a condo development firm that owned a tract of land along the BeltLine. And Mayor Franklin formed a BeltLine steering committee headed by a Cousins business partner.[25]

As City Hall and the BeltLine project came increasingly under Cousins's influence, BeltLine news saturated local media, causing property values to spike even before legislation was passed to move the project forward. Between 2001 and 2006, homes within an eighth of a mile of the proposed BeltLine TAD experienced a 68 percent increase in value, while homes a mile away increased by 32 percent.[26] Gentrifiers and seasoned developers alike scooped up properties. One wealthy developer, Wayne Mason, bought a swath of land comprising one-fifth of the BeltLine route, which he eventually sold to the city for a $45 million profit.[27]

By the time the ADA had a BeltLine TAD agreement drawn up and ready for approval, the pressure to pass it was immense. The Atlanta City Council was first to approve the TAD, in November 2005, at the urging of Franklin and Giornelli. The agreement projected a whopping $800 million coming from city and county property taxes and $850 million from school taxes. APS soon agreed to these terms, but the Fulton County Commission stalled, with one commissioner remarking that Atlanta officials were trying to "cram it down our throat."[28]

Fulton County did join the TAD before the year was over. But during the first bond validation hearing the following June, when a superior court judge was expected to rubberstamp the deal, a real estate lawyer unexpectedly intervened. John Woodham challenged the bond sales, arguing that it was illegal for APS to take part because the state constitution prohibited the use of school property taxes for non-educational purposes. Unfazed, the ADA and its partners continued to lay the groundwork for the BeltLine as the lawsuit triggered by Woodham unfolded. A Fulton County judge dismissed the case, but Woodham appealed to the Georgia Supreme Court, and made oral arguments in September 2007. The next month, volunteers ceremoniously began to clear debris from the first 1.7-mile stretch of the BeltLine.[29]

The gears of the BeltLine ground to a screeching halt, however, in February 2008, when the Georgia Supreme Court ruled that the BeltLine TAD did indeed violate the state constitution, since the project had "little, if any, nexus to the actual operation of public schools in the city of Atlanta."[30]

BeltLine boosters and TAD hucksters were stunned; the ramifications reached well beyond the BeltLine. The ruling meant that no TADs could use school tax dollars for hotels, condos, restaurants, and the like. One attorney who made his living facilitating TAD deals wistfully told *Journal-Constitution* reporters that he didn't know what was going to happen to the Hard Rock Hotel planned for downtown, since he had been banking on a large portion of the $18.9 million it sought from the city's Westside TAD to come from school taxes. That a Hard Rock franchise wasn't an appropriate use for millions of education dollars didn't seem to register.[31]

Those who were disappointed, even devastated, by the ruling didn't have long to worry. Within days, state legislators drafted a resolution creating a statewide referendum to amend the constitution, allowing for school property taxes to fund non-educational projects. Among the resolution's sponsors was Kasim Reed, a state senator and formerly Shirley Franklin's campaign manager. The following year he would succeed her as mayor of Atlanta, and Franklin would transition to heading an organization, Purpose Built Communities, that Tom Cousins launched to replicate the East Lake privatization model across the country.[32]

As legislators were figuring out how to change the constitution to fit the interests of influential developers, Central Atlanta Progress formed a campaign committee called Georgians for Community Redevelopment and began raising money to wage a campaign in favor of the constitutional amendment. By the time the historic 2008 election rolled around in November, it had leveraged $200,000 to convince voters that spending school funds on Hard Rock Hotels was okay. Cousins Properties contributed $25,000, the second largest donation after Central Atlanta Progress. The constitutional amendment passed with 51.5 percent of the vote.[33]

It was a bittersweet victory for those who wanted to spend hundreds of millions of education dollars on remaking the city into an upscale playground for the wealthy. Weeks before the election, the economy had tanked, and property values took a nosedive. Now the profit projections for the TADs were up in the air. The BeltLine TAD was already looking like a bad deal for Atlanta schools and the children they served.

Woodham, the anti-BeltLine lawyer, filed a second suit, this time representing the Fulton County Taxpayers Association, a conservative advocacy group. They challenged the validity of resurrecting the BeltLine TAD with a constitutional amendment. But this time they fought in vain. In October 2011, a trial court ruled in favor of the BeltLine, and the Georgia Supreme Court would eventually do the same. The

BeltLine TAD would come to fruition, and Dunbar Elementary would be in it.

That fall, as the aftermath of the state investigation into CRCT cheating continued to unfold, with pundits pronouncing that teachers had "cheated" the children, the real estate industry was cheating those same kids out of millions of dollars that should have gone toward their education. I was trying to ignore it all. I had bigger things to think about—like getting married.

I I I I I I I I I I I I

Moses popped the question on a warm night over Labor Day weekend in Centennial Olympic Park downtown. Jets of water shot up from spouts in the pavement, lost momentum at about twenty feet, and showered down on squealing kids. Moses and I watched from a dry distance, enjoying ourselves on a walk after a dinner date.

"Do you remember when I first saw you at the pool when we were twelve?" he asked, leading me to a bench where we sat down.

"I remember Shayla told me you were asking about me," I said with a sly smile.

"I said, 'Who's that girl over there? She is fine!'" he teased. We laughed, and he squeezed my hand. Then he turned to me.

"Shani, I always had a crush on you. But in the past year together, I've fallen in love with you." As he spoke, my heart beat faster.

"Having you in my life has changed so much for me. I feel like I have a direction and focus that I didn't really have before. The way we support each other and have fun together and spend just about every day together. . . . I want it to last forever." I tried not to choke up as he crouched in front of me on one knee. He didn't even have to say the words, but of course he did. My answer was, overwhelmingly, yes.

Moses voiced what I had been feeling for some time. In the year since he ventured out on the dance floor with me in spite of his reservations, we had become inseparable. We had such a natural way of being together. We enjoyed the same pastimes: going to movies and restaurants, spending time with each other's families and friends. We shared a passion for social justice and talked about starting a nonprofit; he was considering quitting his job as a financial manager at a car rental company to start a program for underserved youth. We were both adventurous and traveled together. We could discuss anything—books, music, the news, spirituality—and it was always a fresh conversation, sometimes deep, sometimes hilarious, never boring.

As Moses slipped a sparkling ring on my finger, I was elated. The GBI report, the stresses of my counseling job, and all my worries evaporated like water on hot pavement. Of course, water vapor always rains back down eventually. But that night, the storm was far away.

Five days before Christmas, Nathan Deal quietly released the results of the state investigation into Dougherty County Schools, which had the second highest number of suspicious test scores after APS. Like the APS report, this one was long, detailed, and dramatic. State investigators found that cheating occurred in eleven schools (there were fewer than thirty in the district), and that at least forty-nine educators, possibly many more, were involved. The report called the situation "disgraceful" and "a blight on the community that will feel its effects for generations to come." As in Atlanta, investigators said the Dougherty superintendent, a white woman named Sally Whatley, should have known about the cheating, even if they didn't have conclusive evidence to prove that she did. But unlike the APS report, this one did not heap blame onto Whatley. It softened the blow by acknowledging that the Dougherty school district was like many school systems around the country "in that the pressure to meet AYP is constantly present and regularly emphasized by those in leadership positions. . . . Since the enactment of No Child Left Behind, standardized testing has become more about measuring the teachers, principals, and schools than accurately assessing the children's academic progress."[34]

I was stunned to see this important piece of context that was absent from the APS report, which portrayed Beverly Hall as the malevolent origin of high-stakes testing. I was also surprised by the lack of media attention in the wake of the report. Whereas commentators had come out of the woodwork to denounce APS educators, few seemed to think Dougherty warranted the same alarm. There certainly weren't any television news crews hiding in bushes to film Whatley going about her business, as Channel Two *Action News* had done to Hall. I learned that Nathan Deal had even tried to call off the Dougherty investigation prematurely after the APS report was released. It seemed he had already gotten what he wanted at that point, but Mike Bowers urged him to keep the Dougherty case open.[35]

Perhaps Deal was heeding demands made earlier by the Dougherty school district's internal investigator. Channel Two revealed that well before the GBI's involvement, back when GOSA was overseeing internal reviews in school districts across the state, Whatley had hired James Wilson, an education consultant and former superintendent in Fulton and Cobb Counties, to ferret out cheating in the Dougherty school system. Instead, Wilson tried to subvert GOSA's efforts and resorted to intimidation in a meeting with GOSA director Kathleen Mathers, telling her, "I'm not going to give you any threats. But let me tell you, I can get there."[36]

Mathers and Perdue ultimately deemed Wilson's investigation insufficient, but it seemed that under Deal, Wilson's desire for Dougherty's cheating problem to be swept under the rug was realized. Mathers was no longer around to pursue it; she had departed GOSA in the fall to start her own education consulting business. She also joined the board of Latin Academy, a charter school whose CEO would spend the next several years stealing $600,000 from the school's bank account to pay tabs at strip clubs and luxury car dealerships while Mathers and her fellow board members turned a blind eye, until the FBI caught up with them.[37]

Meanwhile, reports continued to surface showing that cheating on state standardized tests was extremely widespread. In March 2012, the *Journal-Constitution* investigative team that had broken the APS cheating story explored test scores nationwide and found improbably high wrong-to-right erasures on standardized tests in 196 school districts. Education Secretary Arne Duncan blandly called the findings "concerning."[38]

By the spring of 2012, real estate tycoons and strippers had easier access to education funds than some schools. Educators were doctoring tests left and right in practically every state. The cheating in Dougherty was quickly fading from public consciousness. But the APS cheating case was metastasizing into the scapegoat for everything that was going wrong.

I was paging through a wedding magazine when I got a phone call informing me that I had been subpoenaed to appear before a grand jury.

It looked like Paul Howard, the Fulton County district attorney, was seeking indictments. But I felt like I was a small fish in a big pond and that they were probably just calling people in to gather more evidence against Beverly Hall.

On the day of the grand jury, I waited in a large lobby within the Fulton County Superior Court and was pleased when Cleveland showed up; we were apparently scheduled to testify back to back. We joked around to lighten the mood, imitating Jack Nicholson in *A Few Good Men*, exclaiming, "You can't handle the truth!" It felt good to let off some steam with Cleveland. I was nervous, even though I already knew what I was going to say. I would assert my Fifth Amendment right to silence ("No person shall be . . . compelled in any criminal case to be a witness against himself") in response to each question the prosecutor posed. I knew this was a standard procedure in criminal cases. Even if you had done nothing wrong, it was better not to give prosecutors any information that they could somehow find a way to use against you.

It was a long wait. Our banter petered out, and I was lost in thought when suddenly Rose Neal entered the waiting area. I jolted to attention and my heart rate quickened as a flurry of thoughts crowded my mind. *I can't believe they scheduled her the same day as us! Did they do that on purpose to put me on edge? Should I say something to her? I want to tell her she's a lying fool. But she looks so pathetic, so tired and worn out. What has she been going through? Why did she get us into this mess?*

Neal avoided eye contact with us and found a place to sit that was far enough away to preclude any interaction. She was called into the grand jury room shortly, leaving Cleveland and me to wait some more and stew in silence.

When it was finally my turn to testify, I had butterflies in my stomach. I took some deep breaths and walked into the courtroom. It wasn't like any court I had visited as an advocate for my teenage clients. The prosecutor, a youngish black woman, pointed me toward a typical-looking witness stand. But instead of a jury bench off to the side and tables for the prosecution and defense in front of me, I faced grand-jury members who were seated across a raised platform, looking down at me.

Even with my plan ready, it was intimidating. Once I was seated, the prosecutor, who stood at my level, perfunctorily swore me in and said, "State and spell your name for the record." She proceeded to rattle off questions as if she were reading a checklist. I answered the basics: the name of my school, what grade I taught. But when her questions turned to the CRCT, I invoked the Fifth Amendment. Like my interviews with the GBI, the grand jury process was nerve-wracking but brief. Soon I was free to go home and get back to wedding planning.

I had no idea how expansive the APS cheating case was becoming. Counter to what I assumed, Paul Howard was not just going after Beverly Hall. He had hired John Floyd, the leading expert on Georgia's version of the Racketeer Influenced and Corrupt Organizations Act (RICO), which Congress passed in 1970 to take down the Mafia and organized-crime rings. One attorney told the *Journal-Constitution* that Floyd was known to "push the envelope" as to how RICO was used. Howard wanted Floyd to determine whether a school system could be treated as a criminal enterprise under that law.[39]

Under RICO, certain crimes that normally carry relatively light sentences can land a defendant in prison for twenty years if the defendant is proven to be part of an "enterprise," which for a long time was understood to mean a group of people that functioned as a "continuing unit" working toward "a common purpose." But in 2009, a US Supreme Court decision authored by George W. Bush appointee Justice Samuel Alito reinterpreted RICO, setting a precedent that made it possible to claim that a defendant was part of an enterprise if they were proven to have engaged in a "pattern of racketeering activity," even if there was no formal organization behind that activity.[40]

What this meant became clear in January 2012, when David Camez, a small-time identity thief in Arizona, was slapped with RICO charges by federal prosecutors. Camez had paid $330 for a fake ID from a website that was basically a criminal version of eBay, where users all over the world could buy and sell illegal products. The user who sold Camez the IDs was a federal agent making a sting. Prosecutors took advantage of the Supreme Court ruling to argue that Camez was part of an enterprise, making Camez culpable for all the crimes committed by the website's nearly eight thousand users, the vast majority of whom he had never interacted with.[41]

What a nightmare, to be held responsible for other people's transgressions, people who you've never met. Such was the nightmare Paul Howard and John Floyd were concocting.

CHAPTER FIVE

The Darker the Night

■ | | | | | | | | | | | | | | | | | | | | | | | ■

WHEN I VOWED TO BE MOSES'S WIFE, for better or worse, I had no reason to believe that the worst would come soon.

It was the middle of summer, July 2012, and it seemed my appearance before the grand jury had never happened. I hadn't heard anything about the case since that tense day a few months prior, and I had become consumed with planning what turned out to be an epic wedding.

The day started at the historic Georgian Terrace Hotel downtown, where my bridesmaids donned their lilac strapless satin dresses and zipped me into my bright white mermaid gown. I met Moses on the hotel's sweeping marble staircase for our "first look." He stood halfway down the stairs with his back to me while I approached him, carefully taking slow, graceful steps to counter the anticipation wracking my nerves. When I tapped him on the shoulder and he turned to me, my jitters broke into giddy relief, his overpowering smile instantly calmed me, and I followed his lead as he leaned in for a kiss and then twirled me while the bridesmaids and groomsmen clapped from the balustrade and the photographers snapped dozens of pictures.

From there we drove to a ballroom outside of the city where nearly four hundred friends and family members awaited our arrival. Several of my former coworkers from Dunbar were there, and even one of my former first-grade students came with his family. Of course, my favorite part of the ceremony was walking down the long aisle lined with white calla lilies and lilac ribbons, up to a beautifully decorated stage where Moses awaited me. At the close of the ceremony, Moses and I "jumped the broom," carrying on an African American tradition that was done during slavery to consecrate marriages that the legal system wouldn't recognize. Then Moses and I walked back down the aisle and out of the ballroom to Stevie Wonder's song "Signed, Sealed, Delivered I'm yours."

After the ceremony was the reception, where Moses and I took the first dance. Later it was my dad's turn, and we performed a routine to a medley that included oldies-but-goodies like the Jackson 5's "Dancing Machine" and newer hits like "Crank That (Soulja Boy)" and "Single Ladies (Put a Ring on It)." By the time we hit our last mark, everyone was on their feet applauding and cheering. Many people asked my dad how he learned all of those moves. He just smiled at them and shrugged. He never let on that I'd had him on a strict practice schedule for weeks until the dance was perfect.

After Moses and I honeymooned in Jamaica, we launched the nonprofit we had dreamed of starting together. Using our own funds, we created a program for underserved teenagers in a community near the neighborhood where we had lived as kids on the eastern outskirts of Atlanta, an area that had been hit hard by the crack epidemic and devolved to the point where our families, and others who could, moved away. We held weekly job readiness and career exploration classes at a public library. We wanted the children who participated to be aware of all of the options available to them post-graduation. We found speakers to talk to the kids about skilled trade careers. We also brought in representatives from local colleges to explain the process of applying to schools.

I was still working for the counseling agency, where I supported teens in foster care and group homes. It was an amazing experience to combine what I had learned as a teacher and counselor to create a program that met kids' needs beyond what they were getting in school and at home. It felt like I was truly stepping into my life's work; I even convinced my parents to go through the lengthy process of becoming foster parents so they could take in a teen girl I worked with in a youth detention center. That fall I started making plans to go back to school to get an advanced degree in social work.

The next time I gave any thought to the APS cheating case was in January 2013, when the US Department of Education's inspector general cleared the DC public school system of cheating allegations. The department had launched the investigation in 2011 after *USA Today* published a report flagging 103 schools in DC for having a suspiciously high number of wrong-to-right erasures on its 2009–10 standardized tests. Shortly after the article appeared, a DC elementary school principal, Adell Cothorne, filed a lawsuit alleging that the district committed fraud by using inflated test scores to get tens of millions of dollars from Race to the Top and other funding programs.[1] The Education Department's inspector general closed the initial investigation and opened a new one focused on Cothorne's claims, at the same time that the local DC inspector general was investigating her case. The local investigation concluded in August 2012, with a measly fourteen-page report that found no evidence of widespread cheating. A *Washington Post* reporter faulted the local investigator for probing only one school, quoting no erasure experts, and kowtowing to the influence of DC Public Schools chancellor Kaya Henderson, who by that point had taken the baton from Michelle Rhee, the infamous crusader for "no excuses" high-stakes testing.[2]

Now the Department of Education was corroborating the DC inspector general's conclusions, with hardly any more scrutiny of the system as a whole.[3] What about the 102 other DC schools flagged by *USA Today*? When I read the news, I marveled at how the DC investigation turned out so differently from the one ordered by Sonny Perdue in Atlanta. It seemed investigations of this sort could produce whatever conclusions were politically convenient to the people in charge. For those in Atlanta, it seemed that smearing public schools could fuel the fervor for private charters, which were playing an important role in lucrative real estate development that uprooted black communities and shepherded in wealthier, white residents.

While the DC cheating case was put to rest, plans were moving forward to incriminate educators in Atlanta. At the end of March 2013, a Fulton County grand jury convened to determine if there was probable cause to file criminal charges against anyone implicated in the cheating scandal. When I heard a legal analyst discussing it on the local National Public Radio station, I flashed back to the day, almost a year earlier, when I testified before grand jury members who looked down at me from their elevated seats. The analyst explained that DA Paul Howard would present the grand jury with findings from hearings that had taken place over twenty-one months.

"The only thing they can charge these people with are serious felony offenses like racketeering. The statute of limitations period has run out on any misdemeanors," the analyst said. *Wow*, I thought, *these people could be in a lot of trouble.*

"I think they're about to get Beverly Hall," Moses said to me a few days later. It was Good Friday, and we were eating lunch at his office. He worked long hours at his new job as a general manager of a finance company, so I often went to see him during his lunch break. Speculation about the impending grand jury decision was dominating the media, and Moses was live-streaming a local news station on his laptop while we ate at his desk.

After lunch, I met up with one of my coworkers from the counseling agency. We often carpooled to see clients in a group home that was a long drive from our other sites. I was happy that it was her turn to drive that day. On the way, we talked about how we wanted our sessions to go, which clients we would see first, and the activities that we would do with them. She was telling me about a breathing exercise she was teaching one of her teenage girls to help her cope with anxiety, when my cell phone rang. Moses's name flashed on the screen.

"Hold on, my husband is calling me," I told my coworker. "Hey, babe!" I answered.

"Hey, don't panic," he said slowly, in a low voice. "I just want you to know that you've been indicted in the cheating scandal."

"What?" I blurted, realizing from the look my coworker shot me that I must have sounded alarmed.

"I saw your name scrolling across the bottom of the screen on the news. They charged you with RICO. You need to call your attorney."

I've heard people talk about "losing time" to describe what it's like to be in shock. There's a point of departure, the last thing you remember, and then you're at a different moment in time, and you can't account for anything in between. I don't know how long I sat in silence, uncomprehending.

"Hello? Are you still there?" Moses's voice jolted me into the realization that my heart was beating too fast and my legs had gone numb. I tried to remember the breathing exercise my coworker had just explained. I was wary of her presence next to me; it seemed she had grown tense too. Straining to sound casual, I quietly said, "Okay, let me call you back."

I told my coworker that a family issue had come up and that I needed to make some important calls and would wait outside while she was seeing her clients. Once I was alone, I called attorney Annette Greene. Then I made a plan to go to her office as soon as I could.

On the ride home with my coworker, I sank into shame and embarrassment. What were my parents going to think? What would my in-laws think about having a new daughter-in-law involved in a racketeering case? I tried to keep a grip on my emotions so that my coworker wouldn't think I was losing my mind.

Family members and friends started calling to find out what was going on. As the humiliation set in, I rushed people off the phone, assuring them that everything was fine. Except for my mom. I told her I was headed to Greene's office, and she insisted on meeting me there. When I spotted her slight frame as she waited on the sidewalk outside of the building, my heart plummeted to see the worry etched on her face, an expression that almost looked like guilt. It hit me that she had been so proud when I became a teacher like her. Maybe she thought this was somehow her fault. I desperately wanted to tell her that everything would be okay, but I couldn't be sure that was true.

After meeting with my attorney, I went to my parent's house and sat in their living room, still in shock, while my mom explained everything to my father. Up until then, I had no idea what RICO was. I vaguely recalled hearing the term on an episode of *Sons of Anarchy* and getting the impression that it was a high-level crime dealing with money. Now my mom was telling my dad that the charge against me could carry a sentence of twenty years in prison.

"She's also charged with one count of making false statements and writing," my mom went on as my dad listened, stone-faced, "which could add another five years. That's about the allegation that she changed answers on those CRCT tests."

"I never changed any answers!" I sputtered, my throat clenching.

"We know," my mom said, putting her arm around my shoulder. I glanced at her and choked back the sobs I felt welling up. Behind her brown-rimmed, oval glasses her eyes looked raw, as if she'd cried and tried to hide it, maybe while she was in the bathroom. Now she had a gentle smile, but it looked precarious, and I thought that if I wept she would break down altogether. I tried to regain my composure.

"So there's a warrant out? What do we do?" my dad asked. He sat forward on an armchair, elbows resting on his knees, looking from me to my mom intently. He usually maintained a tough exterior. I had only seen him cry once, at an aunt's funeral.

"She's going to have to turn herself in on Monday," my mom said, softly rubbing my back. "This is the worst part, Jessie. Her bail is $200,000."

"Oh my God," my dad said, sinking back into the chair and crossing his arms. "This is crazy."

Even with a bail bond, I wouldn't be able to come up with 10 percent—$20,000. I'd be stuck in jail. A television in the corner was tuned to a local news station. As my parents continued talking, I heard a reporter naming my former coworkers: Lera Middlebrooks, the vivacious learning specialist who had worked closely with our principal and served as testing coordinator in 2009; Diane Buckner-Webb, the artistic first-grade teacher I had worked with as a rookie straight out of Teach for America; Pamela Cleveland, the friendly second-grade teacher who took a liking to me; and Gloria Ivey, the fifth-grade teacher who had dedicated decades of her life to working at Dunbar. As the testing coordinator, Middlebrooks had instructed Buckner-Webb, Cleveland, and me to erase stray marks from our students' test booklets in 2009. Rose Neal, at that time a second-grade teacher, had been there too, but she was immune to indictment after having accused us.

As the reporter added my name to theirs, I turned to the television and saw a document displayed on the screen. With horror, I realized that the reporter was describing a letter I had signed, written by the Georgia Professional Standards Commission (GPSC), which licenses teachers. About a year earlier, I had received the letter stating that the commission believed I was involved in wrongdoing. They gave me the option of accepting a two-year suspension, appealing, or facing further sanction if I didn't respond. I had left teaching at that point and didn't even have a teaching license. I had a five-year, nonrenewable certificate that was about to expire, and I had no plans to return to teaching. I knew before signing the letter that to do so would not be considered an admission of guilt, and accepting the two-year suspension seemed like the most reasonable way to bring closure to the matter. I decided to sign because I had no interest in going through an appeal process to save a certificate that was about to expire. I also didn't want to leave the door open for other repercussions for something I didn't do. Now a reporter was describing the letter as if it proved that I had cheated.

Then the reporter started talking about bonus money, implying that we had all cheated in order to get a payout.

"How can they do this?" I protested. "I never got any extra money. My school didn't even meet our district targets!"

My vision began to swim, and the room seemed to contract around me. I closed my eyes, willing myself not to pass out.

There were thirty-five educators indicted in the APS district. Among them were Beverly Hall; her human resources director, Millicent Few; three School Reform Team directors (who were responsible for supervising principals in four sub-districts within APS); six principals; two assistant principals; six testing coordinators; one school improvement specialist, one school secretary; and fourteen teachers, including me.

Agent Rocky Bigham's face flashed in my memory. The day we met in the mall parking lot he had assured me there were no plans to send teachers to jail. Now teachers made up more than a third of the people facing felony charges.

Everyone was indicted on at least one of four charges: false statements and writing (changing test answers or signing official documents verifying that testing protocol was followed); false swearing (lying during hearings with the GPSC, to the GBI, or to the grand jury); "theft by taking" (receiving bonus money for falsified test scores); and influencing witnesses (hushing up colleagues who tried to speak out). I could have been slapped with two additional false swearing charges if I had pursued the appeal with the GPSC and if I hadn't invoked my Fifth Amendment right during the grand jury hearing.

It seemed plausible to me that some of the thirty-five people who were indicted had done some of these things. But the indictment also charged that these acts constituted "a pattern of racketeering activity," because they allegedly had "the same or similar intents, results, accomplices, victims or methods of commission."[4] The language was alarmingly broad. Two teachers at two different schools could take similar actions and have similar intents but have no knowledge of the other person's actions. Under this definition, that scenario could constitute a conspiracy between two people who didn't even know they were conspiring.

District Attorney Howard soon gave a press conference, flanked by Mike Bowers, members of the investigative team, the RICO expert John Floyd, and an APS parent and student.

"What has really driven us are two incidents that I would like to discuss with you today," Howard began, "because we believe that these two incidents and these two Atlanta families really express the crimes that have been committed against the children of the city of Atlanta."

He introduced Justina Collins, whose daughter had attended Cascade Elementary. Howard explained that when the girl was in third grade, she was behind in reading and failed the CRCT practice test. But when she took the real CRCT, she passed with flying colors. Collins knew her daughter couldn't read and wanted her to take third grade again, but, because the child passed the CRCT, school officials wouldn't hold her back or provide academic support. Collins took the matter all the way up to Beverly Hall, but the superintendent allegedly brushed her aside. Now her daughter was in ninth grade, and her reading ability was that of a fifth grader. The story was disturbing, but there was one piece that didn't add up. No educators from Cascade Elementary had been indicted or even implicated in the GBI report from 2011. Why was I taking the fall not only for what Beverly Hall had allegedly done but also for the alleged actions of people who themselves weren't being held to account?

Howard then introduced a former Dunbar student, whose name he mispronounced several times before he was quietly corrected by one of his staff. The girl reported that her teacher, my former coworker Gloria Ivey, had helped students on the 2009 CRCT. She said that when Ivey had approached her, she'd told Ivey that she didn't need help. I braced myself to hear something more, something really damning that Ivey had done, but that was it. Howard concluded this story by noting that the girl currently had the highest reading scores in her eighth-grade class.

While the content of the press conference fell short of its dramatic overtones, the media commentary that followed approached hysteria. "This is nothing but pervasive and rank thuggery," special investigator Richard Hyde told the *Journal-Constitution*.

I stayed glued to the news all weekend, despite the toll it took on my mental health. At one point, the local news stations paused from the cheating scandal story to report that a boy had been killed in a hit and run. The driver was caught, charged with vehicular homicide, and given a $10,000 bail. I couldn't believe that my bail was twenty times higher than a man who had killed a child, and my bail amount was one of the lowest among the defendants. Beverly Hall's bail was set at $7.5 million.

After multiple defense attorneys spoke out, all of the defendants' bails were reduced. But it came at a price. In exchange for lowering our bail, Howard put us under a gag order so that we couldn't give interviews to the media. Millions of people across the nation were suddenly captivated by the cheating scandal, but they would only hear one side of the story.

Mike Bowers soon went on CNN and told host Suzanne Malveaux that educators had cheated in "an attempt to gain bonuses [and] enhance careers without any regard to the little children," even though this patently contradicted the 2011 GBI report he oversaw, which stated that "the monetary bonus for meeting targets provided little incentive to cheat."[5] Not to mention that the "little children" Bowers feigned concern for were the same children he'd called "superpredators" when he ran for governor in the late 1990s.

Bowers's flawed assessment was typical of most of the media commentary in the wake of the indictment. However, there were exceptions. The Reverend Timothy McDonald of the Concerned Black Clergy criticized the district attorney's office to the *New York Times*.

"Show me a white face," McDonald said of the thirty-five indicted educators. "Let's just be for real. You can call it racist, you can call it whatever you want, but this is overkill."

It was true that out of the thirty-five indicted educators none were white, and only one wasn't black, even though there were white educators from majority white schools implicated in the 2011 GBI report. I also noticed that out of the forty-four schools named in the first report, the indicted educators all came from just eleven schools located in or near tax allocation districts that covered some of the poorest areas of Atlanta, the west and south sides. Several schools, like Dunbar, were in the same neighborhoods that for years had been dismantled and neglected by city leaders but now were increasingly the most coveted for redevelopment: Mechanicsville, Peoplestown, Vine City, and South Atlanta, where a Christian nonprofit affiliated with Tom Cousins was attempting to overhaul the community.

The west and south sides of the city also happened to be where the majority of new charter schools in the metro area were clustered. Since Cousins's East Lake Foundation had launched Atlanta's first charter school to attract middle-class families to the area in 2001, the number of charters in APS had steadily increased, thanks to a mostly pro-charter school board and a decidedly pro-charter superintendent.[6] But there were also new charter schools cropping up in Atlanta that were not a part of APS, schools that the local school board never approved. As schools became linchpins for lucrative real estate deals and charters gained a reputation as desirable alternatives to troubled public schools, more and more developers, financiers, and corporate executives were looking for ways to proliferate charters without relying on approval from local school boards. This effort in Georgia had been in the works for years and came to a head a few months before I found myself facing serious prison time. The ensuing battle would demonstrate how powerful the corporate education reform movement had become and how much stronger it could grow as the APS cheating scandal created a crisis of confidence in public schools.

| | | | | | | | | | | | |

From the thunderous applause resounding in the gymnasium of Cherokee County High School on June 24, 2011, passersby might have assumed that a teen athlete had just scored a winning basket. But there wasn't a game taking place in the gym that night: it was a meeting of the

local school board, whose members had just voted 4–3 to reject a charter school petition so controversial that hundreds of people turned out
wearing either red or black T-shirts to signal their stance on the matter.
The petition was backed by Charter Schools USA, a for-profit charter
franchise that had twice before attempted to push through its plan for
a new school in the district and twice had been rejected. Along the way,
the exurban county ("where metro meets the mountains," as its motto
declares) an hour's drive north of Atlanta had unwittingly become a
flashpoint in a battle over charter schools that would have statewide and
even national implications.[7]

The Cherokee County school board first turned down Charter
Schools USA's petition to open a school called Cherokee Charter
Academy in July 2009, doing so without much fanfare and citing a
slew of shortcomings. Board members said the company didn't pro-
pose any unique educational programs; it wasn't clear that the school
would meet the needs of disabled students; there was no transportation
plan, which pointed to a lack of accessibility for low-income students;
and the company's budget had set off alarms, especially its odd plan to
lease a school building for $156,000 more per year than the fair market
value of the property.[8]

Such questionable practices were characteristic of Charter Schools
USA and other for-profit charter operators, which have been found to
hire inexperienced teachers at low rates, avoid enrolling special-needs
students, and implement other cost-cutting measures in order to profit
by way of bloated CEO salaries and land and asset acquisition.[9] Jonathan Hage, founder of Charter Schools USA, readily acknowledged to
a *St. Petersburg Times* reporter that he viewed starting the company as "a
classic business opportunity."[10]

Hage, a conservative politico, served as a researcher for George H.
W. Bush's speechwriters, worked at the far-right Heritage Foundation,
and directed policy research at Jeb Bush's Foundation for Florida's Future, which was instrumental in passing the state's charter school laws,
before launching Charter Schools USA in 1997. Over the next twelve
years, the company spawned twenty-two Florida schools, which critics
derided as "cookie-cutter," and was looking to expand to other states
when it ventured to Georgia in 2009. Though the company reported

revenues of over $100 million that year, only 10 percent of its schools were meeting adequate yearly progress benchmarks.[11]

Charter Schools USA is technically an education management organization; such companies usually provide services to charter schools on a contract basis while functioning independently of the schools. That's because many states, including Florida and Georgia, have laws requiring charters to be run by a nonprofit governing board, so a for-profit company can't operate a school by itself. But Charter Schools USA has skirted these laws by setting up nonprofits to establish charters and then funnel public education funds to the company, which has total control of the schools. In Georgia, the nonprofit petitioning the Cherokee County school board was the Georgia Charter Educational Foundation, an organization incorporated in Fort Lauderdale that shared an address with Charter Schools USA. A strangely high rent payment in its proposed budget was to go to Red Apple Development, which Charter Schools USA has described as a "sister company," also registered at the same address as the charter franchise.[12] Red Apple acquires property and builds schools, often with funding from tax-exempt municipal bonds that enrich investors, and then charges exorbitant rent to Charter Schools USA as a way of channeling more public education dollars to pad the profit margins of the two private companies.

School board members in Cherokee County saw through the scheme, and they weren't the only ones. Atlanta Public Schools and three other metro area districts had already rejected similar petitions from the company. But when Cherokee rejected Charter School USA's petition, they did not have the last word.[13]

Charter Schools USA took its petition to the newly created Georgia Charter Schools Commission, a state agency with the power to override local school districts by authorizing charter schools and redirecting education funding to them. The idea for the commission came from an advocacy group, the Georgia Charter Schools Association (GCSA), which recruited an attorney to help them craft legislation to establish it. The attorney worked for the Atlanta firm McKenna Long & Aldridge, which had carved out a niche serving charter school clients and brokering tax allocation district deals (it has since merged with the global law firm Denton's). The attorney who worked with GCSA also sat on the board of the Georgia Public Policy Foundation, an ALEC-affiliated think tank. During the 2008 state legislative session, GCSA's bill was sponsored by Jan Jones, a Republican representative who headed ALEC's Education Task Force. GCSA lobbied for the bill and saw it passed.[14]

It was a watershed moment for GCSA, which was founded by a group of charter school operators in 2001, with the help of the Georgia Department of Education and the Georgia Public Policy Foundation.[15] GCSA gained steam in 2004 when the Walton Family Foundation awarded it a grant that boosted the organization's revenue tenfold.[16] The Waltons, the family that owns Walmart, are heavy hitters in the corporate education reform movement, donating billions of dollars to charter schools as well as candidates and campaigns that are favorable to education privatization.[17] While GCSA was founded to advocate for the interests of charter schools, it would focus increasingly on the interests of corporations, wooing sponsors in every sector from insurance and real estate to for-profit charter operators by offering access to an "exclusive marketplace" of "charter schools, administrators, and teachers."[18]

By 2008, GCSA had a new director, Tony Roberts, fresh from Texas, where he had been vice president of development at a charter school chain with academic scores as low as its executive salaries were high.[19] Roberts seemed to view locally elected school boards as impediments to such enterprises, and now, with the Georgia Charter Schools Commission intact, those school boards could be sidestepped. A new, corporate-backed, state-run conveyor belt was in motion, rubber-stamping charter schools that local communities didn't want.

The problem didn't lie in the mere existence of commission-authorized charter schools. The kicker was the Georgia Charter Schools Commission's ability to drain money from local districts to pay for the charters. One of the first charter schools authorized by the commission was in a suburb of Atlanta. Ivy Preparatory Academy received nearly $850,000 per year in state funding that would have otherwise gone to Gwinnett County Public Schools, which had denied Ivy Prep's original petition. The school district sued the Georgia Charter Schools Commission, the charter schools it authorized, and state officials in 2009 (surprisingly, Mike Bowers was the attorney representing the school system), charging that the commission had violated the state constitution on two grounds. First, only local school boards and the Georgia Department of Education were legally allowed to create charter schools. Second, only local school districts could levy local tax dollars to fund schools. The state was effectively levying local taxes by providing extra state funding to commission-authorized charter schools proportional to the amount of local taxes they would have received if they had been authorized by local school districts, then deducting that amount from state funding to the local districts where those charter schools were located. As the lawsuit progressed, six more school districts joined, including Atlanta Public Schools.[20]

Meanwhile, Charter Schools USA met with disappointment when its Cherokee petition couldn't even pass muster with the embattled Georgia Charter Schools Commission, which denied it, citing a lack of community support, in December 2009. The company's next recourse was to appeal the local Cherokee County school board decision, so in June 2010, the board reviewed the proposal for the second time.[21]

Again the board voted unanimously against Charter Schools USA, citing several of the same concerns it had identified the year prior, including the issue of the company paying extremely high rent to its partner firm, Red Apple Development.

"This would be a third-party-for-profit Florida firm owning a facility paid for by Georgia taxpayers," school board attorney Tom Roach warned. He also noted that Charter Schools USA planned to spend only 46 percent of per-student funding on classroom instruction, compared to 69 percent in the district's traditional public schools.[22] Danny Brewington, a consultant hired by Charter Schools USA to advocate for proposed charter schools in Georgia and Louisiana, was among the few people at the meeting who spoke favorably of the petition.[23]

Undeterred by the second rejection from the local board, Charter Schools USA took its revised petition back to the Georgia Charter Schools Commission, and in December 2010 it was accepted. The commission's about-face may have had something to do with its new executive director, Mark Peevy, a former GCSA board member. Though it's unclear how close Peevy's ties to Charter Schools USA were beforehand, it's telling that less than a year later he would join the company's hired gun, Brewington, in launching a new charter school consulting firm, Ed Innovations Partners.[24]

Peevy had to leave his post at the Georgia Charter Schools Commission in May 2011, when the Supreme Court of Georgia sided with the Gwinnett County school board and six other districts by ruling that the agency was unconstitutional, which concluded the lawsuit that was launched in 2009. Suddenly, the seventeen schools the commission had authorized, nine of which had opened, were in limbo, with no clear funding source. Charter Schools USA had begun enrollment at Cherokee Charter Academy for the fall, so it made one more last-ditch effort at attaining local approval for the school.

It was the third time in as many years that the Cherokee County school board was faced with the decision, and by that point the public dialogue around the issue had risen to a fever pitch. In describing the crowd that turned out for the school board meeting in red and black T-shirts that summer, an *Atlanta Journal-Constitution* reporter said the issue had pitted neighbor against neighbor. But judging by the crowd's reaction when board members voted down the petition, it was clear that the majority were opposed to Charter Schools USA.[25]

Cherokee County school board member Mike Chapman would later explain in an op-ed for the *Journal-Constitution* that the decision rested on the same shortcomings evident in the Charter Schools USA's previous petitions. "They refused to allow the school board approval of CCA's [Cherokee Charter Academy] annual budget before turning over millions in taxpayer dollars," he stated, "and their records are filled with red flags as far as lack of local control over those dollars, with evidence that Charter Schools USA would really be driving operations with a goal of increasing its profits and real estate holdings."

Chapman went on to bluntly name a largely unspoken reason for Charter Schools USA's appeal to the small number of Cherokee County parents who did support the charter initiative. Comments by those parents, along with initial enrollment data, he said, "reveal the true desire for this school: a tuition-free private school with little to no enrollment of Hispanic, special needs, and low-income students."[26]

As the dust settled in Cherokee County, the matter was hardly at rest in Atlanta. The state supreme court ruling had sent charter school supporters into a frenzy, not only concerning the fate of the seventeen schools that were delegitimized. The ruling called into question the viability of the entire charter school market in Georgia and gained widespread attention. A vice president of the National Alliance for Public Charter Schools told the *New York Times* that the move might have a ripple effect by sending a message to "people who aren't big fans of charter schools" that, "if we can't kill them in the legislature, we can try to kill them in the courtroom."[27] This struck fear in the hearts of those invested in Georgia's reputation as a leader in education reform. The state had been ranked fourth in the nation for the strength of its charter school laws in 2010.[28] And just like the faulty 2009 standardized test scores, Sonny Perdue and his team had highlighted the unconstitutional Georgia Charter Schools Commission in its application for Race to the Top's $400 million grant.

But Georgia lawmakers had experience creating workarounds to the pesky state constitution. They had done it in 2008 when the state supreme court ruled it unconstitutional to use education tax dollars to build Hard Rock Hotels through the tax allocation district financing scheme. So when the legislative session rolled around in January 2012, Jan Jones (the ALEC member who had sponsored the 2008 bill creating the Georgia Charter Schools Commission) introduced legislation creating a ballot initiative to amend the state constitution. It required a two-thirds vote to pass, so it initially looked as though Democrats could quash the measure. But after weeks of amendments, debate, and heavy lobbying by charter school proponents, the best they could do was water down the bill. The amendment would allow an independent state commission to authorize charters but not to redirect local funding to them as the Georgia Charter Schools Commission had done. The new agency would have a nearly identical name: the State Charter Schools Commission. The final bill passed by just two votes.[29]

To rub it in, Governor Nathan Deal signed the bill in a ceremony at Cherokee Charter Academy, the new branch of Charter Schools USA that the local school board had rejected three times. (By that time the

state had allocated funding to the seventeen schools thrown into limbo
by the dissolution of the commission.) "The charter school has received
great community support here in Cherokee County," Deal had the gall
to say before signing the measure.[30]

From there, the race was on to convince voters to approve the constitutional amendment on the 2012 ballot. The Georgia Charter Schools
Association pulled together Georgia's pro-charter forces and out-of-
state interests to form a campaign committee called Families for Better Public Schools. They also launched a dark money group ironically
called the Brighter Georgia Coalition. As a nonprofit, Brighter Georgia
didn't have to disclose its donors or spending, even though its message
and materials were virtually the same as those of the official campaign.[31]

Families for Better Public Schools raised $1.8 million in a matter
of months, with donations pouring in from New York, the District of
Columbia, and elsewhere, revealing who stood to benefit from the State
Charter Schools Commission.

There were the advocates for corporate education reform, like Alice
Walton, Walmart heir, who gave $600,000 to the campaign. Students-
First, the group former DC chancellor Michelle Rhee founded, put up
$250,000.[32] Americans for Prosperity, a right-wing political organiza-
tion founded by billionaire industrialists Charles and David Koch, gave
$10,000 and assigned their state director to support the effort.[33] Ameri-
can Federation for Children, a group created by billionaire evangelicals
Dick and Betsy DeVos (heirs to the scandal-ridden Amway Corporation) spent $72,000 on pro-amendment radio ads.[34]

Charter schools also put money in the game. K12 Inc., the nation's
largest for-profit charter operator, whose virtual schools consistently
rank low and whose cofounder once said that aborting black babies
would make crime rates drop, donated $300,000 to Families for Bet-
ter Public Schools. The Georgia Charter Schools Commission had
approved a K–12 school a year earlier. National Heritage Academies,
which had a commission-authorized charter in Atlanta and a track record of financial mismanagement and poorly performing schools, contributed $75,000 to the campaign committee. And Charter Schools
USA gave $100,000.[35]

Then there were the business interests, the developers and financiers, who stood to profit from charter school growth. A partner at Hamlin Capital Management, a New York–based investment house that is one of the largest holders of high-yield, tax-exempt municipal charter school bonds, gave $25,000. Julian Robertson, a retired hedge fund manager and cofounder with Tom Cousins of Purpose Built Communities, gave $250,000, and Cousins himself chipped in $25,000.[36]

With this war chest, Families for Better Public Schools hired Ed Innovation Partners, the consulting firm founded by former Georgia Charter Schools Commission director Mark Peevy and Charter Schools USA consultant Danny Brewington. Peevy served as the spokesman of the campaign, insisting that it was a grassroots effort despite the deluge of money from billionaires across the country.[37]

The result was an onslaught of direct mailers, television and radio ads, phone-banking, and events aimed at convincing the electorate that a state commission of political appointees should have the power to create new charter schools even if local communities didn't want them because of their abysmal academic track records, shady profit motives, or the likelihood that they would spark a resegregation of the public schools. Of course, that's not how the pro-charter campaign described it. To hear them tell it, the State Charter Schools Commission was simply about giving parents greater choice.

"More choices don't necessarily mean better choices," countered Maureen Downey, the *Journal Constitution*'s education columnist. Choice, she wrote, would not make up for the $5.7 billion the state had cut from its education budget over the previous ten years or for the problems those cuts had caused. Two-thirds of Georgia's school districts had been forced to reduce the number of school days in their calendar year, and many had increased class sizes. Some schools had shrunk their calendar from the standard 180 school days to just 150, while some classes had ballooned to include as many as thirty-seven students.[38] Sure, traditional public schools were struggling, and parents wanted solutions, but it wasn't due to a lack of "choice."

While there were outspoken groups who shared Downey's critique, their resources were no match for the avalanche of money from every corner of the corporate education reform world. Nearly 59 percent of voters approved the constitutional amendment.[39]

In the first few months of 2013, the resurrected Charter Schools Commission was gearing up to authorize charter schools designed to convey public education dollars to private interests while their students did about as well or worse than traditional public-school kids, with underpaid teachers and rote curricula. The whole operation had the support of celebrity reformers like Michelle Rhee, who had narrowly avoided being held to account for a cheating scandal of epic proportions in DC, and Tom Cousins, whose business dealings had long deprived Atlanta's children of better opportunities. Yet the State Charter Schools Commission and its proponents were widely lauded, while I was headed to jail for "cheating the children."

| | | | | | | | | | | | | |

The Monday when I had to turn myself in at the Fulton County Jail approached incredibly slowly. All weekend I stayed in bed replaying everything up to that point in painful detail, searching in vain for a singular fact, a missing link, to plainly show that my indictment was a simple mistake. There had to be something that could make it all go away in a flash. A critical piece of paperwork misplaced, perhaps? Of course, there was no such thing. In reality, my indictment was a very complicated mistake. But I couldn't stop my brain from rewinding again and again to rehash the day in the computer lab at Dunbar, the meeting with Agent Bigham at South DeKalb Mall, the grand jury hearing, and so on.

Then there were my fears about jail. What did it look like? What did it smell like? What were the guards like? Would I be beaten? My imagination ran wild. I hoped that it would be just a book-in, book-out situation, but I wasn't sure.

When Monday finally came around, I was a nervous wreck. All day I watched the news and saw people turning themselves in one by one. It seemed like every media outlet in the city had turned out to document the perp walk, a march of shame that each educator endured from the moment each stepped out of a car until the jail's double doors thudded closed. Some people carried umbrellas to block the cameras, while others seemed to walk in with pride, their heads held high. The footage made it seem like this was the crime of the century, like educators were money-hungry, ruthless criminals who had no shame about harming children.

Around nine o'clock in the evening, my parents and brother gathered with Moses and me in the living room of our house to say a prayer before driving to the jail together. "God, we come to you in prayer," my mother began, holding my hand tight. "We ask that you protect Shani with your almighty love on her journey tonight. We ask for your favor with the media, that they will not use this perp walk to further embarrass and humiliate her. We ask that you bless our family and guide us through our tribulations with your holy grace. Amen."

The Fulton County Jail was nestled in a swath of trees off an industrial road in Bankhead, a rough neighborhood on Atlanta's northwest side, famous for the many rap stars who grew up there. It looked like any other brick municipal building except for the narrow windows and razor-wire-topped fence. Attorney Greene was waiting for us in the parking lot. It was dark, and the media scrum had dwindled. Surprisingly, no cameras bombarded me when I stepped out of the car. Greene locked her arm with mine. I walked toward the front doors with my head held high.

We passed the camera crews, but they weren't quick to capture my perp walk. Some seemed tired or like they were on a break. I noticed only two cameras trained on my face. As we crossed the threshold into the jail, I took a deep breath and mentally prepared for what would happen next. My family waited a few minutes before following us inside.

In the fluorescent-lit waiting area, I saw a few educators who I recognized from the news. They were being handcuffed and taken down a long hallway. My heart skipped a beat seeing the handcuffs go on.

Shortly after Greene registered me at the front desk, an officer called my name to take me back. As I approached the officer, I turned and winked at my family. I hoped that the message, "I got this," would soften the trauma they surely felt seeing me locked up. The officer was a black woman, maybe ten years my senior. She placed the heavy cuffs around my wrists, snapping them into place unceremoniously. The sound brought to mind the crack of a tree branch giving way under an enormous weight. A piece of my humanity breaking off and plummeting.

The officer gripped my arm and walked me down the hallway and into a huge room with rows of plastic seats connected by long, metal bars underneath. It reminded me of a bus station waiting room except for the holding cells lining the walls. One of the cell doors was open; inside I glimpsed the teachers from the lobby. I had to wait in the open area until jail staff called me to a counter to complete more paperwork. Then I was directed to the open cell.

The first thing I noticed when I stepped into the cell was the strong stench of urine emanating from an open toilet in the corner. I scanned the dozen or so women, all black educators, sitting on benches along the walls and felt a wave of relief when my gaze landed on Pamela Cleveland and Gloria Ivey.

"Robinson!" Cleveland exclaimed, waving me over.

"Are you okay?" Ivey asked, making room for me next to her on the bench.

"I'm as fine as I can be," I told her, feeling better by the second in their maternal company.

"I can't believe this is happening," Cleveland said, the outrage in her voice muffled by weariness. She had been there for two hours already.

Our conversation soon merged with others in the group, and I began to hear stories like my own for the first time, and some that were worse. I thought I had it bad when Agent Bigham interrogated me like a criminal, but others had faced greater pressure, even threats, from the GBI agents who interviewed them.

"They didn't read me any Miranda rights, and before they asked me a single question, they told me I would be handcuffed and hauled off to jail, then and there, if I didn't cooperate," Ivey remembered. "They told me I would never teach again, that I wouldn't be able to support my family. They even threatened my pension. I was scared as hell!"

Other women chimed in, saying they too had been told they would lose their pensions if they didn't confess to cheating. One woman said she heard about a GBI agent pulling out his gun and placing it on a table while he interrogated a teacher. I heard another story about a GBI agent warning a teacher that he would take away her children if she didn't cooperate. One of the younger women said she was pregnant when the cheating scandal first came to light. She went into an early labor after being interrogated and believed it was due to the stressful ordeal.

Like me, many of these women did not have an attorney present during interrogations.

"We had no prior warning," Cleveland recounted. "Those GBI agents came to Dunbar and pulled us out of class and took us down to the music room. It was spur of the moment."

Like me, they signed the GBI's pre-written statements attesting that what they said was true, never imagining they could be charged with a felony for "false statements and writings" as a result.

"You know you should read stuff before you sign it," Cleveland lamented. "And I read it, sure. But you know, I didn't have time to really study it with them breathing down my neck. You're facing the big folks! Somebody who is standing in for the governor. And it feels like they'll put a target on your back if you don't sign it."

Even though we were stuck in a jail cell, I found immense comfort in being around these women. Up to that point, I had only talked about my plight with family and friends, none of whom had experienced what I was going through. In the jail cell, it was almost like being in a group therapy session.

Even the jail staff offered words of encouragement. Officers passing our cell told us, "Keep your heads up," "It's going to be all right," and "It's a shame what they're doing to y'all." It was the first time I'd heard that kind of affirmation from strangers; I had been so inundated by the talking heads on television insisting we had "cheated the children" that I had begun to believe the whole world was against us.

We talked for hours, and, as midnight approached, the last defendants came trickling in, including Diane Buckner-Webb. The stories continued, and we speculated about what went down when the GBI interrogated Rose Neal, the coworker who accused us.

"I bet she was just trying to get herself out of trouble," Buckner-Webb mused.

Someone else said her lawyer was at the DA's office when Neal arrived to give her confession. According to the lawyer, Neal was "shaking all over and spouting off all kinds of nonsense, like she would agree to say anything."

Finally, in the early hours of the morning, officers began calling our names as our bonds were processed. When it was my turn, they handcuffed me again to walk me back down the long hallway. This time the handcuffs felt a little bit lighter.

When I made it to the waiting area where all the family members and attorneys were gathered, everyone started clapping and cheering. My family embraced me, and I rode home with them in a daze. I went to bed just before dawn and slept harder than I had in a long time.

In the weeks following my night in jail with the other educators, revelations of cheating in school districts across the country would amplify the absurdity of our criminalization. First, a journalist for PBS's *Frontline* obtained a memo concerning the DC public school system, written in 2009 by an independent analyst hired by the district to investigate cheating allegations. The memo implicated 191 teachers in seventy schools and was presented to DC school officials, although former chancellor Michelle Rhee said she didn't recall receiving the document. The school district never acted upon the alarming findings. This was the same school system that had been dogged by cheating allegations since 2011 (and earlier, according to the newly discovered memo) but had been cleared of wrongdoing by the DC inspector general and the US Department of Education, sweeping a lawsuit filed by a DC educator under the rug. While the memo cast a shadow on their conclusions, neither agency seemed in a hurry to investigate further.[40] Nor did federal education officials see fit to take a second look at Georgia's Race to the Top grant, awarded in part based on the test scores that were now the focus of overzealous news coverage nationwide. I thought surely there would be some discussion of revoking at least part of the grant, but that never materialized.

Then a report by the US Governmental Accountability Office found that forty states had reported allegations of standardized test cheating over the past two school years, and thirty-two had "cancelled, invalidated, or nullified test scores as a result of cheating."[41]

Yet nowhere else were teachers dragged to jail, paraded before news cameras, or slapped with felony charges punishable by decades in prison. That treatment was reserved for the black educators of Atlanta. The procession in and out of jail was just the beginning. Soon I would have to make my first appearance in court and meet the judge who would determine my fate.

CHAPTER SIX

Between a Rock and a Hard Place

❚❘❘❘❘❘❘❘❘❘❘❘❘❘❘❘❘❘❘❘❘❘❘❘❘❚

"WE MAY HAVE TO RENT an abandoned Kroger to fit everybody. This case is going to be crowded," Judge Jerry Baxter quipped in his distinctively throaty half-drawl.[1] A native of Atlanta, where Kroger grocery stores are ubiquitous, Baxter's good ol' boy Georgia accent was tempered by a lifetime in a diverse city. His sense of humor, on the other hand, seemed oddly unbridled for a judge.

It was early May 2013, my night in jail a little more than a month behind me, and I was crammed in a downtown courtroom with more than sixty people—most of the thirty-five defendants and their lawyers, plus a swarm of reporters who filled the jury box. It was our arraignment, our first appearance in court, where each defendant had to enter a plea. I was there to plead not guilty, and so was everyone else.

The process was straightforward. Our names were called, and our lawyers answered for us. It started with former superintendent Beverly Hall, who by now had taken on the mythos of a mob boss in the popular imagination. Much of the media attention was on her. Within about half an hour, the rest of us had pleaded.

Baxter then turned to another issue. The district attorney's office wanted him to place a gag order on the defense lawyers, prohibiting them from speaking to the media. This was in addition to the agreement defendants had made to not give interviews in exchange for having our bonds lowered. With this gag order, even our lawyers wouldn't be able to speak to reporters on our behalf.

To my delight, Baxter was incensed by this. "These folks have pretty much been vilified and tried in the court of public opinion, and your office has been leading the charge," he spat at a deputy district attorney, taking care to express his particular disdain for the press conference in which Paul Howard had trotted out parents and students for show.

"My goal, and I think my obligation, is to ensure the presumption of innocence is involved," Baxter declared as he denied the gag order. "I think everybody understands that I'm going to be very upset if this case is tried anywhere but in the Kroger or wherever we go."[2]

Get 'em, judge! I thought to myself, holding back laughter at his fixation on the grocery store chain.

Then an attorney for the *Journal-Constitution* and WSB-TV asked Baxter to strike the conditions in our bond agreements that prevented us from speaking to media. Prosecutors protested, but Baxter was resolute. "I'm striking that," he said flatly.

I was exuberant when court adjourned. Baxter's comments had me convinced that the case would eventually be thrown out, even though he had set a trial date for May 2014, one year away.

Outside the courtroom, I gathered with my codefendants from Dunbar. Lera Middlebrooks, the testing coordinator who had instructed us to erase stray marks on students' test booklets, was imposing as ever. She had a shock of platinum-blond hair styled in a short wave, eyelashes out to here, chunky jewelry, and a look to kill.

Middlebrooks fumed about how Principal Greene had told investigators that she didn't know we were erasing stray marks, saying she felt like the principal had basically thrown her under the bus to get the GBI off her back.

"Well, we're all under the bus now," said Diane Buckner-Webb, my former co-teacher.

"Yeah, but I think that judge is on our side," I interjected. "He was telling those prosecutors off."

Middlebrooks heaved a sigh and pursed her lips, as if she wasn't so sure.

The trial was a year away, but the defense lawyers quickly began filing motions, and pretrial hearings kicked off in June. The stakes were soon as high as any trial's.

Some of the motions would have turned the odds in our favor, like one brought by Pamela Cleveland's lawyer that sought to take the case away from the Fulton County District Attorney's Office because of Paul Howard's conflict of interest. His wife, Petrina Howard, worked at an elementary school that had come under the scrutiny of Sonny Perdue's special investigation back in 2010. Six of her colleagues confessed to cheating. Howard had assisted the testing coordinator and was among those who handed out and collected the tests. But neither she nor anyone else from her school was indicted.

Prosecutors argued that this was because the school had only a moderate level of cheating compared to other schools. They also said that Paul Howard had put up a "Chinese wall" to insulate himself from his department's investigation into his wife's school. But his staff had worked with the special investigation team that produced the GBI report and had relayed information to Howard during that time. He also had dinner with the men heading the investigation, Mike Bowers, Richard Hyde, and Bob Wilson, to discuss the investigation "in general terms," while it was underway. Despite the glaring conflict of interest, Baxter denied the motion.

The most important motion Baxter considered was one that all defendants signed on to, which held the promise of the outcome I anticipated. Soon, I thought, all charges would be dropped.

Brian Steel, the attorney representing former middle school principal Lucious Brown, tried to have the entire indictment overturned due to prosecutorial misconduct. According to Steel, many defendants gave statements to investigators under the threat of losing their jobs. In a series of hearings in the middle of June, he presented a letter that Beverly Hall wrote to APS employees at the start of the state investigation in 2010, instructing them to cooperate with investigators or "risk being found insubordinate." In a follow-up letter, Hall specified that insubordination could lead to termination.

This, Steel argued, flew in the face of the law established by *Garrity v. New Jersey*, a 1967 case in which the US Supreme Court ruled that evidence obtained by compelling public employees, including teachers, to incriminate themselves under threat of termination could not be used against them in a criminal prosecution.

"This entire process is so poisoned," Steel said. "The entire indictment must be dismissed."[3]

RICO expert John Floyd, who had volunteered to work on the prosecution team even though he was a private attorney, claimed that *Garrity* didn't apply because none of the defendants made a self-incriminating confession; we all denied wrongdoing in our interviews with investigators.

"Well, they made a statement which they have been indicted for," Baxter retorted.

It was true that many of the defendants were indicted for "false statements" or "false swearing," because investigators thought they lied when they denied cheating. While I was charged with false statements and writings, it wasn't because of what I said to the GBI, it was for allegedly changing answers on the CRCT.

Floyd also claimed that attorneys had accompanied educators during interviews with investigators, implying that we couldn't have been coerced in their presence.[4] While that was true for some, I couldn't believe he would make such a generalization. There was no lawyer sitting in that sedan with Agent Bigham and me in the mall parking lot.

Prosecutor Fani Willis presented additional letters from Hall and the APS general counsel that were issued after the letters that threatened termination for insubordination. These letters informed APS employees that they had a right to legal representation and could invoke their Fifth Amendment right against self-incrimination.

But Steel called Mike Bowers to the witness stand and showed that even when educators were accompanied by attorneys and attempted to invoke the Fifth Amendment, investigators still used threats to try to get them to talk. Steel asked Bowers to read transcripts from the investigative team's interviews with Lucious Brown. Bowers read part of a conversation between himself and Brown, in which he warned Brown that his principal's certificate, and thus his job, could be in jeopardy if he pleaded the Fifth.

"You are still telling Dr. Brown that by invoking his Fifth, he is going to suffer the civil consequence of potentially losing his certificate, do you realize that?" Steel asked when Bowers was done reading.

"Yes. I realize that, and I can't change that," was Bowers's response.

When I heard this, I remembered the conversations from my night in jail, how my fellow educators had recounted the sundry threats investigators had made to pry information from them.

The absurdity and unfairness of the whole ordeal was finally being exposed, just like I knew it would. Baxter agreed with Steel and said so in his characteristically emphatic style.

"The fastest way they thought to get to the truth was to go in like a bull in a china shop," he said about the investigators.[5]

When the hearings concluded, Baxter hinted that he was ready to throw out the indictment, telling prosecutors, "I am seriously concerned about your case." But he put off making a final ruling until the following week.

In the meantime, the *Journal-Constitution* reported these developments as a great disappointment, with headlines like "APS Case Appears at Risk" and "How Did APS Case Run into Trouble?" Why, I wondered, couldn't they write headlines like "At-Risk Teachers Appear Close to Freedom" and "How Did Lawyers Save Maligned Educators?" It was likely because the coverage till then had drummed up the public to eagerly expect a bloodletting.

"If this case gets dismissed, I'm going to be brokenhearted," sniffed a parent interviewed by a *Journal-Constitution* reporter. She was a white woman whose children attended a school with a relatively large proportion of white students, a school that had never been implicated in cheating.

Another white parent, Cynthia Briscoe Brown, told the reporter she wanted closure. "We need to see those who were responsible suffer the consequences of their actions," she said.[6] Brown's son attended North Atlanta High School, an APS school in Buckhead, the northernmost and wealthiest Atlanta neighborhood. This school was also untouched by the cheating scandal. In fact, at that moment, it was in the limelight for a posh makeover. The school district had just shelled out $147 million to retrofit an eleven-story office tower, situated on fifty-six wooded acres, into the school's new state-of-the-art campus, featuring skyline views, a spring-fed lake, a video production center, a food-court-style cafeteria with a smoothie station, and an indoor shooting range. Meanwhile, in Atlanta's West End neighborhood, at Booker T. Washington High School, where Martin Luther King Jr. matriculated, raw sewage was seeping through the floor, and mold had destroyed the band uniforms. APS dragged its heels in replacing the uniforms for so long that media mogul Tyler Perry eventually stepped in and donated cash to replace them.[7] It seemed that people with the fewest problems in their school zone were most eager to see black teachers behind bars.

At the end of June, Baxter decided not to dismiss the case based on *Garrity*. I was stunned. It had seemed like his mind was made up in our favor. What had changed? In his ruling, he wrote that "there were no expressed threats to the Defendants that he or she would lose their jobs." It seemed that the second round of letters from Hall and the APS attorney, which Fani Willis presented, had convinced him that the school district didn't intend to fire anyone for refusing to answer investigators' questions. However, Baxter wrote, defendants may have subjectively believed that their jobs were at risk, even if they weren't. So he invited defendants to make individual motions to exclude from trial the statements they made to investigators, based on *Garrity*.

Baxter also denied my attorney's request to dismiss my RICO count on the grounds that I was only charged with one "predicate act," which is a crime carried out for the purpose of committing an even bigger crime. For me, the "false statements and writing" count was the underlying charge that enabled prosecutors to make this a RICO case. But historically RICO charges could only be applied if there were at least two predicate acts, since RICO charges require a *pattern* of racketeering activity. In 2001, there was a change to the law allowing just one predicate act to underlie a RICO charge. However, Georgia courts and federal courts still applied the two-predicate-act rule in most cases. Floyd, the RICO expert, told Judge Baxter that as long as I had made "some kind of agreement" or "some kind of effort to join in the conspiracy" I could be charged with RICO. Of course, I hadn't made any agreements, I definitely wasn't part of any conspiracy, and I couldn't see how a single "false statements and writing" charge, itself bogus, could amount to such. It was the craziest thing I had ever heard.

My confidence was dashed, but not for long. The next great hope on the horizon was a trial slated for September in which one of the indicted educators, Tamara Cotman, would fight her charge of "influencing a witness." Like the rest of us, she had been slapped with a RICO charge on top of that one. Baxter had granted her a speedy trial on the condition that it would concern only the "influencing a witness" charge, and not the RICO.

Cotman was a School Reform Team director who supervised twenty-one schools within APS. The charges against her stemmed from a meeting she convened of the principals under her watch. In an interview with investigators, Cotman explained that in the meeting she had conducted a "stress relieving exercise" for staff who were demoralized by the cheating investigation.

"I had talked to principals who were extremely frustrated," she said. "I had talked to teachers who had been cursed at, had been threatened to have their children taken from them if they didn't say what the investigators wanted to hear. There was a lot of anger."[8]

Cotman passed out copies of a memo labeled "Go to Hell." The memo was a spoof on office culture, the kind of thing that you would find in a shop for gag gifts. It included check boxes indicating how the recipient might fulfill the memo's directive; via "a handbasket," "good intentions," and "a flaming chariot" were some of the options. Cotman told the principals they could use it to write a note to anyone they wanted. The memos wouldn't actually be delivered; Cotman explained that the exercise was inspired by an article she read online that suggested that simply writing an angry letter could relieve stress.

One principal interpreted the exercise as a warning against cooperating with the investigation. That was the basis for the "influencing a witness" charge. But another principal said she wrote the name of her mortgage company on her "Go to Hell" note and said she didn't recall Cotman mentioning the GBI specifically.[9]

The trial lasted two weeks. It was viewed as a "dress rehearsal" for the RICO trial. For my codefendants and me, it seemed a bellwether of our fate.

My heart soared when the jury returned the verdict: not guilty. "There was a lack of evidence for the charge that was brought on this person," one juror told a *Journal-Constitution* reporter, noting that the prosecution had presented much convincing evidence that cheating had happened in the district but not enough to conclude that Cotman had intimidated her subordinates.[10]

Tamara Cotman wasn't the only one seemingly off the hook that month. About a week after her trial, Dougherty County District Attorney Gregory Edwards announced he would not prosecute any of the forty-nine educators accused of cheating in that county's school district. Dougherty had the second-highest percentage of schools flagged for suspicious scores after APS and was the only other district investigated by Bowers and the rest of the team assembled by Governor Perdue.

Edwards explained that firings and revocations of teaching certificates would suffice because there was no "top-down conspiracy," just "individuals . . . working independently."[11] Even so, Edwards could have charged educators with felonies like "false statements and writings" without indicting them for racketeering and conspiracy. Why were the black educators of Atlanta being dragged through the mud in an unprecedented, unparalleled fashion?

In November, *Garrity* was back on the table for defendants who decided to pursue it individually: several defendants tried to have their interviews with investigators stricken from the record on the grounds that they had been coerced to talk under threat of being fired. This could have led Baxter to drop their charges of "false statements and writings" and "false swearing." I didn't use this tack, since I wasn't working for APS at the time the GBI interrogated me, and so I hadn't been afraid of being fired for not answering their questions. But I followed the hearings, and that's when I really began to worry.

Gloria Ivey, my former fifth-grade co-teacher, took the stand and described, as many defendants had, receiving the letter from Beverly

Hall instructing employees to cooperate with investigators or "risk being found insubordinate." Then Ivey repeated the story she had told me during our night in jail.

She said that in one of her interviews with GBI agents, "Before the questions were asked, I was told that I would immediately be locked up in handcuffs and taken to jail if I didn't cooperate. They told me that I would lose my job. They told me that I would be indicted. They told me that they would take every penny that I own. I wouldn't be able to support my family. They told me they would take my pension. They would report me to the Professional Standards Commission, and I wouldn't be able to teach for the rest of my life."

Several defendants testified to this sort of bullying by investigators during the November *Garrity* hearings. But prosecutors shut them down with an underhanded move. In Ivey's case, it was prosecutor April McConnell who presented her with the prepared statement GBI agents had proffered in their meetings. It was the same document I had signed in the mall parking lot with Agent Bigham. McConnell had Ivey read the paragraph attesting that she did not take part in or know about cheating. Then McConnell asked Ivey to read the statement at the top of the page: "I declare that the following admission is truthful and made of my own free will."

In earlier *Garrity* hearings, this exercise had the intended effect of putting defendants between a rock and a hard place. They were claiming to have been coerced into talking to investigators, but here was a document they had signed saying that they gave their statement voluntarily. Some defendants faltered, seemingly trying to explain what Pamela Cleveland had plainly stated when we talked in jail, "You know you should read stuff before you sign it, but you're facing the big folks!" It was clear no one wanted to admit that they hadn't carefully scrutinized what they had signed.

Ivey had a different take. "I read that," she said. "I told the investigator, I pointed out[,] that this was voluntary. And I said, 'I don't have to sign this statement.' She said I had to sign it or else I would be sent to jail."

"Ms. Ivey, is your position that that wasn't the truth?" asked McConnell, referring to the portion of the statement that denied cheating.

"Excuse me?"

"Why would you feel forced to sign a statement that you contend is true?"

Ivey was confounded. I shuddered at this exchange. It was a catch-22. The way McConnell framed it, Ivey either had to claim she cheated and was coerced into making a false statement to the contrary or that she didn't cheat and wasn't coerced. Neither scenario would meet the threshold for the *Garrity* argument, so Ivey's charges were not dropped. Neither were anyone else's.

Of course, reality was more complicated than McConnell made it out to be. Ivey and some of the other defendants had been wary of signing the statement declaring that they didn't cheat, not because it wasn't true but because they sensed it had the potential to draw them into the very trap in which they now found themselves. But they signed anyway because they were compelled by the investigators' bullying tactics and the edict from Hall to cooperate.

It was becoming clear to me how prosecutors could twist information to turn our own words and actions against us. Even Tamara Cotman's victory, which had buoyed my hopes, was under attack. Prosecutors planned to go ahead and try her for RICO with the rest of us, using the same evidence they had deployed in her speedy trial, despite her lawyer's protest that this constituted double jeopardy.

Judge Baxter's attitude had shifted too. Where he once used a sharp tongue on the prosecutors while championing fairness for defendants, he now sided with them on almost everything and treated us with a sort of fatalism. After Ivey's hearing, he reminded us that the deadline to enter a plea deal was coming up in January. "And I would suggest everybody start talking to the prosecutor, unless they want to go on this long journey to possible bad outcomes," he said.

Four days earlier, teacher Lisa Terry had become the first indicted educator to take a plea deal. She admitted to letting her students change their answers after testing was over and agreed to testify in the trial, pay back the meager $500 bonus she received in 2009, and read a letter of apology in court. In exchange, her felony charges were dropped and replaced with a misdemeanor obstruction charge for which she received a year of probation and 250 hours of community service.

"The truth is finally out," crowed DA Paul Howard to a *Journal-Constitution* reporter. A legal expert interviewed for the same article gave a crasser assessment. "Let the games begin," he said.[12]

No doubt, it was tempting to envision a possible twenty-five-year prison sentence reduced to some community service and probation. Some defendants were facing even more time—up to forty years. For the older defendants, that was practically a life sentence. *Should I lie just to lift this burden from my life?* I wondered. Then again, didn't Terry's plea deal expose the absurdity of this case? If the punishment for an alleged crime could range from nearly half a century in a cage to a few months of volunteerism, wouldn't people see that the scales of justice were more than a bit off-kilter? It was like the prosecution had a greater goal that they were trying to get to, and they wanted most of us out of the way or working for them. I mean, they couldn't have cut a sweeter deal. It was like they were screaming, "Just say you cheated! We don't care! You can go back to life as usual!" They wanted Beverly Hall, I figured. They didn't care what happened to the rest of us. But that was hardly justice.

Shortly before Christmas, I heard the news about Lera Middlebrooks. She had agreed to a plea deal. She told prosecutors that she had given Dunbar teachers answer sheets after testing was completed and that she believed we had changed incorrect answers. I was devastated.

Later I would read a transcript from one of her earlier interviews with the GBI in which Middlebrooks denied wrongdoing, and it would strike me how different her tone was from the false confession she ultimately made. Her words jumped off the page; I could hear her voice rising with indignation as she went to bat not only for herself but also the rest of us, talking over the agents who called her boastful, telling them, "You don't even know me." That was the Middlebrooks I knew and admired. It was strange. I didn't feel angry at her for throwing us under the bus the way she said Principal Greene had done to her. I only felt depressed. They were breaking us.

‖‖‖‖‖‖‖‖‖‖‖

As the fabric of APS frayed, education profiteers descended on the city, perhaps sensing opportunity in the mistrust much of the public now felt toward the public school system. That November, while the

Garrity hearings were underway, Atlantans were tasked with electing new school board members for the first time since the cheating scandal broke. Unlike any local election in the city before it, this school board race became a feeding frenzy for investors and education reform advocates from across the country who swooped in to stack the board with their preferred candidates.

Alumni of Teach for America were running for four of the nine seats on the school board. In 2008, shortly after I joined their teacher training boot camp, TFA spawned an offshoot called Leadership for Educational Equality (LEE) to help corps members get elected to public office once they completed two years in the classroom. It was part of TFA founder Wendy Kopp's original vision that people in powerful positions would have the experience of teaching at impoverished schools, making them more likely to enact policies and decisions that benefited those schools. But TFA alumni brought more than their classroom experience to these positions; they were imbued with an ideology about education reform that favored corporate interests. Even if TFA alumni like me questioned parts of the organization's philosophy, LEE brought them further into the sphere of corporate influence.

At the time of the 2013 Atlanta school board race, TFA's board included people like Arthur Rock, a California venture capitalist and partner in Rocketship Education, a for-profit charter school chain that relies heavily on computer-based instruction and unsalaried classroom aides instead of traditional teachers. Greg Penner, a member of the Walton (Walmart) family, was on the board too, and so was Joel Klein, former chancellor of New York City public schools, who oversaw an era of rampant charter school proliferation before departing to the private sector to head an education technology company that produced tablets for K–12 schools. All three donated thousands of dollars to the four TFA candidates running for the Atlanta school board. So did numerous other hedge fund managers, investors, and CEOs of major corporations based in New York and California, people with no connection to Atlanta Public Schools other than the TFA and LEE network.[13]

Altogether, the TFA candidates were able to raise far more than their opponents. One ran unopposed and still racked up nearly $37,000, which was more than that accrued by any of the candidates squaring off against the other three TFA alumni. Courtney English, who was in my TFA cohort, raised over $100,000, outgunning everyone in the race except for Mark Riley, the former school board member and Cousins-affiliated developer who was attempting a comeback. English had gone straight from teaching to running for the school board in 2009 and was now up for reelection. If he realized that one of his fellow corps members was standing trial in the cheating scandal, he never mentioned it.[14]

The unusual level of outside spending made headlines and thrust the issue of charter schools to the fore, driving one of the TFA candidates to protest, "People shouldn't be concerned that there will be some radical change or that there's a conspiracy theory of privatization."[15]

But the moment was ripe for a turn toward privatization if a willing school board emerged from the election. Atlanta charters were attracting more and more students in the wake of the cheating scandal; that fall, one in twelve APS students was enrolled in a charter school.[16] It seemed that the logic of disaster capitalism was at play. Although the crisis of the cheating scandal was in many ways the result of years of corporate-driven education reforms, it was often construed as a problem of government corruption and an argument for privatizing the public sector.

That wasn't the view of Erroll Davis, the superintendent who had taken the reins from Beverly Hall in the midst of the cheating scandal and planned to retire at the end of the year. Davis had put the brakes on new charter schools in response to a pension fund dispute. He thought charter schools should pay into the teacher pension fund, while charter operators argued that since their teachers didn't receive pensions, they shouldn't have to contribute.

And though the previous year's election had ushered in the State Charter Schools Commission, which could override Davis's decision to deny new charters, it wasn't clear that the commission would in fact serve as the rubber stamp its promoters had intended. The commission had only approved one school out of the sixteen that had applied after it began operating the previous March. This had groups like the Georgia Charter Schools Association, which fought tooth and nail for the commission, up in arms.[17] While GCSA's director decried the situation with the usual rhetoric of "school choice," the board chairman of a proposed

charter school that Davis opposed had a different take, one that illumi-
nated the motivations underlying the charter trend. "It's bigger than
Atlanta Public Schools," he said. "We want our city to be an attractive place for businesses because of our public schools. That's what's
at risk."[18] That risk could be averted if a charter-friendly school board
replaced Davis with a pro-charter superintendent when he retired.

With local business interests at stake, it wasn't just corporate executives and hedge fund managers in New York and California investing
in the school board election. Homegrown business leaders turned education reformers put their money in the race too. Chief among them
were Lillian and Greg Giornelli, the daughter and son-in-law of real
estate developer Tom Cousins. Greg Giornelli was now president of
Purpose Built Communities, the organization Cousins founded with
hedge fund manager and charter school investor Julian Robertson, to
replicate the East Lake model of privatizing public housing and public
schools together.

Upon its inception in 2009, Purpose Built set its sights on New
Orleans, where the devastation of Hurricane Katrina drew privatizers
hungry to preempt the city's rebuilding its public infrastructure by ped-
dling plans for privately owned and operated replacements. Charter operators took over a majority of the city's public schools, and TFA corps
members replaced many of the thousands of teachers who were laid
off after the storm. In the chaos after the hurricane, city council members voted to demolish the city's four largest public housing units, even
though tenant groups and housing justice advocates contended that the
buildings were not severely damaged. Purpose Built proposed replacing
the St. Bernard housing project with a mixed-income complex called
Columbia Parc, built and managed by the same company that transformed East Lake in Atlanta. While St. Bernard comprised 1,464 public
housing units, Columbia Parc would have a total of only 900, and only
a third of those would be for low-income families.[19]

The Columbia Parc proposal mimicked East Lake in that it included
plans for a charter school and a "championship" golf course and club. It
also followed the East Lake model in adopting an approach to social engineering based on a pathological view of poverty. On a tour of the area,
Cousins declared, "Children who grow up here are going to be good

citizens—tax payers, not tax users," implicitly maligning the former residents of St. Bernard.[20] When Columbia Parc was completed, low-income residents were subject to strict regulations intended to correct their presumed deficiencies: work requirements, criminal background checks, and rules governing guests, sitting on porches, and playing music.

By 2013, Purpose Built had propagated its model in numerous cities where it was involved in privatization efforts. Though Cousins scorned "tax users," the developers who worked with Purpose Built Communities were happy to use millions of dollars in tax credits to finance the mixed-income complexes and charter schools that replaced public housing and traditional public schools. Purpose Built's neighborhood redevelopment in Indianapolis leveraged funding with more than $19 million in tax credits, some of which came from the New Markets Tax Credit Program, a federal handout to private investors who put their money into projects in low-income neighborhoods.[21] In addition to low-income housing, charter schools are eligible for the lucrative New Markets Tax Credit financing, making it one of the driving forces for charter school growth and a favorite tool of investors eager to profit from public education.[22] With the 39 percent tax credit offered by the program, on top of interest, lenders can double the money they invest in new charters in seven years.[23] As the Atlanta school board race was underway, the Cousins' East Lake Foundation was expanding Drew Charter School, building a high school with $34 million in New Markets Tax Credit funding.[24] Interim superintendent Erroll Davis took an unpopular stance against the expansion, saying that with other APS high schools under-enrolled, a new one wasn't needed.[25]

Investors and developers in Atlanta were also happily taking subsidies in the form of public education dollars redirected to private development through the tax allocation districts that Greg Giornelli had helped create as head of the Atlanta Development Authority. By the end of 2013, the city had allocated over $450 million in TAD funding for the construction of a slew of high-end condos and upscale office buildings. The only education-related project funded by the TAD program was a $648,000 grant to Corinthian Colleges, a national chain of for-profit colleges with more than a hundred campuses across the country, including four in Atlanta, and revenues totaling over $1 billion, derived mostly from federal student loans and grants.[26] Five years after receiving the TAD grant, Corinthian went bankrupt as lawsuits in twenty-one states and a federal probe found that the company saddled students with astronomical debt, provided subpar educational programs, lied about job placement rates, and used illegal tactics to collect on the high-interest loans it pushed on students.[27]

Not only was APS losing millions of dollars to sleazy, profit-driven ventures, the school district wasn't even getting what it was contractually owed from the biggest TAD deal. When the BeltLine TAD was created in 2005 to turn a twenty-two-mile loop of defunct railroad into an "emerald necklace" of green space, bike paths, and light rail transit, the deal stipulated that while $850 million in property taxes would be diverted from APS, the district would receive annual fixed payments totaling $150 million over twenty years beginning in 2011. Before the TAD could go into effect, it was shot down by a state supreme court ruling that found it unconstitutional to spend education funds on anything besides education. As a state senator, Kasim Reed sponsored a constitutional amendment that passed in 2008 to change that. In the meantime, the stock market crashed, sending the real estate market into a tailspin and property tax revenue plummeting.

So, in 2009, the same year Reed was elected mayor, APS renegotiated the TAD deal with the Atlanta Development Authority. A series of amendments increased the annual payments to a total of more than $162 million over eighteen years and pushed the start date back to January 2013, among other provisions. But by the time the school board race rolled around in November that year, the Atlanta Development Authority, which Reed had rebranded "Invest Atlanta," had yet to make its first payment to APS. The overdue payment would finally come in December but without interest. Invest Atlanta would again fail to make its January payment in 2014, and by the following summer it would be $19 million in arrears and seeking another renegotiation with the school system.[28]

The defunding of APS by the city's development agency garnered little attention during the school board race. At that point, the school board was trying not to ruffle feathers in the mayor's office, even as he flouted the terms of the TAD agreement. So, instead, the cheating scandal dominated the discourse, creating a smokescreen that distracted from everything else going on in the school system. In fact, one of the newcomers to enter the race was Cynthia Briscoe Brown, the Buckhead parent whose child attended the most expensive public school in the state and who had told a reporter that the indicted educators should "suffer." She beat Mark Riley, who had more campaign cash and local business connections than anyone but had been on the school board when the cheating happened.

Tied to the cheating scandal was the issue of charter schools and privatization, but a robust public debate about it never really materialized. The TFA candidates trod lightly on the subject. Courtney English expressed his support for charter schools by stating simply that children "should not be forced to go to a bad school."[29] The $100,000 he collected from venture capitalists, Walmart heirs, and education technology CEOs raised eyebrows, but it also paved the way to victory. English won handily, and the three other TFA candidates made the cut as well.

The election produced a major turnover on the school board. When the dust settled, seven out of nine board members were new. But while the slate was clean, it remained tethered as ever to the business interests that spurred the policies and practices that had birthed the cheating scandal.

1 1 1 1 1 1 1 1 1 1 1 1 1

"I'll be glad when this trial is over," I told my dad. It was an afternoon just before Christmas, and I had stopped by my parents' house for a short visit between errands. We sat in the wood-paneled den filled with African art and chatted while he peeled and ate an orange.

I caught my dad wince at the word "trial." I knew my parents were incredibly stressed by my predicament, and the longer I delayed my decision about the plea deal, the more they worried. Ever since they saw me handcuffed, I could tell there was a desperate fear that they were trying to suppress. It came across as a constant uneasiness. They were living every black parent's worst nightmare. I could make it go away if I took a deal. Indecision gnawed at me. As much as I wanted to dissolve my parents' distress, the indignity of the lie I would have to assume fueled my desire to fight the charges. But in that moment, my father gave me pause. He usually seemed younger than his age; his lanky body emanated a boyish energy, his easy smile framed by a black goatee with just a sprinkle of gray hairs, eyes flashing with interest behind rimless glasses. Today, though, sitting hunched forward on the couch in silence, bits of orange peel cupped in his hand, he looked worn down. *Maybe I just need to bite the bullet*, I thought.

The phone rang, and Dad reached to the side table to answer it.

"Hello? Yes, this is Jessie. Yes, my daughter is here." Looking confused, he handed the cordless receiver to me. "It's a nurse from my doctor's office," he said. "She wants to speak to you."

"Hello?" I said, taking the phone.

"Ma'am, your father's test results have just come back," said a stern voice on the other end. "If you don't get him to a hospital right now, he could die."

I don't remember that drive to the hospital. It was like the day I learned I was indicted but worse. Numb legs, short breaths, prayers, reflexes.

At the hospital, doctors put Dad on emergency dialysis. There was a buildup of fluid in his kidneys. He would need a series of surgeries, they said, and he would have to remain in the hospital for several days, but he would likely pull through. I was on pins and needles. My dad had never been so ill in his life.

Family began to arrive, and I gradually felt relieved as my dad perked up. Before long, we had crowded his room with my mom and brother, Moses, and my godfather, Uncle Rudy. He had been a close friend to my parents since long before I was born, when they all lived in the same apartment complex and went to church together. His daughters were my godsisters, and we were raised together like family. I grew up with Uncle Rudy bringing us fruit from his garden and fish that he caught, tinkering with things that needed fixing (he was an engineer), and filling our home with his jovial presence. As my dad stabilized, we joked and told stories to lift his spirits. At some point in the conversation, Uncle Rudy leaned back in his chair and started snoring.

"Wow, he must be really tired," my brother, Jamal, said.

Rudy's snoring got heavier and louder, and I noticed his tongue slipping out of his mouth. Something was wrong.

I jolted from my seat and ran down the hallway, calling for help. I frantically waved doctors and nurses toward my dad's room, shouting, "It's not the patient!"

When I got back to the room, Uncle Rudy was on the floor, and the doctors and nurses had started CPR. "Code blue!" the nurse said. "He doesn't have a pulse."

I backed into the hallway and paced near the door in a frenzy, begging God to bring Uncle Rudy back to life. I pictured Rudy's daughters, my godsisters, Arlissa and Patrice. They would be devastated. This can't happen, I thought. The doctors started using a defibrillator to shock his heart.

"Still no pulse," another nurse said.

Words rushed out of me without forethought, determined prayers that came from a deep hope I felt grounding my feet to the floor. I stopped pacing and prayed furiously.

"He's awake!"

I darted back into the room. Uncle Rudy's eyes were saucer-wide.

"What happened?" he mumbled.

"You just went into cardiac arrest, sir," a doctor told him. Uncle Rudy didn't remember a thing about the ordeal.

Later that night, after Patrice and Arlissa arrived at the hospital, we all sat together in Uncle Rudy's recovery room. He smiled at me and said, "So what happened, Shani? Did I just go to sleep?"

"Yes, a deep sleep." I said. "Don't you *ever* do that to me again!"

Arlissa asked, "So, what did you learn from this experience, Dad?"

"Well, I learned it's easy to die," he joked.

"I learned it's easy to come back to life," I retorted.

Maybe not always easy, I thought, but possible. Things can turn in your favor, no matter how bad it looks, if you have faith. And a bleak situation may lead to a miracle—after all, if my dad hadn't fallen ill, Uncle Rudy wouldn't have been in the hospital when his heart failed and likely wouldn't have survived. I thought about how bleak my own situation seemed.

I was facing twenty-five years in prison for something I didn't do. I could make a false confession and receive a lesser consequence. But I would have to live with the reality of my good work ruined. On top of that, no one would know the truth of what really happened, how a broken and biased system had railroaded innocent people. If I stood up for myself and won, maybe that system would be held to account. Maybe it would be harder for a travesty of justice like this one to happen again in the future. I knew there was only one choice I could make with a clear conscience. I would not accept a plea deal. I was going to trial.

At the dawn of 2014, I had a new attitude. I had unwavering faith that I was going to be vindicated. I meditated and prayed almost every day, requesting wisdom, guidance, and protection from God and from my ancestors. Where before I had been reluctant to talk about the case with anyone outside of my immediate family, I now reached out to others for help and distanced myself from some people who I could tell did not support me.

Mine became an increasingly lonely position as other defendants began to enter plea deals. The first week in January, six educators took deals, including Gloria Ivey. The DA's office had contacted her lawyer three times to encourage her to take a plea bargain. Her attorney pointed out that, in her GBI interviews, Ivey had said she'd sometimes told kids to "rethink" an answer while they were taking the CRCT. He explained to her that that was considered cheating, and Ivey decided to take a plea deal. Otherwise she would have faced thirty years in prison.

"If I wasn't still grieving my daughter's passing, I might have fought it," Ivey would later tell me. Her daughter died from breast cancer a few months after the GBI report was released to the public. Around the same time, Ivey received a letter from Errol Davis, the interim APS superintendent, stating that she had to retire, resign, or be fired. "I think about all the dedication of the years I taught," Ivey said. "The money I spent helping kids, buying clothes for their graduation when they couldn't afford nice outfits. The sacrifices I made. I sit back and think, 'God, why did this happen to me?' There must be a lesson in it."

Ivey received 250 hours of community service and one year of probation. After thirty-seven years teaching, she was forced to retire. She and the other five defendants had to read letters of apology to Baxter, whose demeanor remained decidedly cold, practically the opposite of the friendly, fiery manner he'd displayed between our arraignment and the first *Garrity* ruling, when he decided not to overturn the indictment.

In response to one teacher's letter he said, "I'd give that about a D as far as an apology."[30]

With that, half of the defendants had pleaded guilty, and only seventeen were left facing trial. Baxter extended the deadline to January 24, clearly hoping that more plea deals would follow. He seemed increasingly disgruntled with the impending trial, which promised to be impossibly unwieldy. Prosecutors originally presented him with a witness list of twenty-four hundred people. Baxter called it absurd and forced them to whittle it down to four hundred. He'd also had to field arguments between defense lawyers and prosecutors over a "data dump"; the prosecution team had handed over terabytes of documents that weren't organized in any way to enable the defense to identify what was relevant. On one occasion, Baxter grilled prosecutor Fani Willis about it, demanding, "Have you read all these documents you have dumped?"

"I have not reviewed every single document within the hard drive. It would probably take a lifetime," Willis admitted.

"Do you understand my point?" Baxter persisted. "That is a strategy, to just dump and make people spend a lot of unnecessary time."[31]

But it was becoming rare for Baxter to put prosecutors in the hot seat like this. Instead he seemed to think that the way to make the trial manageable was to reduce the number of defendants. As he pushed defendants to accept plea deals, he grew ever more irate at those of us who remained. I later learned that prosecutors told some of the people who had already taken plea deals to convince the rest of us to do the same or else face conviction.

When the deadline for plea deals came and went, there were thirteen people left to stand trial. The superintendent, Beverly Hall; three School Reform Team directors, Sharon Davis-Williams, Tamara Cotman, and Michael Pitts; one principal, Dana Evans; one assistant principal, Tabeeka Jordan; two testing coordinators, Donald Bullock and Theresia Copeland; and five teachers, Angela Williamson, Dessa Curb, Diane Buckner-Webb, Pamela Cleveland, and me.

Then the trial, originally set for May, was postponed until August due to Beverly Hall's health. She had stage-IV breast cancer and was too sick to appear in court.

Then Tamara Cotman's lawyer, Benjamin Davis, moved to have Baxter removed from the trial. Davis had appealed Baxter's refusal to dismiss Cotman's racketeering charges on double jeopardy grounds after she was acquitted of her other charge of "influencing a witness" the previous fall. As an appeals court reviewed the case, it informed Davis that Baxter had made multiple phone calls to the appeals court clerk, "urging quick action." Davis told reporters, "I was just dumbfounded. Judges are prohibited from trying to contact a judge on the Court of Appeals or trying to communicate with a judge through the clerk's office." Baxter fired back with his own comments to the press. Every defendant signed on to Davis's motion to have him removed from the case. A legal ethics expert supported the effort with an affidavit saying that Baxter's actions created the appearance of partiality.[32]

Again, it seemed the case was falling apart. If a new judge were appointed, there was no telling how long it would take her to catch up or how she might approach the ordeal differently. But in June, a Fulton County superior court judge ruled that Baxter wasn't out of bounds when he called the clerk.[33] The trial would go forward, beginning in September.

That same month, a different APS issue grabbed headlines for once. People were finally starting to pay attention to the massive debt that Invest Atlanta owed to the school system for the BeltLine project.

At that point, the nonprofit that Invest Atlanta created and tasked with developing the BeltLine had spent $350 million, from both public and private sources, to construct a few miles of disjointed bike paths, impractical for commuting, and a smattering of parks, with no headway on the light rail, which had been reconceived as a future streetcar. The project was looking less like a transportation solution and more like a thoroughfare of pedestrian leisure that catalyzed cutthroat gentrification in the neighborhoods through which it passed. BeltLine hype had spurred more than $1 billion in private development, mostly high-end condos and boutique retail. Increasingly common on real estate websites were posts advertising homes for sale in historically black BeltLine-area neighborhoods with pitches like: "This great investment or starter home sits on the Atlanta BeltLine. . . . Tenant occupied, however the tenant will be evicted."[34]

Invest Atlanta was $19 million behind on its BeltLine payments to APS, and outgoing superintendent Erroll Davis was threatening legal action. In response, Mayor Reed threw a tantrum, telling Davis at a BeltLine board meeting, "Nobody's going to negotiate at the end of a gun. So, if you're going to take hostages, you'd better be ready to shoot the hostages." But he didn't stop there. His next statement belied all the concern he and his ilk had expressed about how educators had "cheated the children." "The Atlanta BeltLine is the most popular public project in the entire city of Atlanta," he said, "a lot more popular than APS."[35]

Who's cheating the children now?, I thought. Nineteen million dollars was far more than any bonuses that educators supposedly reaped from fraudulent test scores. And the same impoverished children whose well-being was of grave concern when it came to standardized testing suddenly didn't matter when their families were evicted to make way for the designer stroller set.

APS's popularity got something of a boost that summer with the hiring of a new superintendent, Meria Carstarphen, who left her post as head of the Austin, Texas, public school system in a cloud of controversy. The school board there had just voted not to renew her contract due to intense community pushback against heavy-handed reforms, including turning a number of schools over to charter operators. Atlanta's reformer school board, stacked with Teach for America alumni, had found their perfect match. So had Atlanta's business elite.[36] Though her official start date was in July, nine corporations donated $260,000 to cover her salary and a transition team to begin work two months ahead of schedule. She was wined and dined by city leaders who practically swooned over her take-charge attitude, her proclaimed commitment to "turn around" the school district. It was not unlike the scene fifteen years earlier when Beverly Hall had arrived in Atlanta. But unlike Hall, Carstarphen did not hedge expectations with a warning not to anticipate miracles. "I can implement anything," she declared. "Be careful what you ask for, because it will be done."[37]

As the dog days of summer trudged toward the trial, I was busy readying myself mentally for what lay ahead. Just as my attitude had shifted at the beginning of the year, I now felt a physical change. Early one morning in August, a drugstore test administered in my bathroom revealed the cause. I was carrying a child. Moses and I were ecstatic; we had been trying. Having a child during this time wasn't ideal, but it seemed as if the perfect moment would never come. We had spent over a year waiting for the case to blow over, but it never did. Now there was no telling how long the trial would take, and we weren't willing to put our lives on hold any more.

Days later, a police officer in Ferguson, Missouri, with no reason at all, shot to death a black teenage boy whose body bled for hours in the street. As angry crowds congregated, Michael Brown's mother was bombarded by reporters who wanted to know what her son's life, and now death, meant. Of all the things she might have told them, she uplifted his education. He had just graduated high school and was headed to college. "Do you know how hard it was for me to get him to stay in school and graduate?" she demanded. "You know how many black men graduate? Not many."[38]

Across the country, communities convulsed with this latest of countless state-sanctioned assaults on black lives. Ferguson was a war zone, with militarized police facing down young people who cried, "Hands up, don't shoot!" and "Black lives matter!" In Atlanta, five thousand people marched on CNN to protest the network's racialized portrayal of Michael Brown as a thug. Night after night, in seemingly every city, people flooded the streets with a resolve for change, taking action that hadn't been seen in some time.

Two days after the slaying, and on the first day of school, with a new black life in my womb, I arrived at the Fulton County Courthouse to face a jury of my peers.

CHAPTER SEVEN

Getting Cold

■‖‖‖‖‖‖‖‖‖‖‖‖‖‖‖‖‖■

MORNING SICKNESS and jury selection did not mix.

I rabidly tore open a granola bar wrapper and wolfed down the snack to ease my churning stomach, willing myself not to vomit as Judge Baxter gave instructions to the first fifty prospective jurors on how to fill out long questionnaires designed to determine whether they could be fair and impartial. Over the coming weeks, six hundred prospective jurors would file in and out of the courtroom as lawyers and prosecutors tussled through the process of arriving at just twelve jurors and eleven alternates.

"In this case, we have been inundated for several years with news stories, television stories, community conversations about the Atlanta Public School system," Baxter told each group. "I'm instructing you that you have to presume that the defendants are innocent of the charges until the state, if it can, proves the charges to you beyond a reasonable doubt."[1]

Four days a week, my codefendants and I were in the courtroom watching from the sidelines. Beverly Hall remained notably absent; she was in treatment for cancer and would stand trial separately, whenever she was able. Our lawyers would introduce themselves and us to the prospective jurors, and then we sat in silence until the next group arrived and we repeated the process. I kept snacks lined up on the table in front of me; eating was the only thing that quelled the nausea.

Sometimes it got so bad, all I could do to keep from gagging was lick salt off of my hand. I was trying to hide my pregnancy for as long as possible, but clearly I would have to let the cat out of the bag soon.

I began getting to know the other defendants during lunch breaks, when some of us would sit in the courthouse library and read motivational quotes and scriptures from the Bible to lift our spirits. There was Donald Bullock, a round-faced, soft-spoken man in his sixties who chatted with me often. He had served as a testing coordinator at Usher–Collier Heights Elementary School. Angela Williamson, who looked younger than her forty-eight years, with stylishly highlighted curls framing her slender face, usually joined us. She was formerly a teacher at Dobbs Elementary, along with Dessa Curb, the eldest defendant, who seemed frail but had a friendly demeanor. Sharon Davis-Williams, a former School Reform Team director, typically led us in a collective prayer. She had a colorful style, often sporting bright lipstick and cropped hair, dyed reddish-blond.

Other times, I used the break to try to get some work done. Because of the trial, I had quit the counseling agency. But I was still working part time for one of the group homes I had served, mostly doing administrative work remotely.

By the third week of jury selection, prosecutors and defense lawyers had reviewed scores of questionnaires, and Judge Baxter began fielding requests from prospective jurors who wanted out, due to various hardships they would suffer by participating in a trial that was expected to last three months.

As the jury pool shrank, defense attorneys protested that too many black people were being struck. Bob Rubin, who represented former Dobbs Elementary principal Dana Evans, had filed a motion arguing that black people were underrepresented in the jury pool from the get-go. As prospective jurors were dismissed, that already small number was dwindling further. Baxter brushed the concern aside, saying, "I'm looking at all these people individually, black, white. I haven't seen any purple yet."[2]

In early September, Baxter held a hearing on Rubin's motion, which stated that African Americans were underrepresented in the jury pool by 11 percent compared to the population of potential jurors in Fulton

County. A jury composition expert took the stand and testified, "This didn't just happen because of luck of the draw. This happened because something systematic is going on."[3] The expert further stated that, according to his analysis, more than sixty thousand names of potential jurors had been erroneously deactivated in the county's database, meaning that those people would never be summoned for jury duty unless they were reactivated.

Rubin asked the expert to explain the 11 percent racial discrepancy in terms of standard deviation. That was the statistical method that erasure experts had used to show how far from the norm the number of wrong-to-right erasures deviated on CRCT tests. Anything above three standard deviations was considered impossible without human intervention.

"Well, we are five standard deviations too low on the African Americans," the jury composition expert replied.

"If the jury list were an APS teacher, it would be indicted," Rubin concluded.[4]

But a state prosecutor argued that Rubin had to show that black people had been intentionally excluded from the jury pool. Rubin maintained that he only had to prove the exclusion was systematic, not intentional. A Fulton County jury clerk testified that a vendor handled the database, so she had no idea how the names had been deactivated or what had caused the racial discrepancy in the jury pool for this trial. In the end, Baxter denied Rubin's motion, saying the jury pool was "fairly constituted."[5]

So the jury selection process slogged forward. Days later, my co-defendants and I were directed into an assembly hall within the courthouse for something called "the reading of the indictment." I had no idea what it was, so I wasn't prepared for the humiliation that ensued.

We filed into a big auditorium where Fulton County Commission meetings were usually held. The remaining prospective jurors, still hundreds of them, were seated in ascending rows of theater chairs. We took our places on the floor below them, in the commissioners' seats behind a long dais table. It felt like one of those nightmares people have about being shamed in front of their entire school. We were to sit there while prosecutors read the ninety-page indictment enumerating our charges.

Before they began, Baxter explained to our audience that what they would hear was not evidence of guilt. He also warned that "if you feel like driving a nail through your hand, you know, I don't blame you."[6]

He wasn't kidding. For the next two hours, prosecutor Clint Rucker droned through page after page, starting with the counts against us, which consisted of dense legal jargon like "as described below, and incorporated by reference as if fully set forth herein." Eyes were already glazing over by the time Rucker got to the second section, in which he defined terms like "Criterion-Referenced Competency Test" and "adequate yearly progress" in excruciating detail. Eventually Rucker came to a section titled "Overt Acts in Furtherance of the Conspiracy."

Here the indictment became slightly easier to follow, as it described in plain language what some of the defendants had allegedly done to warrant the charges against them. Prospective jurors who were in a stupor seemed to revive and listen more closely. They heard a lot about Beverly Hall, her top administrators, and School Reform Team director Michael Pitts, who oversaw Parks Middle School. Parks had the highest prevalence of cheating in the state and some of the most lurid stories, including alleged sexual harassment by the principal, Christopher Waller, who had taken a plea deal long ago. Pitts, a tall, sturdy man with a shaved head and a mustache, was there on the stage with us, facing trial. As the executive director of the schools in School Reform Team 2, which included Dunbar, he was Principal Greene's direct supervisor. A few other schools and their School Reform Team directors were mentioned in this section of the indictment but not in any way comparable to the exhaustive account of what transpired at Parks. Administrative wrongdoing was also recapitulated in detail, with stories of Beverly Hall and her human resources director, Millicent Few (who had taken a plea deal), retaliating against whistleblowers, hiding information, and ignoring clear signs of cheating.

As Rucker read the damning accounts, I felt hundreds of eyes fixed on me, as if I were the subject of what Rucker described. But my name never surfaced in "Overt Acts in Furtherance of the Conspiracy," nor did any other teachers' names. Would jurors be able to distinguish us as individuals? Would they lump my school in with Parks, even though nothing like that happened at Dunbar? Did they remember that Baxter said that none of this was evidence? Or was the information overload rendering us an indiscernible bunch of cheaters in their view? After a couple more hours of reading, punctuated by bathroom breaks, we would find out.

When the reading finally concluded, the crowd applauded, and Baxter promised everyone they would never have to endure that again. Then he asked if anyone had formed an opinion about whether or not we were guilty. About sixty hands went up, and a case manager recorded them, then gave instructions. Nine prospective jurors would be interviewed that afternoon, and the rest would follow in the days to come.

Those interviews revealed a cross section of how the world saw our case and the assumptions that jurors brought to it. A middle-aged woman said that ever since news of the cheating scandal broke, she had thought we should all be locked up. Another said she thought we were guilty because, "hearing all the different charges this morning[,] . . . there is so much against them." On the contrary, a nervous woman proclaimed that she had been raised by a schoolteacher and principal, so unless educators "rape, beat, or kill somebody, I'm not going to find them guilty of anything." An older, neatly dressed black gentleman gave a moving statement of support for us.

"When I retired from the federal government in 2000, I took a position as a substitute teacher with APS," he began. "And the people that I worked with, I found that they were dedicated, professional, had integrity, [were] hard workers, underappreciated, underpaid."[7] He went on to say that as a black male, his mother had instilled in him that he needed an education. His third-grade teacher made him believe he could accomplish anything. When he heard about the RICO charges against us, he couldn't believe it; he associated those charges with gangsters. He finished by declaring that the trial was a waste of taxpayer money. "The money that is being used could be used to give teachers raises and give them more resources in the classroom."

I wanted to give the man a standing ovation, but I kept still. He was dismissed.

Once all of the people who claimed a bias were interviewed, the rest of the prospective jurors were called in for questioning. Throughout the process, defense attorneys and prosecutors sparred in private over who to keep and who to let go. Finally, after six weeks, we were left with a jury of four white men, one white woman, three black women, two black men, one Asian woman, and one Hispanic woman. They were mostly older, with children who were either grown or in high school if they had any. And they were overwhelmingly middle-class professionals; one even worked as a wealth adviser for "ultra high net worth" clients of Goldman Sachs. Three of the jurors worked in the public sector, and just one had a low-paying service industry job.

In their interviews, they all said they could be impartial, though several mentioned things that gave me pause. A Transportation Security Administration worker (and former prison guard) recalled when reporter Monica Pearson tailed Beverly Hall in Hawaii on the evening news, one of the more sensational moments in the media coverage of the scandal. A small business owner said that while listening to the indictment he had tried to maintain the presumption of innocence, "But man, you know, you listen to that, and you're like, well, how can they come up with all that stuff?" An IRS manager acknowledged that he knew District Attorney Paul Howard; their kids went to school together, and they'd chatted at a football game once. Would any of these factors influence their understanding of the case? Only one juror, an older black woman who worked as a medical assistant, said anything that could be construed in our favor. She thought standardized tests were unfair.

On the final day of jury selection, Judge Baxter gathered these twelve people and their alternates to provide instructions. Testimony would start the following week. "This is not going to be boring," he said. "I have been dealing with this case for a long time, and it is not like watching grass grow."

As trial moved forward, the cheating scandal served as fodder for education machinations in Atlanta and across the state. There was the BeltLine dispute that had flared up earlier in the summer; now lawyers for APS and the city were exchanging angry emails, with the latter using the cheating scandal to justify its refusal to pay the millions of dollars owed to the school system.[8] Meria Carstarphen, the new APS superintendent, promised to create a culture change that would restore confidence in the school district as she made moves to revamp it into a charter system.[9] And Governor Nathan Deal was running for reelection with an education agenda focused on adopting Louisiana's Recovery School District model, which enabled that state to take over most New Orleans schools and convert them into charters after Hurricane Katrina. At the time of Deal's campaign, 90 percent of New Orleans schools were charters.

While our jury selection was underway, Louisiana's governor stumped for Deal at a campaign event where Deal announced his intention to replicate the state takeover model, saying, "We're continuing to put money into school systems that continue to fail."[10] Meanwhile, he tried to avert the controversy that had plagued his first gubernatorial campaign by selling his car salvage company, which had profited enormously from a state-funded program that he had, perhaps illegally, worked to keep in place while he was in Congress. Deal netted $3.2 million from the sale, as did his business partner, only to face a fresh wave of controversy when it turned out the buyer was a company that owed the state $74 million in back taxes. But it caused barely a hiccup in Deal's campaign.[11]

Three days before prosecutors gave opening statements against us, the governor was the subject of fawning praise as he pandered to black families in a bizarre photo-op with rapper Ludacris at Utopian Academy, a nearly all-black charter school in an impoverished corner of southeastern metro Atlanta. It was the first charter school authorized by the State Charter Schools Commission that Deal had fought hard to resurrect in 2012 and that, it was becoming clear, had laid the groundwork for the state takeover district Deal was now proposing. Later I would hear from a friend who taught at Utopian that some grade levels didn't have textbooks for all subject areas. That bleak reality seemed to matter as little as Deal's shady business practices. That fall, there was nothing anyone could do to be as maligned as the APS educators standing trial.[12]

ııııııııııı

"They changed answers from 11 o'clock in the morning to 11 o'clock at night and ate fish and grits! I can't make it up!" prosecutor Fani Willis exclaimed as she paced in front of the jury, holding forth like a fire-and-brimstone preacher.

It was September 29, 2014, and opening statements were underway. A petite black woman in her mid-forties with a penchant for dull blazers, Willis had emerged from the gaggle of prosecutors working on the case to become one of a few who would carry the trial. Her opening statement was a lengthy theatrical production pocked with such absurdities as the claim about fish and grits, which the media ate up.

Willis might have been the ringleader, but there was also a clown at the trial—Judge Baxter. Shortly after convening the court, Baxter announced that he'd been to Walmart where he'd purchased a T-shirt and some iron-on letters. "I have hand made a Dubious Achievement Award. . . . I'm hoping that nobody gets it," he said, holding up the shirt, which read "I'm talking and I can't shut up."[13] It was his way of encouraging brevity among the attorneys.

Willis's opening statement was hardly brief. She began her diatribe with a protracted story about the Cascade Elementary student whose mother, Justina Collins, had spoken at Paul Howard's press conference announcing the indictment more than a year earlier. No one from Cascade was on trial, nor was Beverly Hall, who had allegedly denied Collins's pleas for help when her daughter mysteriously scored high on the CRCT, despite being unable to read. But this story, which ended with her daughter lacking the help she needed, showed the harm of what Willis termed "a cleverly disguised conspiracy."[14] She would repeat this phrase again and again, as if she were trying to lodge it in juror's brains. Another phrase she repeated was "magic elixir."

"Dr. Hall was hired because she sold herself as having a magic elixir!" Willis bellowed. She was implying that Hall had proffered false promises from the start, which was hardly the case. All of this, she said, was a plot to reap financial rewards. Over ten years, Hall had received over $500,000 "because she fixed these CRCT results," Willis claimed. Again, her statement wasn't totally accurate. Hall had received bonuses for meeting a long list of goals set by the school board, which included CRCT targets, among other measures. Then Willis made the bizarre claim that Hall had developed a "data-driven system" in order to foster cheating. But using student data to shape instruction was a nationwide trend, hardly an evil tool of Hall's invention. Throughout the trial the prosecution would treat "data-driven" as if it were a code phrase for cheating.[15]

"They stole," Willis somberly went on, referring to all of us. "There was a financial benefit to the children doing well on the CRCT . . . it was bonus money."[16] This was key to the state's argument; they had to prove financial gain in order to convict us under RICO. Of course, I never received a bonus.

Once Hall was sufficiently painted as a villain with a "magic elixir," Willis went on to describe how the superintendent's top administrators aided in the supposed conspiracy by covering up evidence of cheating, shredding documents and the like. None of them were on trial. Then she got to the defendants, portraying us as Hall's lackeys as she described what each of us allegedly did. When she arrived at my name, she rattled off several points. "She was a first-grade teacher and a young teacher in 2009. She had 15 students. She was making $66,000 her first year there."[17]

My jaw hit the floor. That was $22,000 more than my salary. One of the first things the jury heard about me was an absolute lie.

Finally Willis began to wrap up with an explanation of RICO. "The act of one conspirator is the act of all," she gravely stated. She added that people don't have to meet in person or agree on anything to be conspirators. "But what you do have to do is all be doing the same thing for the same purpose." That shared purpose, she said, was to illegally inflate test scores.[18]

I craned my neck to try to get a look at the jury on the other side of the room. Because there were so many defendants, we couldn't occupy the usual defense table up front where the jury could see us. Instead we filled several rows of tables where benches for observers would normally be. The prosecution table, however, was right next to the jury box. My lawyer had asked Judge Baxter to change the seating arrangement so the jurors could see us better, but he had declined. Now they had been instructed to treat each of our cases individually, but they were also hearing that "the act of one is the act of all." I could only hope that they would pay close attention and realize that the case against me was riddled with holes.

Attorney Greene said as much in her opening statement. She informed the jury that my first graders' test scores didn't count toward the adequate yearly progress benchmarks or APS targets, that I did erase stray marks but never answers, and that I received "not a penny worth of bonus money."[19] I stood right next to Greene before the jury so the members could see me as an individual as she spoke. My baby bump was visible at that point, and I heard cameras clicking furiously as the press realized I was pregnant.

Several other defense lawyers gave opening statements, not without their own dramatic flair. Attorney Bob Rubin, who had challenged the racial makeup of the jury pool, displayed an image of Disney villain Cruella de Vil on an overhead projector to illustrate how the prosecution had depicted his client, Dana Evans, the sole principal on trial. I'd heard that she transferred to Dobbs Elementary, an impoverished, mostly black school, from a wealthier, whiter school because she'd felt driven to work with kids who had the greatest needs. Now Rubin told the jury that Evans had been accused because she had "ruffled feathers" when she made reforms at her school. Her accusers were a teacher who Evans fired for being late sixty times and another she wrote up for calling her students the N-word and for addressing her students with racial slurs and other inappropriate labels.

Lawyers for two Dobbs teachers, Angela Williamson and Dessa Curb, gave opening statements as well. Curb's lawyer noted, "If she's a cheater, she's the worst cheater because her kids didn't even pass."[20] Her classroom was never flagged in any of the erasures analyses.

Theresia Copeland's lawyer gave an opening statement that similarly laid bare the scant evidence against her. Copeland, a middle-aged woman who was as chatty and friendly behind the scenes as she was unflinching in court, was the testing coordinator at Benteen Elementary in 2009. Some of her colleagues told investigators they had seen her pushing a cart full of tests, as if there was something suspicious about that: it was part of her job. She also had an independent monitor shadowing her all day, someone who investigators had never interviewed, her lawyer said.

Attorneys for Bullock and my former colleague Diane Buckner-Webb also gave opening statements. Bullock's lawyer challenged the idea of the conspiracy, saying that "there was no common objective" and noting that his client didn't have access to his school's testing materials because he had a doctor's appointment on the last day of the test in

2009. Buckner-Webb's lawyer described the lack of credibility of the witnesses against us, explaining how Rose Neal had made conflicting statements at different times. And like me, Buckner-Webb had never received a bonus.

The rest of the defendants opted to withhold their opening statements until the prosecution had presented its case.

That evening, the *Journal-Constitution* ran an article on its website misquoting my lawyer, who had given an interview when opening statements concluded. It said that Greene told the reporter that I was instructed to erase answers. Luckily, after my lawyer's quick call to the paper, the reporter was able to correct her quote to say that I had erased stray marks. The correction was made before the printed edition of the paper went to press, otherwise countless people would have thought my own lawyer had labeled me a cheater. I had been frustrated with the media coverage up to that point, but that day I lost all hope in the newspaper.

The next day, the state began presenting evidence. This time Clint Rucker took the stage. A stocky, bespectacled, and goateed black man with a sonorous voice that slipped easily between formal and folksy deliveries, he was the other lead prosecutor alongside Willis.

Rucker started by bringing Justina Collins and her daughter each to the witness stand to rehash what they had stated in Paul Howard's press conference about trying to root out the reason for the girl's impossibly high CRCT scores, only to reach a dead end with Beverly Hall. No one from the child's school was on trial, and neither was Beverly Hall for that matter. The only slightly relevant defendant was School Reform Team director Sharon Davis-Williams, who was copied on a letter to Collins from Hall's office concluding that there was no information to indicate why the child's scores had skyrocketed. But Collins acknowledged that she never had any conversations with Davis-Williams about her daughter.

The final person to testify that day was Norman Johnson, the former school board member who worked closely with the Atlanta Housing Authority to privatize public housing and public schools, beginning with Fowler Elementary and Techwood Homes, the nation's first public housing complex. It wasn't entirely clear why Johnson was on the stand, since he had left the school board by the time of the cheating scandal, and several defense lawyers objected to his testimony on that basis. But this was not before he had talked generally about the ills of "concentrated poverty." Rucker prodded Johnson to offer the opinion that the suspicious test scores in 2009 must have been produced by cheating, until a defense lawyer protested that Johnson's opinions weren't grounded in fact but instead comprised "just general hocus-pocus." Testimony wasn't exactly off to a strong start.

For the rest of the week and much of the next, prosecutors focused on the schools that were under the watch of School Reform Team director Michael Pitts. It seemed that, in Hall's absence, he was now their main quarry.

There was a lengthy examination of Reginald Dukes, a private investigator APS hired in 2006 to look into cheating allegations at Parks. Dukes claimed that he presented his findings, that there had been cheating, in a meeting with Hall, human resources director Millicent Few, and Pitts. But according to a sign-in sheet from the APS central office for the day in question, the meeting never happened.

Pitts's lawyer produced the sign-in sheet, which showed that Dukes had signed in and then signed out only twenty-two minutes later, though Dukes testified that the meeting had lasted at least an hour. He had also written on the sheet that he was there to meet with another APS employee, not Hall, Few, or Pitts. The back-and-forth on this issue devolved to the point where Rucker sought to bolster Dukes's account, which included mention of Hall eating chicken wings, by calling a caterer to testify about what she had served at the APS central office that day. Her records showed that she did in fact serve chicken, at which point defense attorney Gerald Griggs cross-examined her with just one question, "How many different ways are there to prepare chicken?"[21] Her answer: about fifty.

Such antics quickly became commonplace, laying bare the ridiculousness of the trial. But there were also dramatic moments in which the whole case seemed to be spinning out of control.

The day after the chicken-related questioning, Armstead Salters, a seventy-six-year-old former principal of Gideons Elementary, was set to testify that Hall and Pitts had pressured him to direct teachers to cheat. He had been indicted with the rest of us but agreed to testify in exchange for a plea deal. However, his testimony quickly ran off course. When Rucker asked why Salters had instructed his testing coordinator to return completed tests to teachers, Salters said it was so they could ensure that the students had bubbled in the answer sheets correctly. He said nothing about changing the answers. Clearly taken aback, Rucker doubled down.

"Did you ever personally erase a wrong answer on an answer sheet and change it to the right answer?" he demanded.

"I never touched the tests," replied Salters softly, looking pitiful hunched on the witness stand in an oversized gray suit. I couldn't believe it. The state's witness was recanting.

Frustrated, Rucker stumbled for several minutes, trying to ask questions that would steer Salters back to the script outlined in his plea agreement. When that went nowhere, Judge Baxter declared Salters a hostile witness and instructed Rucker to cross-examine him, ignoring protests from the defense lawyers. In the middle of the fracas, one of the defense attorneys called out Prosecutor Willis for making faces and gestures at the jury, as if she were trying to influence them. The jury was eventually sent out, and defense lawyers argued vehemently for a mistrial, which Baxter denied.

When the jury returned and questioning finally resumed, Rucker presented Salters with his plea agreement and read each statement, pressing Salters to confirm its accuracy. Salters avoided giving a yes or no answer about whether he had instructed the testing coordinator to give answer sheets to teachers, whether he knew they intended to change the answers, and so on, repeating, "I took the blame."

That is, until Rucker said, "Based upon the pressure you received from Pitts and Hall, you felt you had no choice but to encourage and aid cheating on the CRCT at Gideons."

"Mr. Pitts nor Dr. Hall ever encouraged me to cheat," Salters replied, nearly whispering.

The courtroom went still. The prosecutors looked stunned. Salters's testimony was supposed to help them nail Pitts and Hall, but now it was doing the opposite.[22]

"Listen, I made a mistake initialing this," Salters said, gesturing to the plea agreement. "This was impacting on me. I was getting sick from it. And I did what was in the best interest of myself, and maybe I did it the wrong way. Maybe I made a mistake. But they didn't put pressure on me for anything." Rucker made a few last-ditch attempts to turn the ship around, but Salters just dug deeper.

"I may have to go to prison for it, but they never placed any pressure on me to cheat under any circumstances," Salters said definitively.

I could have fallen out of my seat. Here was a key witness admitting he had succumbed to pressure from investigators and prosecutors and lied to get a plea deal. Looking at the diminished old man who had spent nearly fifty years of his life as an educator only to end his career in shame, I held no hard feelings toward him. I just wondered how many others had done the same thing, how much of this trial was based on trumped-up accusations and lies told under the gun.

I didn't have to wait long to see that Salters was not an anomaly. Over the next two days, his testing coordinator, Sheridan Rogers, was a witness for the state. She upheld the allegations and confessions she'd made in her plea agreement: that Salters ordered her to give teachers the students' testing materials so they could change the answers from wrong to right. But during cross-examination, Pitts's lawyer drilled her with questions about her initial statements to the GBI, in which she denied having ever spoken to Salters about cheating. When offered a plea deal that reduced her felony charges to a misdemeanor punishable with one-year probation, a fine, and community service, Rogers had changed her story.

"So, all you got to do is show up today and testify," Pitts's lawyer said, "and not only are you done, this is wiped from your record. . . . That's what you bought with your testimony, isn't it?"[23]

Rogers wouldn't admit that she either lied to the GBI or lied in her plea deal, leading Baxter to revoke her probation, along with Salters.

Unfortunately, it wasn't Salters recanting or Rogers committing perjury that made the biggest news splash that week. "Witnesses differ over eating fish and grits while cheating," read the *Journal-Constitution* headline about testimony from former Gideons employees. Willis had promised and delivered. Two former teachers from Gideons testified the same day as Rogers and said that after she gave them the tests, they went to a teacher's house to change answers. One claimed the host had prepared fish and grits, while the actual host claimed they had gone out to eat at a burger joint. I just shook my head at the article. *Chicken wings, fish, and grits—why not throw in some watermelon while you're at it,* I thought.

The tomfoolery continued the following week, when the focus shifted to schools under School Reform Team director Tamara Cotman's purview. Willis asked a state witness to point Cotman out, but she couldn't identify her. Willis told her she could walk around the courtroom to find Cotman, and the lady set off wandering. After a few moments of this ridiculous display, Judge Baxter told her, "You're getting cold."

"Seriously?" one of the defense lawyers blurted at Baxter.

"Seriously. She is cold."

"You can't do that, Judge."

The witness never recognized Cotman and eventually returned to the witness stand to finish her testimony. Silly as it was, Baxter had tried to aid a witness in identifying a defendant, an act of judicial misconduct that was no joke.

Hijinks aside, the trial became monotonous. For the next two weeks, a stream of witnesses who had worked at various APS schools told stories that at this point were mind-numbingly familiar. Their students scored suspiciously high on tests. They faced retaliation for reporting suspected cheating. Their higher-ups put immense pressure on them to raise scores. They participated in cheating. But none could produce a smoking gun that proved that any of the defendants condoned or encouraged or took part in cheating. Defense lawyers conducted cross-examinations that called much testimony into question based on contradictory statements witnesses made and the coercive nature of the immunity deals and plea deals they had received.

All in all, it seemed the prosecution's strategy was to cobble together a mish-mash of suspicious activities into a conspiratorial constellation, but the dots just weren't connecting. Or maybe it was to wear down jurors by piling on so much information, only a fraction of it relevant, that they would throw their hands up and declare the whole system rotten.

That's how it felt to me. By the last week of October, I was working hard to keep my mind from wandering during the long, dull hours of testimony that never got straight to the point and rarely seemed revelatory.

Then Lucious Brown took the stand.

Brown was the former principal of Kennedy Middle School, located in Atlanta's most destitute Westside neighborhood, where thriving black communities had been systematically dismantled. It was his lawyer who had brought the *Garrity* motion that had nearly killed the case the previous year. When that didn't work, Brown eventually took a plea deal, stating that he had orchestrated cheating in response to pressure from School Reform Team director Sharon Davis-Williams. But when Brown testified, in a repeat of the Armstead Salters episode he retracted his accusation. He said that pressure had stemmed from the Georgia Department of Education, which had threatened to close his school when it hadn't made adequate yearly progress under No Child Left Behind for seven years straight. Regardless, he said, the decision to cheat was his alone. Clint Rucker pushed him like he had Salters.

"Are you trying to communicate to the jurors you are taking this all on your back?" Rucker asked.

"No one asked me to do it," was Brown's reply.[24]

Again, Baxter declared the witness hostile, and again the defense attorneys clamored for a mistrial to no avail. Brown's testimony dragged out for two days before prosecutors moved on to Clarietta Davis, another principal who worked under Davis-Williams. Davis admitted to changing answers with members of her staff, but there was a discrepancy between her account and that of another witness, which became a sticking point. Her employee stated that Davis had worn gloves while she changed answers. Davis insisted she had not.

One of the defense lawyers implored Judge Baxter to strike the testimony since one of the witnesses had to be lying. "A conviction cannot rest upon perjured testimony," he said.

"Perjury is being committed daily here," Baxter responded with resignation.[25]

I couldn't believe his admission. If Baxter knew witnesses were perjuring themselves it was his responsibility to declare a mistrial or at least strike their testimonies. But he did neither.

I I I I I I I I I I I I I

By November, it was clear that everyone had woefully underestimated how long the trial would last. The state was nowhere near resting its case. And whenever they finally did, twelve lawyers would have to present twelve separate cases. It was hard enough to maintain my emotional and physical well-being, and now the trial was starting to take a serious financial toll on my life.

I never expected to have to pay legal fees for full-time work for months on end, but Judge Baxter had prohibited the defense attorneys from taking on other cases, so we were their only clients. My legal fees were piling up, and I barely had an income. Because the trial was all-consuming, I'd reduced my administrative work for the group home to just a few hours a week. To keep up with all the expenses, my parents used their retirement fund, my husband assisted with payments, and I maxed out every credit card I could apply for. My mother even came out of retirement and got a job teaching at a private school.

Staying positive under these circumstances was a feat. I sometimes wondered whether depression might have overwhelmed me without my pregnancy to keep me focused. I knew that physical symptoms of stress and anxiety could affect my child in utero, and so Moses and I developed strategies to stay as happy and calm as possible. We rarely talked about the trial outside of court. We filled our weekends with dinner dates and funny movies and things that made us feel like a normal couple. One day I came home, and there in the living room was a beautiful little aquarium with a betta fish. Moses had read somewhere that it could have a relaxing effect. I often marveled at our young marriage and how it was standing up to this test. The duress of the trial might have driven a wedge between us, but instead we were growing ever closer.

My parents also supported me beyond financial matters. My dad had recovered steadily in the months since his medical emergency. Now he was in court nearly every day, observing, taking notes, and spending breaks with my codefendants and me. My brother, mother, mother-in-law, and godsisters joined him when they could. My father-in-law lived in another state but would call regularly to check on me.

I needed all the support I could get during the first week of November, when one of the greatest hypocrisies of the cheating scandal was on display. Over the course of three days, Kathleen Mathers testified for the prosecution. Mathers had served as the head of the Governor's Office of Student Achievement under Governor Perdue and now ran her own education consulting firm while serving on the board of Latin Academy, a charter school whose CEO was siphoning hundreds of thousands of dollars from the school's bank account to pay for luxury items and strippers.[26] Mathers had led the charge on the erasure analyses that originally flagged high numbers of wrong-to-right erasures on the 2008 summer school CRCT retests at Deerwood Elementary and later called into question the 2009 scores in 191 schools throughout the state. Rucker and Willis focused much of their questioning on Mathers's interactions with Beverly Hall, trying to draw out evidence that the superintendent had behaved conspiratorially.

But defense lawyers grilled Mathers on a glaring problem with her crusade against cheating, one that never made it into the public dialogue surrounding the scandal. Mathers and Perdue had touted the 2009 test scores in their application for a $400-million grant from the federal Race to the Top program *after* their erasure analysis suggested the scores were fraudulent.

"Did you submit in the application that the reason that the CRCT results had increased was because there were higher standards, and harder assessments, accompanied by effective professional development for teachers?" asked Attorney Benjamin Davis.[27]

"Yes," Mathers replied, "across the entire state of Georgia." She went on to justify the language in the application by saying that because 80 percent of schools in the state were not flagged for cheating, the statewide CRCT scores remained valid, as if a decrease in scores from 20 percent of schools wouldn't have had an effect.

Davis asked why she hadn't at least mentioned the investigations in Atlanta or Dougherty County in the application.

"There was no reason for me to mention that," she replied coolly.

Davis also asked about a meeting in Washington, DC, where Mathers, Perdue, and other state officials fielded questions from the Race to the Top selection committee. Why, he wondered, weren't they transparent about irregularities in the CRCT scores at that point?

"I don't believe we were ever asked a question about irregularities," was Mathers's response.

My mind raced with comebacks that I wished Davis would deploy. Did Mathers really think the Race to the Top selection committee wouldn't care to know that she was undertaking the largest, most expensive investigation in Georgia's history to determine the validity of the same scores they were considering in this application? With $400 million at stake, Fani Willis's accusation about using illegally inflated scores for financial gain might as well apply to Mathers too, I thought. But Judge Baxter was satisfied with her responses and told Davis to move on.

Next, an analyst from the Georgia Department of Education's testing division gave testimony that corroborated Mathers's testimony on the analysis of Deerwood's 2008 CRCT retests. This was the school where one of my codefendants, Tabeeka Jordan, worked as an assistant principal. The school had six times the number of wrong-to-right erasures compared to a control group made up of demographically similar schools from other parts of the state. That wasn't a shocker. But his cross-examination undermined testimony given a couple of weeks earlier by a Deerwood teacher who claimed that check marks had been placed on the answer sheets that were to be manipulated. Now Jordan's lawyer presented the analyst with Deerwood's answer sheets from 2008 and asked him to identify check marks. There were none.

These were the tests that sparked the whole investigation! I glanced at Jordan, a woman in her forties with a youthful pixie haircut. She'd been weathering the storm longer than any of us. In that moment, I felt hope. There was just no way the jury would move to convict with so many blatant flaws in the case against us.

As I left court that Thursday, I braced myself for the following week when former governor Sonny Perdue, the man responsible for blowing the cheating scandal wildly out of proportion, would be on the witness stand. But before that could happen, a different scandal erupted.

On Friday, when court was not in session, District Attorney Paul Howard called Judge Baxter on his cell phone with a request. Reginald Dukes, the investigator Beverly Hall hired in 2006 to look into cheating at Parks Middle School, had informed Howard that someone had left him a threatening voicemail in response to his testimony. Fox 5 Atlanta had found out and was preparing a story about it. Fearing the story would have a chilling effect on future witnesses, Howard frantically appealed to Baxter to issue an order barring the station from airing the story, and Baxter complied.

Monday morning, his courtroom was in an uproar. The *Journal-Constitution* had reported that Baxter had unconstitutionally silenced the media, and lawyers for Fox 5 had filed a motion to overturn the order. Reporters for both outlets were there, arguing with Baxter as he tried to kick them out in order to have a closed hearing with the defense lawyers who were furious that he'd had an ex parte conversation with the prosecution. Judges are not supposed to communicate with one party in a lawsuit without informing the other. This was Baxter's second time engaging in a questionable phone call; he'd almost been kicked off the case the previous spring when he called a court clerk in an attempt to influence the judges presiding over Tamara Cotman's appeal.

Baxter eventually caved, allowing the media to stay in the courtroom while he heard from the lawyers, who were incensed that they hadn't been contacted.

"It wasn't ex parte contact with the district attorney," Judge Baxter tried to explain.

But as the defense attorneys argued, Baxter grew red-faced and short-tempered, snapping at one of the attorneys who tried to speak, "You were jaywalking this morning! I caught you jaywalking on the street. If I see you doing that again, I'm going to have you cited."[28]

Another attorney steered him back to the issue at hand, saying, "Mr. Howard, Ms. Fani Willis, and all these people know how to get in touch with me. We could have been gotten on the phone."

Still defending himself, Baxter admitted he'd broken the rules. "Well, sometimes you can't do this job without every blue moon having an ex parte conversation," he exclaimed.

Then he challenged attorneys to show how the conversation with Howard harmed their clients. Theresia Copeland's lawyer moved for a mistrial, explaining, "If she's convicted, if you put her in prison, it comes back on this conversation, that you were favoring the state."

"I think you are a grandstander is what I think," Baxter snarled, "You like to see yourself in the media. You prance around the courtroom. And I'm moving you to the back . . . because you seem to be a peacock that likes publicity."[29] With that, he denied the motion for mistrial and recessed to his chamber.

When Baxter returned, less flushed, he convened court, and the state called Perdue to testify.

The former governor, a rotund, balding man from Middle Georgia, gave testimony that was mostly uneventful. Rucker's examination seemed to focus on providing background for the jurors as to when and why and how he and Mathers had decided to investigate suspicions of cheating. Rucker also delved into detail about Perdue's interactions with Beverly Hall, and, like Mathers, Perdue described Hall's reluctance to take cheating allegations seriously.

"I got the distinct feeling that she essentially just wanted us to go away," Perdue said.[30] But Perdue acknowledged that she wasn't the only one with power and a desire to suppress the investigation. This was a rarity, since the prosecution had placed Beverly Hall on the highest rung of the conspiratorial ladder. Perdue recounted a breakfast at the governor's mansion where Mathers presented the erasure analysis to members of Atlanta's business elite, many of whom held significant sway over Hall and APS. Indeed, some of the people in that meeting took charge of APS's internal investigation, instructing Hall on the formation of the blue-ribbon commission. In his testimony, Perdue said the report had the semblance of a "cover-up." It was practically the only time in the trial when Hall wasn't held solely responsible for that report.

Defense lawyers tackled the issue of the Race to the Top funding as they had with Mathers. Unfazed, Perdue readily conceded that he ordered a special investigation into Atlanta's and Dougherty County's 2009 CRCT scores two days after winning the $400 million Race to the Top grant, which, defense attorneys pointed out, was based in part on the veracity of those very scores.

After Perdue came GBI director Vernon Keenan and Robert Wilson, who headed the state investigation with Mike Bowers and Richard

Hyde. Much of their testimony added to the background Perdue provided, detailing how their investigation was conducted. In that, there were some revealing moments.

Keenan confirmed that several teachers had complained of being "abused" by GBI agents who intimidated them. He noted the allegation that an agent placed a gun on the table during an interview but said it hadn't been substantiated. Later, several defense lawyers posed questions that exposed how the investigation encouraged false confessions and rewarded those who cheated.

"Immunity became a golden opportunity," challenged attorney Bob Rubin.

"They were safe from criminal prosecution if they told the truth," Keenan explained.

"And the people that determined what the truth was, [were] Mr. Bowers, Mr. Hyde, and Mr. Wilson, or the Fulton County DA's office, correct?" Rubin asked. Keenan agreed.[31]

Attorney Ben Davis asked if Keenan was aware that many witnesses gave one story and then, after receiving immunity, gave a different story. Keenan said he was.

"You might look at that person and their credibility as suspect, true?" Davis followed.

"It does bring their credibility into question, but it is not uncommon for that to happen," Keenan replied.

In Bob Wilson's testimony, he reiterated an important fact from the GBI report that had been all but lost in the years since its publication. Rubin was questioning him about the district's system of targets and bonuses.

"The bonuses had little to do, from what we could determine, as to why cheating occurred," Wilson stated.[32]

I wished that someone would write his quote on the wall. The RICO charge hinged on supposed financial incentives, but here was one of the lead investigators of the cheating scandal saying that bonuses were not a factor! Too often, critical points like this one were difficult to decipher in the moment, as they were buried in hours of roundabout questioning and answering.

Another important detail from Wilson's testimony came as a surprise to me. In discussing the chain of command at APS, Michael Pitts's attorney asked Wilson if he was aware that the Atlanta school board, not Hall, had ultimate authority over the system. I had wondered why no school board members were implicated in the cheating, so my ears perked up.

Wilson replied that during her tenure, Hall held more decision-making power than any other superintendent in the state, thanks to an amendment to the city's charter created by Kasim Reed when he was a state senator. It was another fact that muddied the prosecution's depiction of Hall as a lone super-villain. To the extent that cheating happened, there were many people, policies, and trends that enabled it. But few were actually being held accountable.

In fact, certain conditions that enabled the cheating scandal were being exacerbated. As the trial dragged on through November, the Georgia Education Department introduced a new teacher evaluation system, encouraged and paid for by the Race to the Top program, that rated teachers based on student test scores. In an ironic twist, the millions of dollars that Mathers and Perdue procured using inflated CRCT scores were being used to raise the stakes of standardized tests even higher, making it that much more likely that educators might respond to the pressure by cheating. While much of the public thought the problems wrought by the cheating scandal were being vindicated in the courtroom, they were actually proliferating in the education system.

The distracting drama of the trial was giving a boost to advocates for school privatization too. The ills of the cheating scandal were increasingly counterposed with the promise of charter schools, in stories like one published that month by *Journal-Constitution* reporter Bill Torpy, who called the trial "a reminder of all that was sordid about Atlanta Public Schools," while characterizing Drew Charter School as a symbol of "hope and renewal."[33]

Meanwhile, the midterm election had come and gone, with Nathan Deal reelected governor. In his acceptance speech, he claimed to have invested in education during his first term, making no mention of the billions of dollars he had cut from the state's education budget.[34]

The last two weeks of November finally afforded some breathing room, as several days of court were canceled due to one lawyer's illness and another with a death in the family. Then came Thanksgiving, a welcome reprieve. But I didn't have long to recharge. Dunbar was next on the prosecution's agenda. When court reconvened, the state would present its case against me.

CHAPTER EIGHT

Not the Brightest Bulb in the Box

■ | | | | | | | | | | | | | | | | | | | | | | | | ■

THE FIRST DAY OF TESTIMONY AGAINST ME began with a wild lie that I never saw coming.

It was the morning of December 2, 2014, and before court convened, prosecutor Linda Dunikoski, who worked alongside Willis and Rucker, informed Judge Baxter that while reviewing Lera Middlebrooks's plea agreement with her the day before, Middlebrooks had added new information to the story she planned to tell on the witness stand.

Attorney Greene was indignant. "Your honor, I'm asking for that statement to be excluded," she demanded. "This is our first time hearing this."[1]

Originally Middlebrooks had said that when Sonny Perdue's investigation was underway, she had told Rose Neal and Pamela Cleveland that she would sue anyone who mentioned her name. Now she had suddenly added that Cleveland had responded, "Well, Shani Robinson is being interviewed over at DeKalb Mall right now. I need to call her and let her know she needs to stick to the script."

Stick to the script? I was livid. Hadn't she done enough to drag us through the mud? It made no sense. No one knew I was being interviewed while I was with Agent Bigham. I hadn't spoken to Cleveland for months at that point. It was right after the interview that I stopped by her house on an impulse to see if she could tell me what was going on. I thought back to the party Middlebrooks had thrown at the end of that school year. How she had cornered me and asked if I'd spoken to the GBI. I told her all about it, including my visit to Cleveland's home afterward. Did she somehow mix that up in her head to produce this false claim? Or was she flat-out lying?

As he attempted to sort the situation out, Baxter went on one of his tangents and surprised everyone when he said, "I'm a little bit doubtful, somewhat doubtful, about the RICO." For a moment, my heart soared to imagine that he might, after all we had been through, dismiss the charges. When the state rested its case, defense lawyers would have the option to argue that prosecutors hadn't sufficiently carried the burden of proof, and Baxter could "direct a verdict," ending the trial and setting us free.[2]

But my heart crashed right back down as Baxter went on to deny my attorney's request to exclude Middlebrooks's new statement from testimony, saying that Greene would have time to interview Middlebrooks at lunch and make any necessary adjustments to her defense strategy. We were not off to a good start.

Before the state began presenting evidence on Dunbar, they brought in Christopher Waller, the former principal of Parks Middle School, to finish his testimony from the day before.

Waller was the self-described "poster child" of the cheating scandal, and he was called in to testify against Pitts. It was Waller's school that had the highest number of classrooms flagged in the state and where some of the most outrageous acts allegedly took place. Numerous former Parks employees portrayed the situation at the school as a hot mess, with affairs, sexual harassment, and infighting among the staff. On the stand, Waller acknowledged that he'd had affairs with four of his employees and admitted to orchestrating cheating for three years, due to pressure to raise test scores.

Interestingly, in response to questioning from one of the defense attorneys, Waller said that the pressure stemmed more from the threat of school closure than a need to meet district targets. Parks had been sanctioned under the No Child Left Behind law because it had failed for several years to meet the statewide adequate yearly progress benchmarks mandated by the federal government. Parks was at risk of being shut down by the state if the scores didn't improve.

When it was finally time for testimony about Dunbar, my nerves were buzzing with anticipation. Gloria Ivey took the stand, looking tired but composed, with her hair neatly swept over her head into a side bun. She seemed resolved to get her testimony over with. It didn't implicate anyone else, so I didn't have my hackles up yet.

Ivey admitted to telling students to rethink incorrect answers and pointing to the correct answers a few times. She also admitted that she tried to assist the Dunbar student who spoke at Paul Howard's press conference when the indictment was announced. She clarified that she had tried to help the student on the Grade 5 Writing Assessment, which was unrelated to the CRCT but was still a testing violation. Ivey said she had acted alone and never told any of her coworkers what she was doing. She stated that she felt pressured by Principal Greene to increase her students' test scores. And when it came to the question of changing answers on the tests, Ivey was adamant that she never did such a thing; she hadn't even erased stray marks on her students' answer sheets.

Ivey claimed to have lied to GBI agents when she initially denied cheating, and during cross-examination the defense lawyers pressed her on this.

"Are you lying now?" Buckner-Webb's attorney asked her, to which Ivey gave a curt no. Credibility was in question to some degree with every witness who had been indicted and then taken a plea deal in exchange for reduced charges and an agreement to testify. But credibility was about to go off the rails when Middlebrooks testified.

I felt my blood rising to my face when she entered the courtroom and took her seat on the witness stand. As always, she was styled to a T, this time with her hair in chin-length black waves parted down the middle and gold eye shadow behind square, black-rimmed glasses. Linda Dunikoski led the prosecution. An angular, middle-aged woman with loosely curled brown hair and an underbite, Dunikoski had a smart-aleck attitude that reminded me of the kind of student who has more awards than friends.

Dunikoski began by having Middlebrooks relay her version of what happened at Dunbar during CRCT testing in 2009. Middlebrooks explained that our principal, Betty Greene, had a meeting with School Reform Team director Michael Pitts, and afterward she asked Middlebrooks to serve as testing coordinator because they badly needed to meet targets.

"If not, there were going to be changes to her job, my job," Middlebrooks claimed. Later in her testimony she would concede that Greene never asked her to cheat, but she felt "it was implied."[3]

Dunikoski produced the testing schedule that Middlebrooks created and questioned her about a portion that outlined when teachers would check the tests for stray marks.

"What was the intent or purpose for meeting with the teachers and having them inspect the documents?" Dunikoski asked.

"To cheat."

"And how did you carry it out?"

"I called first and second grade teachers to the computer lab."

"So who was that?"

"Ms. Cleveland, Ms. Robinson, Ms. Webb, Ms. Neal, and the PE teacher, Mr. Samuel Hill, was in there."[4]

I jerked my head up from taking notes and shot a confused look at Cleveland, who was sitting to my right. The bewilderment on her face almost made me laugh out loud. We knew Middlebrooks had a tendency to run her mouth, especially when she was upset or nervous, but now she was introducing a new character to her story who had never appeared in any of her previous accounts to investigators or prosecutors. The PE teacher was certainly not in the computer lab when we were there. What on earth possessed Middlebrooks to pull his name out of thin air?

Dunikoski seemed caught off guard for only a moment before plowing ahead. She went on to ask Middlebrooks to describe the layout of the computer lab and where we were all sitting. Middlebrooks said there was a long table with three computers facing her and three facing the back wall. With a cool confidence, she said that four of us—Neal, Hill (who was not there), Cleveland, and I—were sitting on the side nearest her, while Buckner-Webb sat on the opposite side of the table. Middlebrooks said that she had been sitting at the desk at the front of the room. During a break in the court proceedings, Cleveland, Buckner-Webb, and I would debate where we all sat and conclude that if we couldn't remember, it wasn't likely that Middlebrooks's mental image was spot-on either.

When Dunikoski asked Middlebrooks what we did in the computer lab, she responded that she saw us erasing.

"Did you see the pencil tips go down?" Dunikoski urged.

"I saw them erase," Middlebrooks stumbled. "I can't say that I saw the pencil lead go down."[5]

It was a strange admission, because we certainly had used both ends of the pencil—we had written on the test booklets while filling in our students' names and other information—but more so because the rest of the time Middlebrooks made painstaking attempts to concoct details that would bolster her allegations against us. Watching her testify was like seeing a contortionist try to fit in a box. Whenever she seemed to realize that her story wasn't adding up, she would embark on a vigorous ramble, bending and twisting the details to fashion something that might work.

When Dunikoski asked Middlebrooks how long we remained in the computer lab, the answer should have been simple. She had told investigators about thirty minutes and said the same in her plea agreement. But now for some reason Middlebrooks launched into a monologue about how she wasn't wearing a watch and what time the after-school bus came before finally stating that we could have been there for up to two hours. I wondered if it had dawned on her that thirty minutes would not have given us enough time to review and change the answers to seventy questions, including thirteen reading passages, on at least fifteen tests each.

Finally Dunikoski arrived at Middlebrooks's claim, that she had talked with Neal and Cleveland about the state investigation. Neal had made a similar claim, telling GBI agents that Middlebrooks had said, "If any bitch mentions my name . . . I'm gonna put liens on bank accounts." Neal had also said that she was afraid she would "get my ass kicked at the car." Middlebrooks's version was less aggressive. She maintained that she had only jokingly threatened to sue for defamation.

Dunikoski approached the subject by asking, "Did something happen around April 12th of 2011 that involved some teachers back at Dunbar?"

Middlebrooks told her version of the story, including the new addendum that she had fabricated just a few days earlier.

"And so Cleveland said that she is going to, you know, contact Shani, because Shani had told her that she was supposed to be meeting the GBI at South DeKalb Mall parking lot. And so she said, I'll get the message to Shani, you know, that all of us stick to the story."[6]

Hold on, I thought. *They're saying this happened in April 2011?* My interview with the GBI agent at South DeKalb Mall happened in October 2010. Didn't Dunikoski know that? What the hell was going on?

"What story?" Dunikoski asked, apparently expecting Middlebrooks to reveal our "cleverly disguised conspiracy." Instead Middlebrooks had another contortionist moment.

"Whatever you told the GBI," she stammered. "Meaning that all of us need, you know, that's why we all asked each other 'what did you say?' So if we are questioned—I was the only one that didn't cooperate with the GBI. I didn't say anything. I didn't call anybody's name."[7]

As she trailed off incoherently, I felt smug. There obviously was no "story." Only the truth, which Middlebrooks had foregone in favor of a plea deal when she was faced with a possible thirty-five-year prison sentence.

Over the next two days, my lawyer, along with Cleveland's and Buckner-Webb's, cross-examined Middlebrooks at length. They produced the state's CRCT manual for first- and second-grade teachers, highlighting the instructions for erasing stray marks and writing in student information, proving there was a legitimate reason for us to work on the test booklets.

They questioned her about the third-, fourth-, and fifth-grade teachers who were not indicted but whose tests had higher standard deviations than ours. Was it her position that they had changed answers too, and, if so, how? Middlebrooks said she had given them the opportunity to cheat that same day after school (which further undermined her claim that we were in the computer lab for two hours), except that they had come to her office and she'd only handed out their Scantron sheets, not the test booklets. How then, our lawyers wondered, did those teachers change answers on a Scantron sheet without knowing what the questions and answer choices were? Did she provide them with an answer key? Middlebrooks maintained that she didn't know how they had done it; she'd just given them the opportunity.

In addition to such threadbare explanations, blatant discrepancies surfaced. Asked what motivation first- and second-grade teachers would have to cheat, Middlebrooks claimed our students' scores counted toward adequate yearly progress, which everyone by then knew was not true. She claimed that Ivey changed answers, even though prosecutors acknowledged in Ivey's plea agreement that she didn't.

Then there was the matter of the Grade 5 Writing Assessment prompt that Middlebrooks had allegedly shared ahead of testing time with a friend who was a reading consultant in another part of the state. APS had investigated that and prohibited Middlebrooks from being testing coordinator again.

As the questioning cast doubt over Middlebrooks's version of events and her general trustworthiness, Middlebrooks became increasingly theatrical, going on long-winded rants about minutiae that veered far from whatever question was posed, desperately avoiding giving a straightforward answer. Several times when she seemed almost caught in a contradiction, she would say that her "lightbulb" had switched on and she now remembered some previously unmentioned bit of information that she would use to try to rationalize her position. At some points, Middlebrooks seemed to perhaps have a guilty conscience; she would make a statement and immediately insist "I'm not lying" before the defense lawyer could even suggest as much. At one point, she concluded a monologue about how she was just a pawn for Principal Greene with a dramatic flourish, saying "And I stand on that, on everything that I love."[8] Again I had to suppress laughter. *"On everything I love?"* She might as well pinky-swear the jury!

The redirect examination was peppered with attempts by Dunikoski to get her case back on track. At one point during the proceedings, I noticed Willis and Dunikoski conferring quietly over some documents at the prosecution table and looking like they had just struck gold. Then Willis turned and looked right at my attorney with a big grin on her face.

When it was Dunikoski's turn, she displayed a page from one of my students' test booklets. There was a huge, dark drawing that wasn't completely erased. Dunikoski argued that I clearly must have been cheating, since I hadn't thoroughly erased all the stray marks. I was furious. I knew I probably hadn't erased every stray mark completely, especially since the very dark ones were hard to eliminate. But it didn't mean I changed answers. Although I was beginning to suspect who had. During the re–cross-examination, my attorney took the same booklet Dunikoski used and displayed other pages to show where I had indeed erased stray marks.

By the end of her testimony, Middlebrooks was plainly making things up. Out of nowhere, she said that she had spoken with Buckner-Webb on the phone about cheating several times over the years, something she had never claimed before.

"Ms. Middlebrooks," Buckner-Webb's lawyer fumed, "about three minutes ago is the very first time in the universe that you have ever said anything about having a phone conversation with Diane Buckner-Webb?"[9]

"I'm just talking," she replied. "I'm just saying, because the light-bulb, yeah, I mean everything is fresh now. So might be some other, ask me some questions. Maybe some other stuff come on out. I don't know."

No way could a jury convict us based on that nonsense. I thought that surely the state's case against the Dunbar teachers was dead in the water. And with Rose Neal up next, I didn't have to worry about it being resuscitated.

The week before, one of Buckner-Webb's lawyers, Kevin Franks, had tried to convince Judge Baxter to exclude Neal as a witness because her story changed, more than any other witness, each time she was interviewed. Franks even said that Dunikoski agreed with him that Neal was unreliable.

"The court cannot allow a witness who is clearly perjuring [herself] to stand as the basis for a conviction of any defendant," he argued.[10]

"The jury will be there to determine her credibility," Baxter said dismissively. Franks tried to convince the judge to change his mind, but Baxter eventually cut him off saying, "I just want to go to lunch."[11]

Now I was face to face with Neal in court, and it was even more difficult than listening to Middlebrooks's lies. Neal was our original accuser. If she hadn't lied and said that Cleveland, Buckner-Webb, and I changed had answers with her, we likely would not have been indicted. But even though Neal had escaped the threat of prosecution by wrongfully naming us, she still seemed worse for wear. She arrived, looking beleaguered, in a wheelchair. Her testimony sounded discombobulated from the beginning as she struggled to remember basic details, like how many children were in her class in 2009. "I'm retired and my mind has gone," she said as she wracked her brain.[12]

Dunikoski led her through a similar line of questioning as she had with Middlebrooks, to get Neal's account of that day in the computer lab. Immediately there were discrepancies. Neal said that Cleveland and I were sitting with Buckner-Webb across the table from her with computer monitors between us. She claimed she could see us changing answers through the spaces between the monitors. Not only did this contradict Middlebrooks's description, it didn't match what Neal herself had told the grand jury. During cross-examination, Buckner-Webb's other lawyer, Keith Adams, would ask Neal why she originally said that we sat at desks "turned all which way."

"There might have been some type of mix-up in my mind," Neal replied. "I think more or less I may have been alluding to my classroom."[13]

I couldn't believe it. I was indicted based on Neal's grand jury testimony, which was apparently so nonsensical that she had botched the one thing that we could all agree on: that we were in the computer lab.

Neal also told Adams, when he asked her what conversation was going on in the room while this supposed cheating took place, that she "wasn't paying the other teachers any attention."[14] If she wasn't paying attention to us, how could she claim to have seen us changing answers?

When Dunikoski asked if anyone else was in the room, Neal didn't say anything about Coach Hill. Instead she said that the school librarian briefly came in to ask Middlebrooks a question and caught Neal by surprise. She claimed that she cried out, "Oh, shit!

I was starting to feel like we were in a sitcom whose writers were revising the script over and over, trying out new settings and characters with each attempt.

Dunikoski tried to settle the Coach Hill issue by asking directly if he had been there too. But Neal wouldn't give a straight answer.

"I can't remember him being in that room. I'm not saying he wasn't in there, but I just can't remember." Later she would tell the defense attorneys that she was "leaning toward no" on the Coach Hill question.[15]

While the "who" and the "where" did not match up, Neal echoed Middlebrooks when it came to the "why." She claimed to have cheated because she wanted to raise her students' scores to meet targets. But of course, the first- and second-grade scores didn't count toward targets, just like they didn't count toward AYP, which my attorney would later demonstrate by presenting a document that outlined Dunbar's projected targets between 2001 and 2010. Each year it listed CRCT targets only for third through fifth grade.

Neal's tale diverged from Middlebrooks's again when Dunikoski questioned her about the conversation in April 2011. Neal reiterated what she had told the grand jury, that Middlebrooks had threatened retaliation against anyone who mentioned her name to the GBI.

"What did Ms. Cleveland say in response?" Dunikoski asked.

"I don't remember her saying anything," Neal said, confirming that Middlebrooks had made up the bit about Cleveland calling to tell me to "stick to the story."[16]

When Dunikoski was done with her examination, our defense lawyers grilled Neal, who became increasingly distraught. While Middlebrooks had a lightbulb to help explain away her inconsistencies, Neal blamed memory loss and even menopause when her story seemed to be falling apart.

My attorney brought up the fact that Principal Greene had placed Neal on a professional development plan, essentially probation, because she had problems with classroom management. And Neal had filed a harassment claim against the principal with APS's Office of Internal Resolutions. Neal admitted that she had hoped to transfer from Dunbar, and Attorney Greene suggested that perhaps she cheated because she thought that scoring higher would get her off probation and placed in another school.

Attorney Adams focused on Neal's purported history of cheating. Dunikoski had asked Neal if she had ever cheated before 2009, and she said yes, though she wasn't sure what year and didn't remember who she might have cheated with. Adams pointed out that when she first confessed to GBI agents, she told them that she had never cheated before.

"At that time I possibly did not remember that," Neal said.

"Right, but you sure remembered it when you went before the grand jury and you told them no you hadn't cheated before," Adams pressed. "And they said, 'Listen, you know, you're under oath and we could prosecute you.' Sure enough, your memory got really good then."[17]

But perhaps the most astonishing moment came when Adams put Neal's test booklets on the overhead projector to show the jury the handwriting in the section for the student's name, their school name, and so forth. This was to counter something that Dunikoski had tried to prove. She had shown that the district provided preprinted labels for student demographic information. We didn't have to fill in that information ourselves if the booklet had a label, which many did. Dunikoski presented this as if it showed that there was no reason for us to be writing on the booklets. But Adams showed that there was a section on all the booklets where we had to fill in other student information; there was no label for that section. As he was explaining this, Neal said something that stunned everyone.

"This part—the teacher, school system—is not my writing," she said. Adams paused.

"That's not your handwriting?"

"No. That's not me."

A hush fell over the courtroom. I glanced at Willis and Dunikoski to see their faces frozen in looks of shock. It was plain that the writing on the booklet belonged to an adult. Adams showed Neal a few more booklets, and she claimed that the handwriting belonged to someone else on those too.

"Who is it that came behind you and had access to the tests such that they would write in this information?" Adams asked.

"Now, that I wouldn't know," Neal replied.

"You don't know what amount of access Lera Middlebrooks had to these tests after you got done in that room, do you?"

"No."

"You don't know what, if anything, Principal Greene did to these documents after you were in that room, true?"

"True."[18]

I could have jumped for joy. This revelation seemed to prove that someone else had the opportunity to tamper with the tests. It felt like the final blow to the state's shaky case against me and my Dunbar colleagues.

With Middlebrooks's and Neal's testimonies over, a weight lifted from my shoulders. I no longer had to sit quietly and listen to falsehoods leveled against me. The rest of the week was taken up with testimony concerning Dobbs Elementary, but the following week Dunbar was under the microscope again when prosecutors dragged in poor Coach Hill to respond to Middlebrooks's accusation. He flatly denied going to the computer lab with us, and he was quickly dismissed.

That day, a bit of drama unfolded that left me seriously questioning whether we were getting a fair trial. In the morning, before court was in session, Angela Williamson's lawyer told Judge Baxter that Williamson's sister saw prosecutor Willis making faces and gesturing at witnesses who had testified against Williamson the day before. Williamson's sister had been sitting along the wall on the defendant's side of the courtroom, where she had a good view of the prosecution table. Several family members, including my father, sat in that area. Baxter brushed the accusation aside and instead became angry that family members were in the defense area, ordering them to move to the spectator area.

But apparently he started paying closer attention to Willis, because later that day, when Williamson's lawyer was cross-examining one of her former students, Baxter interrupted him to admonish Willis.

"Ms. Willis, you're going to need to stop making facial expressions toward the jury," he snapped. Willis didn't bother denying it. "Okay," she muttered.[19]

I wondered how long this prosecutorial misconduct had gone unchecked. A few months prior, attorney Theresa Mann told Judge Baxter that she saw the prosecutors nodding and shaking their heads "as nonverbal communication to the jury." Willis denied it. Later I would learn that this wasn't the first time Willis was accused of such behavior. In 2012, an official grievance was filed with the State Bar of Georgia about her unethical conduct during a murder trial involving four young black men. The grievance letter alleged that Willis had coached a witness out in the hallway with an exhibit that had already been admitted into evidence and therefore shouldn't have been out of the courtroom. Willis denied the accusations in a letter to the State Bar. The woman who filed the grievance, a family member of one of the accused, told me she also saw Willis nodding her head "yes" and "no" at the state's witnesses while they were testifying.

Later in the week, the former Dunbar librarian came in to testify about whether she had been in the computer lab momentarily while we were erasing stray marks, as Neal had claimed. She was a quirky, older white woman named Oreta Taylor, who looked exactly the way I remembered her when I taught at Dunbar, with long, gray hair and floor-length skirts. When she arrived to be vetted by prosecutors, she ran into Cleveland, Buckner-Webb, and me on our way into the courtroom. She scurried over to hug us, right in front of Dunikoski, who visibly bristled. During our lunch hour that day, Buckner-Webb, Cleveland, and I sat in the courtroom with Taylor, catching up on old times and what we had been doing over the past few years. Someone from the prosecution team came in the courtroom to keep tabs on our conversation. We didn't care; we just kept right on talking. It felt like a tiny act of defiance to show that we were real people with colleagues who respected and cared for us, even as they were forced to testify against us.

In her testimony, Taylor said that she remembered stopping by the computer lab during the CRCT testing week in 2009. She opened the door to ask Middlebrooks a question, but Middlebrooks told her, "Not now." She said she remembered that there were teachers in the room but couldn't recall who.

With that, Dunbar testimony concluded, and the court adjourned for Christmas break.

My family tried to have a cheerful holiday, but there was no denying that we were all worn down. Plus, money was tight. We never placed as much importance on gifts as we did on traditions, like the big Christmas party at my parents' home and the trivia game I always put together, but the skimpy assortment of presents under the tree was a visual reminder of what a hard year it had been. No matter, the best gift I could receive came from my ob-gyn. Shortly before Christmas, I went in for a checkup and learned that despite the taxing trial, my baby was healthy—and a boy. Moses and I made the announcement at

Christmas dinner, and everyone raised a glass. We had chosen to name him the Yoruba word meaning "strength." Moses's father's side of the family is Yoruban.

"Amari," we all said in unison, our glasses clinking.

After the New Year, and before the trial resumed, a prayer vigil was held at the church of one of my codefendants. To my surprise, a local television news station showed up to cover it. I was shocked that they were willing to do a positive story about us. Even though Moses and I had developed tactics for simulating a normal life and ignoring the trial when I wasn't in court, I still kept up with the media coverage. Most of the footage shown on TV was people crying on the stand and short clips from the prosecutors' examinations. Rarely was any substance from the defense's cross-examination covered. And while Baxter had lifted our gag order, he warned the defendants that he thought we shouldn't talk to the media. To try to stay in his good graces, as if that were possible, we kept our side of the story to ourselves.

It didn't help that the only news station with a camera crew in the courtroom was WSB-TV, owned by the same company, Cox Enterprises, that owned the *Atlanta Journal-Constitution*, the only newspaper providing daily coverage of the trial. Cox, a huge media conglomerate, is owned by one family, whose matriarch was the wealthiest person in Georgia. Besides owning newspapers, television, and radio in numerous states, its subsidiary, Cox Communications, is one of the country's largest Internet and cable providers. And in the years leading up to the trial, another subsidiary, Cox Business, had expanded into the K–12 education market with a slate of virtual learning products and services it sold to more than five thousand schools. At the same time, the company's foundation was donating to charter schools (including Drew Charter in Atlanta), Teach for America, and the BeltLine. The company itself has been involved in ALEC, sponsoring its annual conference and participating in the organization's Communications and Technology Task Force. I wondered if Cox's corporate interests could affect the trial coverage.[20]

January 5 came too quickly. We were back in court, with no end to the trial in sight. Judge Baxter seemed to be down to his last frayed nerve, frequently holding his head in his hands, rolling his eyes, and snapping, "You need to move on!" when the questioning was going slowly, which was most of the time.[21]

For the first two weeks of the trial in 2015, much of the focus was on Dobbs Elementary. Former Dobbs principal Dana Evans and former teachers Angela Williamson and Dessa Curb were on trial. Former Dobbs employees who had been indicted and taken plea deals testified against them. When prosecutors examined these witnesses, the jury heard stories that, by that time, were par for the course about allegedly feeling pressured to cheat, witnessing cheating, and facing retaliation for supposedly trying to expose cheating. But during cross-examination, their testimonies were undermined by their deeply flawed track records and inconsistent statements, which defense attorneys brought to light.

Parents had complained that one witness called students the N-word and accused the students of coming to school just to get a free lunch. Other witnesses, it came out, had been punished for transgressions including being chronically late, choking a special education student, shoving a spoon down a child's throat, and falling asleep in class while three students engaged in sexual activity.

The accusations unraveled further when Dessa Curb's lawyer showed that her special education class was never even flagged for having a high number of wrong-to-right erasures and that many of her students had failed the CRCT.

After the last Dobbs witness testified, the prosecution turned to Benteen Elementary and its former testing coordinator, Theresia Copeland. For two days, testimony centered on the minute details of whether, where, and when Copeland had pushed a cart of testing materials down a hall. Either way, it didn't seem to prove anything, since it was Copeland's job to transport the testing materials, and no one testified to having seen her change any answers on any of the tests.

Usher–Collier Heights Elementary was next. Donald Bullock, a fatherly man who asked me daily how my baby was doing, had served as testing coordinator there. Even though several teachers at the school had high numbers of wrong-to-right erasures in 2008, before Bullock worked there, he was the only person from Usher–Collier Heights indicted for allegedly enabling cheating in 2009.

The most fascinating moment from the testimony against him was when prosecutors brought Brittany Aronson to the witness stand. Unlike many of the APS employees who had testified, Aronson was white.

It turned out that Aronson had more wrong-to-right erasures in her class than any of the teachers on trial and even some of the highest in the district. Her standard deviations on the various sections of the CRCT ranged from 30.7 to 38.1. By comparison, my standard deviations ranged from 11.8 to 13.5.

Despite her extraordinarily high standard deviations, the GBI agent who interviewed Aronson did not threaten or bully her as they had done to so many black teachers. Quite the opposite.

Paraphrasing the agent's words from the interview transcript, one of the defense lawyers said, "If you are erasing answers in a room and erasing so much that you have to go and pick up a new stack of erasers and erase the answers, that's all right with us. That's what the agent told you, right?"

"Yes," Aronson replied.

"And of course, at that point, they weren't like beating you down or browbeating you or threatening you with jail or anything like that because of this erasure analysis, were they?"

"No."

"You told them, I'm not lying; I don't know anything about that, right?"

"Yes."

"And that seemed to be enough for them, right?"

"Yes."[22]

After just one interview, the investigators let Aronson off the hook.

Toward the end of January, prosecutors brought in Melissa Fincher, who oversaw testing for the Georgia Department of Education, to talk about testing protocol. But since she was involved in the state's Race to the Top grant application, which garnered $400 million based on the same 2009 CRCT scores the state was then investigating, defense attorney Ben Davis questioned her as he had Sonny Perdue and Kathleen Mathers in the fall.

"So Georgia never sent to the federal government an update invalidating part of the CRCT numbers, right?" he asked.

"Actually, we did look at the impact of the identified schools for APS on the statewide numbers, and it had no impact," Fincher said with a matter-of-fact twang.[23]

Kathleen Mathers had testified that they took into consideration all the schools that were flagged for a prevalence of wrong-to-right erasures—20 percent of schools statewide—and somehow concluded that discounting their scores didn't affect the state average. But now Fincher was saying that they only took APS schools out of the equation. No matter what, it looked like state officials had knowingly used falsified test scores to reap hundreds of millions of dollars while condemning educators for allegedly falsifying scores in order to obtain bonuses of a few hundred dollars. It was the height of hypocrisy.

While Fincher was on the stand, Cleveland's lawyer took the opportunity to ask her about protocol for dealing with a testing coordinator under investigation for violating testing rules, as Middlebrooks was when she was in charge of Dunbar's CRCT. Fincher said that the Georgia Department of Education had no policy on the books about that but that their recommendation to the school district would have been to remove the testing coordinator until the investigation was complete. So Middlebrooks should never have been administering the CRCT in the first place.

As the trial extended into February, Judge Baxter's temper became even shorter, and this led to a tantrum during Millicent Few's testimony. Few was one of the state's high-profile witnesses. She had served as Beverly Hall's human resources officer, a top administrative position. Her testimony bolstered the allegation that Hall knew about cheating and tried to cover it up.

When it was time for cross-examination, defense attorneys, as usual, brought up the witness's plea deal. When Few was indicted, she faced twenty years in prison for racketeering. In exchange for her guilty plea and an agreement to testify, Baxter gave her twelve months of probation, an $800 fine, and 250 hours of community service. Dessa Curb's lawyer, Sandy Wallack, broached the subject first.

"Was one of your motivations the concern of statements made by Judge Baxter that any defendant who went to trial, was found guilty—"[24]

"Objection," prosecutor Clint Rucker called. Baxter ordered the jury out of the room.

"What are you doing?" he thundered at Wallack.

"I was asking her if one of her motivations for entering a guilty plea [was] statements made by the court that defendants who went to trial and were convicted faced severe consequences. The court has made that statement several times," Wallack responded in a measured tone, which only prompted a tirade from Baxter.

"I'm not allowing it! It is true I have made those statements in court, begging people, if they are responsible, to take responsibility. But, you know, it is totally in my discretion, the sentence, if somebody is convicted in this case. And you are not to go into that."

Wallack cited case law that states that questioning witness bias or motivation is proper during cross-examination. But Baxter dug in his heels. "If somebody does it again, I will send them to jail," he said. "I will. If somebody broaches this subject with me involved about sentencing in this case, then I'm going to send you to jail for contempt."

Soon Cleveland's lawyer, Angela Johnson, challenged Baxter's wrath head-on. This time he had slighted her when she asked him to speak louder. He'd gone on a tangent during a pause in testimony and ended up telling a story about when he was a young prosecutor, addressing his reminiscences to the jury. He wasn't speaking into the microphone, and Johnson couldn't tell what he was talking about, which she called to his attention.

"I wasn't talking to you!" he snarled.[25]

The next day, before court adjourned, Johnson demanded that Baxter apologize to her in front of the jury.

"To be quite honest with you, some of the ways that I have seen you behave not only with me but some of my colleagues in court . . . you disrespect people by yelling at them in front of the jury. You diminished me in the eyes of the jury," she told him.[26]

After hemming and hawing, Baxter eventually agreed to apologize when the jury came in. I fiercely hoped that the way Baxter treated the defense counsel wasn't having the negative effect on the jury that Johnson suggested.

It was getting harder and harder to keep my spirits up as the prosecution at last began winding down. They only had a few more witnesses, and then it would finally be time for defendants to present our cases. I started having a recurring nightmare about losing my son. In those dreams, I was in a hospital room, giving birth. My baby would emerge, but, before I could hold him, someone snatched him away and I was taken to jail.

As my sleep suffered, I had trouble staying focused during the trial, and the last few testimonies passed in a blur. But there was one that grabbed my attention.

Former APS board member Yolanda Johnson testified about what was happening with the school board as the cheating scandal unfolded. Prosecutor Dunikoski started by asking her questions that established that Beverly Hall was generally concerned about board members micromanaging and that she discouraged them from getting involved in the operations of the school system. In 2010, when then governor Sonny Perdue required school districts across the state that had classrooms flagged for excessive wrong-to-right erasures to conduct internal investigations, Johnson had little say in planning the APS investigation. But neither did Hall. Rather, members of the Metro Atlanta Chamber of Commerce worked with select board members to put together the "blue-ribbon commission," a team of mostly corporate executives who hired a firm to conduct the investigation.

By the time the commission finished its investigation and completed a report, Perdue's deadline was long past. Board members received the report at the eleventh hour, and Johnson felt that she didn't have adequate time to review it before the board was to vote to approve it. Johnson was part of a narrow majority that voted to pass it along to the governor's office but without the board's stamp of approval. At that point, the board was split almost evenly between a minority that generally accepted Hall and the Chamber of Commerce's influence, and a majority that did not. Johnson testified that after that vote, the majority faced immense pressure to back the commission's findings.

"Who was putting the pressure on you?" Dunikoski asked.

"Other board members," Johnson said. "People from the mayor's office."

"The mayor's office? Kasim Reed?"

"Correct."[27]

My ears perked up at this detail. Ultimately Governor Perdue portrayed the blue-ribbon commission report as an attempt to cover up the cheating. And now the mayor was being named on the witness stand as part of that cover-up. This was the second time during the trial that Mayor Reed's involvement in APS was scrutinized. Johnson went on to say that Reed personally showed up at a school board meeting and tried to prevent the majority from voting out the chair, who had sat on the commission. Johnson's testimony showed that people much more powerful than Hall had used APS to benefit politically and financially for years, and now they were continuing business as usual while the rest of us were hung out to dry.

On February 11, six months to the day after the trial began and 133 witnesses later, the state rested its case. The last witness, like the first, was meant to elicit an emotional response from jurors. It was a child whose test scores had been changed, her grades wrongfully inflated. She spent three years in the sixth grade as a result. But no one from the school where her tests were doctored was on trial.

When prosecutor Fani Willis said, "Your honor, it's a great honor. The state rests," the jurors applauded.

Baxter sent the jury out on recess and then turned to the defense. With more pep than usual, he said, "Well, all right, let's get started."[28] It was time for the defense lawyers to argue for a directed verdict, which would effectively end the trial and acquit us.

"You just need to get directly to the point on why I should take this case away from the jury, and exactly where the state had failed to carry their burden," Baxter instructed. Something about his tone gave the impression that this was going to be a mere formality.

Sure enough, each defense attorney made a fairly quick argument, only to have Baxter reply, "Okay, well, I deny your motion." Buckner-Webb's lawyer, Keith Adams, made an argument that Cleveland's lawyer and mine signed on to, since our cases were so similar.

"Essentially what the state has alleged in their indictment, is that by allegedly changing answers on the test, she endeavored to get bonus money," Adams said. "But you will remember from the state's witnesses, or from the evidence that's been uncontroverted that's been put up, that as a second-grade teacher, the test results on the CRCT do not count toward AYP or APS targets . . . there is no way that anything she did in regard to those tests can have an impact upon the purported conspiracy." *It can't get much plainer than that*, I thought.

Adams went on to point out that the witnesses who testified against us did not sufficiently incriminate us. Middlebrooks only described our doing what was part of regular testing protocol. Rose Neal said she saw us erase and change answers, but she also said she wasn't paying us any attention, couldn't remember if Coach Hill was sitting right next to her, and described her classroom, not the computer lab, to the grand jury as the room where the supposed cheating took place.

Yes, our standard deviations were high, Adams conceded, but there were other people who had access to the tests who could have changed the answers.

"Okay, well that's something you're going to need to argue to the jury," Baxter interjected. Adams continued to argue, but Baxter ultimately denied the motion for all of us. We were not out of the woods yet.

Several attorneys took shots at the RICO charge that could have changed the game for all of the defendants. Dessa Curb's lawyer, Sandy Wallack, argued that there was no conspiracy at all, saying, "The law requires that the state prove first that a conspiracy existed in one of the two manners that are alleged in the indictment . . . secondly that Ms. Curb knew the illegal purpose or objective of that conspiracy, third that she intentionally agreed to be a part of that, and fourth that she acted purposely with a specific intent to violate the law. The evidence, I would assert, would show that the state did not prove that there was an overall conspiracy."

But RICO expert John Floyd, who had worked with prosecutors throughout the trial, stepped in to counter that the charges underlying Curb's RICO charge showed a "pattern of racketeering activity by her alone, which is one of the ways in which agreement to a conspiracy can be established."

It was a mind-boggling assertion, that someone acting alone could be agreeing to a conspiracy. Baxter deferred making a decision on a different count in Wallack's motion, and he did the same with part of the motion brought by Dana Evans's lawyer. The rest he denied. Trial would go forward, with each of our attorneys presenting our defense in turn.

⊦⊦⊦⊦⊦⊦⊦⊦⊦⊦⊦⊦⊦

The same day that the state rested its case, Governor Nathan Deal unveiled the plan he had been crafting to clone the Louisiana Recovery School District (RSD), which turned over a majority of New Orleans schools to private operators in the wake of Hurricane Katrina. While our lawyers argued for our freedom, Deal issued a press release introducing legislation to create an Opportunity School District that could take over "failing" schools and turn them into charters. The plan would make possible what the state supreme court had prevented the Charter Schools Commission from doing: levying local tax dollars for charter schools not locally authorized.[29]

In a sweeping asset grab, Deal's Opportunity School District (OSD), led by a governor-appointed superintendent, could seize schools and everything inside them (while requiring the local school district to continue paying for major repairs and renovations) and apply to convert them into charters via the State Charter Schools Commission. The commission could choose education service providers to contract with the school, everything from consultants to education management organizations. And, most importantly, OSD schools would receive a per-student share of federal, state, and local education funds, forcing local school districts to pay for schools they would have no control over and enabling charter operators to use public assets for their private enterprises.[30]

That very day, before legislators had time to review the proposal, leaders of Georgia's house and senate education committees held a joint hearing in which two leaders from the Louisiana RSD presented. Paul Pastorek, the former head of the RSD, had been sent around the country by the Eli and Edythe Broad Foundation, one of the most aggressive foundations pushing for corporate education reform, to consult with state leaders about replicating the model. At the hearing, Pastorek explained that as the RSD reconstituted schools, it worked to "remove barriers and restrictions and empower the new leaders of these schools."

The barriers, he said, were "local school boards, collective bargaining agreements, and [teacher] tenure."[31]

Neerav Kingsland, the former CEO of New Schools for New Orleans, followed Pastorek and described how his organization funneled millions of philanthropic dollars to the RSD. He left out the fact that many of the philanthropists who donated to New Schools for New Orleans were venture capitalists, education technology companies, and investment firms that likely saw their contributions as opening up a lucrative market for their business.

That day, as legislators were introduced to Deal's solution to "failing" schools, the media were abuzz with news of the APS cheating trial milestone. Reporters recapped the worst allegations against us as they announced that the state had rested its case. Intentionally or not, they did Deal a great favor by painting a grotesque picture, the epitome of the "failing" schools that he insisted could only be saved with drastic measures. We were everything wrong with what he called the "status quo." We were among the barriers to the corporate model of education reform, and we were being removed.

CHAPTER NINE

Speak of the Devil

∎׀׀׀׀׀׀׀׀׀׀׀׀׀׀׀׀׀׀׀׀׀׀∎

"HOW MANY MORE OF THESE WITNESSES do you plan to put up?"

It was only the fifth day of defense testimony, and Judge Baxter was already tired of hearing our side.

Bob Rubin, former Dobbs principal Dana Evans's lawyer, was in the middle of examining a witness when Baxter interrupted to pose the question. "A full day today," Rubin replied.

"A full day of the same testimony?" Baxter petulantly asked.

"I don't expect it all to be the same," Rubin said in astonishment. Baxter never complained about prosecutors bringing a whopping 133 witnesses. Rubin had so far called nine.

"Okay. At some point, I think you reach the point of diminishing returns," the judge badgered. A stormy expression came over Rubin's face.

"I sat here for six months listening to evidence," he rejoined.

"Okay," Baxter said, backing off. "I'm just making an observation. Go ahead."[1]

The state had rested little more than a week earlier, and since then Rubin had brought a string of witnesses to testify about Evans's character and accomplishments. Former teachers said she never pressured the staff to raise test scores. Her former assistant principal confirmed that the prosecution's witnesses were some of the most problematic employees, who likely held grudges after being disciplined for legitimate reasons. And of the twenty witnesses that Rubin would call, all who had worked under Evans maintained that her leadership was "visionary" and that there was no indication that she or the other Dobbs defendants were involved in, or aware of, cheating.

Rubin concluded his examination on February 23, and then it was my lawyer's turn. I had decided not to present evidence because bringing witnesses was a big risk. One of my potential character witnesses, a family friend, told prosecutors that she thought I worked as a teacher for only one year and that she didn't know why I resigned. She had some wonderful things to say about me, but getting even mundane details like that wrong could inadvertently give prosecutors ammunition. And testifying in my own defense could be risky for the same reason. I knew it was not uncommon for the defense to rest without presenting evidence and that my side of the story would come through during closing arguments. I was hopeful that, despite Baxter's antagonism, despite the slanted media coverage, if the jury was even half-awake during Middlebrooks's and Neal's testimonies, I would come out on top. The case against me and the other Dunbar teachers was just that flimsy.

Many of the defendants took this approach. Rubin was an exception. Michael Pitts's lawyer brought one witness, Dessa Curb's lawyer brought a few, and Williamson's lawyer brought five. Everyone else rested without presenting evidence. The entire defense lasted less than two weeks, and then we were free for a spring break. Closing statements would commence in March. But before that could happen, the cheating scandal reached a tragic point.

On March 2, I heard the news that Beverly Hall had died of breast cancer. Now we would never know her version of events. State witnesses testified that Hall knew about cheating and tried to hide it. However, having been falsely accused myself, I viewed all of the prosecution's evidence with skepticism. Regardless, nothing that the prosecution presented indicated that she had directed anyone to cheat or orchestrated a coordinated effort to cheat, which is what many people now believed. Unlike Hall, I was not a proponent of high-stakes testing or some of the other corporate-inspired reforms that took place under her leadership. But it was sad that the positive things Hall had done throughout her career were forgotten. It was also troubling how the powerful people who had once praised her and used the high CRCT scores to bolster business in Atlanta cast her off as soon as she became a liability to them. Now there were few left who would eulogize her. It was one thing for a career to end in disgrace. It was even darker for a life to end that way.

Hall's demise hung like a shadow over us when we filled the court for closing statements on March 16.

As with the opening, the state went first. Whereas Fani Willis had led the charge before, sermonizing like a preacher at a tent revival, Clint Rucker now stepped up. Rucker was a smooth talker and usually struck a formal tone with a sprinkling of carefully calculated vernacular to reach the jury. But now Rucker went whole hog in an effort to yank jurors' heartstrings as hard as possible.

"They robbed them kids!" he shouted at the jury so forcefully I could practically see veins bulging on his shaved head. "Changed their answers from wrong to right. Passed them on from one grade to the next. Just set them up for failure!"[2] This we had all heard before, if in less fiery terms. But where Rucker went next required an unusually imaginative leap.

"Why is crime so high? Why you scared that somebody gon' hit you on the back of your head and take your car? Who's breaking into your house? What are they supposed to do? They helpless? Hopeless? And they got uneducated. . . . These defendants and them others, they failed our kids," Rucker yammered.

If anyone's been hit on the head, I thought, *it's Rucker*. Was he serious? Blaming us for poverty and violent crime? Forget about racialized dis-investment and the intentional destruction of black neighborhoods, the influx of drugs and militarized policing, the dismantling of the social safety net, budget cuts to public education and billions of dollars redirected to the for-profit education market and real estate schemes. Which of these factors were even mentioned during trial? None of the above.

I expected Rucker to review the facts of the case against us, but his performance was more like a morality play than an exercise in logic. He called for "redemption," which would only come when those who cheated agreed to "take responsibility." He told a long story about James Farmer Jr., founder of the Congress on Racial Equality, whose grandparents were slaves and whose father was so determined to get an education and rise out of poverty that he walked from his South Carolina hometown

all the way to Massachusetts, over one thousand miles, to go to college.
On the overhead projector, Rucker showed a photograph of Farmer in a
group of civil rights leaders, including Martin Luther King Jr., discussing the Civil Rights Act with President Lyndon B. Johnson.

What the hell does this have to do with our case? I wondered as Rucker
spun his tale for the enraptured jury. As if in answer to my unspoken
question, Rucker's voice began to reach crescendo.

"A man whose grandparents had been slaves, because of the quality
education that he got, was able to do something that affects everybody
in this room today. That's what this case is about, and that's why what
they did is so bad, and that is why I am asking you all to have the cour-
age to tell them that we're not going to let you get away with it."

Cleveland, Buckner-Webb, and I looked at each other like, *I can't
even believe this.* There was a depressing irony in a black man co-opting a
piece of civil rights history to convict black educators for something we
hadn't done and that wouldn't even warrant the severity of the charges
against us if we had.

When Rucker finally got around to talking about our case, he was
hardly more specific.

"How about the Dunbar three that's sitting over here in court?" he
hollered, swinging an arm toward Cleveland, Buckner-Webb, and me.
"Friends to the end. Lera Middlebrooks, the testing coordinator who
pled guilty, who came in here and told you she just couldn't hold it in
no more . . . and she told you, listen, we talked about it. We said, hey,
you better stick to the script when you going over there and meet with
the GBI."

There it was, the lie about "sticking to the script." It was so clearly
a lie because Middlebrooks claimed that in April 2011 I was on my way
to meet the GBI at the mall when Cleveland called me and told me to
"stick to the script," or the "story." But my meeting with the GBI at the
mall happened in October 2010. Prosecutors should have recognized
the discrepancy, but here Rucker was framing it as the linchpin of the
case against us.

He brought up Rose Neal's testimony too, conceding that her details were "a little fuzzy" but claiming that she had sufficiently covered the basic facts of what happened. "Fuzzy" was perhaps the greatest

understatement of the entire trial. Neal had said that her mind was "gone" and repeatedly stated that she suffered from memory loss, which she bizarrely chalked up to menopause, while changing her story with practically every sentence she uttered.

Rucker's bit lasted a couple of hours and touched on each of the defendants, as well as the overall themes of the trial (wrong-to-right erasures, bonus money, cover-ups), with the verve of someone telling ghost stories by a campfire. Toward the end, he addressed the actual charges and the legal standard the evidence would have to meet for the jury to convict. That's when Rucker's spiel turned outright confusing.

Rucker placed a copy of the indictment on the projector and turned to the page where the RICO count was explained. It was a paragraph of legalese that broke the charge down into two parts: a) endeavoring to acquire money by engaging in a pattern of racketeering activity, and b) using APS to conduct racketeering activity.

"The law allows us to charge them in two different ways based on two different kinds of conduct that they did," Rucker began. "Okay, there is A and there is B. We charged them two different ways in a single count. What the law says is that we don't have to prove that they committed the crime in each way." This was odd, given that the indictment stipulated that we did both A *and* B, and it was the prosecution's job to prove the indictment true. But Rucker had a solution to that.

"All them words up there, that's a long way of saying this right here 'and' means 'or.' So in the indictment, where it says A *and* B, what that really means is *or*. That's just some lawyer stuff," he told the jury, with a straight face.

"And" means "or"? That's what they teach in law school? The implication was alarming. One juror could decide that I had violated RICO one way, and another juror could find that it happened a different way. Based on Rucker's instructions, they wouldn't have to reach a unanimous verdict to convict.

Rucker then finished by comparing the defense lawyers to an octopus squirting ink to make the water "murky and cloudy, hard to see through." Somehow he had taken us from the Civil Rights Act to an octopus in the ocean, with a bunch of lies and half-truths about the Atlanta Public Schools cheating scandal in between.

When Rucker was done, RICO expert and special prosecutor John Floyd took over, introducing himself as "more of a professor" compared to Rucker's "preacher." Floyd's job was to explain to the jury just how easy it was to convict us of RICO. He echoed Rucker's point, saying, "Just remember, 'and' equals 'or'," and went on to say that if we were guilty of just one act that furthered the "conspiracy" to inflate test scores, then we were guilty of RICO, regardless of whether or not we knew the other "conspirators" or what they were up to. As long as there were two or more people who shared a "common plan or purpose" and agreed to one or more acts that furthered the plan, that was all it took. The agreement, Floyd said, didn't have to be explicit; it could be "an unspoken, tacit understanding between two conspirators." According to Floyd, though, there was a spoken agreement between the other Dunbar teachers and me. Like Rucker, he invoked Middlebrooks's claim that Cleveland had told me to "stick to the script."[3]

When Middlebrooks told this lie during testimony, I thought it was just another falsified detail among many. I didn't realize how significant it really was. Now it was dawning on me that the state was relying on this detail to convict Cleveland, Buckner-Webb, and me on the RICO charge. I thought back to how prosecutor Linda Dunikoski had argued for Judge Baxter to admit this addition to Middlebrooks's statement the morning she was scheduled to testify. How she told him they had reviewed her plea agreement the day before and Middlebrooks happened to supply this new information. *Is that how it went down?* I wondered. Or had Dunikoski gone fishing, asking leading questions until Middlebrooks said what she thought the prosecutor wanted to hear? I couldn't know for sure, but based on how the investigation and prosecution had played out so far, I wouldn't be surprised.

When Floyd finished, it was time for the defense lawyers to give their closing statements. Each defendant would have one hour, starting with Buckner-Webb. Her attorney, Keith Adams, approached the podium carrying a trash can and declared, "This case is garbage. All right. It is a garbage case. It's a RICO case that means nothing."

That certainly set the tone for the arguments that followed, stretching out over three days. Adams and Buckner-Webb's other lawyer, Kevin Franks, hit many of the points that came up during the testimony about Dunbar: we had erased stray marks and filled in demographic information following testing protocol; the witnesses against us had lied in order to avoid prosecution themselves; we had never received bonus money; and our students' test scores hadn't even counted toward adequate yearly progress or targets. They asserted that Buckner-Webb did not participate in a conspiracy but also that there was no conspiracy going on, period. Beverly Hall, Adams said, "never told or encouraged anyone to cheat. No dispute about that, right? But because she set high standards and goals she is liable for anyone who decides that they are going to cheat. . . . It's the most ridiculous thing to say."[4]

The other lawyers similarly dissected the evidence against their clients while taking stabs at the overarching problems with the state's case. Ben Davis returned to the issue of Sonny Perdue's Race to the Top application, in which the governor said the heightened 2009 CRCT scores were the result of "higher standards and harder assessments . . . accompanied by effective professional development for teachers," even though an erasure analysis had cast doubt on the veracity of the scores in 20 percent of schools across the state. "So you will either have to conclude that the governor is not telling the truth or [the scores are] valid," he said.[5]

Sandy Wallack talked about the "witch hunt mentality" of the GBI investigation, and Hurl Taylor characterized it as "shoot first and whatever you hit, call it the target."[6] Akil Secret expounded the power imbalance inherent in the scandal, saying that in thirty-five years of practicing law, "Never have I seen the power of the state wielded like I have in this case . . . millions of dollars spent in resources," to prosecute people whose resources were miniscule in comparison.[7] Gerald Griggs underscored the general lack of credibility among the prosecution's witnesses with the contention that "this is the first trial I have ever seen where every single witness said something completely opposite of the other witness."[8] Teresa Mann pointed out the absurdity of the idea that we cheated for money, when the twelve remaining defendants had garnered a total of only $1,500 in bonuses. My attorney, Annette Greene, said, "I have had to make sense out of nonsense."[9]

In her closing, Greene echoed the points that Buckner-Webb's lawyers made and argued that someone else had changed the answers on our tests. She reminded the jury about the mysterious handwriting on Neal's test booklets and questioned why the prosecution hadn't subpoenaed our principal to testify.

"Who had access to these tests [is] very important to answer. All of the other times that question was posed, the state brought in the principal to answer who had keys to the vault, who she gave those keys to, how secure the tests were," Greene said. "We don't have that in this case. You know, Principal [Betty] Greene is sort of like 'Where is Waldo?' She wasn't brought in."[10]

Cleveland's lawyer, Angela Johnson, drove home the same facts and pointed the finger at Middlebrooks, reiterating something that Melissa Fincher, who oversaw testing for the Georgia Department of Education, had said on the witness stand. According to the best practices stipulated by her department, Fincher stated, Middlebrooks should have been removed as testing coordinator once she was under investigation for leaking the Grade 5 Writing Assessment prompt. "That never happened," Johnson said. "She was accused in early March and she was allowed to stay and coordinate the CRCT the following month."[11] With everything else under consideration, Middlebrooks seemed the most obvious culprit.

The last defense lawyer to give a closing was George Lawson, who challenged the evidence against Michael Pitts and then made a stunning declamation about the deeper conflict underlying the trial.

"It is not just APS that is on trial here today," he said. "You see, public education is on trial today. It was on trial when we started in August. Public education will be on trial for some time, because there are those in our community and in our state who would believe that the dollars and the cents that we put into public education [are] not worth it because the benefit received is nothing."[12] It was a breath of fresh air to hear someone allude to those who stood to benefit from a manufactured crisis in public education such as this trial.

When Lawson concluded, Rucker was afforded the last word with a final closing argument that was nothing less than apocalyptic.

"America will never be destroyed from the outside!" he yelled, his veins popping again. "If we falter and lose our freedoms it will be because we destroyed ourselves. The philosophy of the schoolroom in one generation will be the philosophy of the government in the next."[13]

Now we were apparently responsible for the very downfall of democracy.

Rucker made huge mental leaps that defied logic to try to save his case. He claimed that it didn't matter whether or not we had received bonus money because the indictment said we endeavored to obtain "US currency," which he suggested could refer to our salaries. He said the immunity agreements and plea deals weren't a recipe for false accusations, they were simply an opportunity for "good people" who "did a bad thing" to seek redemption.

Rucker hastily rattled off rebuttals to each defense argument. When he arrived at Dunbar, he brought up the fact that my test booklets still had some stray marks that were never erased.

"What were they doing in there?" he said, feigning wonder. "If you weren't erasing stray marks, you was erasing answers. Shani Robinson was promoted to the fifth grade. Promotion!"

I felt like someone had thrown a bucket of freezing water on me. Where did that come from? I wasn't "promoted" to the fifth grade. I had no title change or pay increase, and I didn't even want to teach fifth grade. Principal Greene simply moved me. And this hadn't come up in trial. Rucker was introducing this idea for the first time. It seemed to be another ploy to get around the obvious fact that I had no motivation to cheat. He was trying to make it look like I had done it to get promoted. That was the last thing the jury heard about me, a bald-faced lie.

l l l l l l l l l l l l l

The cavernous north atrium of the George State Capitol rang with the chants of teachers, students, and parents who crowded the massive bifurcated stone staircase, waving signs with slogans that all drove home one message: no school takeover.

It was the first day of jury deliberation, and while the jurors were cloistered in a room somewhere in the Fulton County Courthouse deciding my fate, legislators were deciding the fate of Georgia's public education system. Governor Nathan Deal's Opportunity School District legislation had made it past the senate and was expected to pass the House Education Committee, whose members were debating as protesters registered their concern.

The committee had heard directly from OSD opponents during a hearing the week prior, when closing arguments in the cheating trial were underway. About a dozen people gave public comment against the OSD, which would enable the state to take control of "failing" schools, without consent from locally elected school boards, and turn them over to charter operators. According to Deal, 139 schools were eligible for takeover, though the legislation provided only a vague definition for what constituted a failing school.[14]

If the school takeover legislation passed, it would still have to be approved by voters in a statewide referendum to amend the constitution. While that added an extra hurdle, public school advocates had seen the process play out before, first with the constitutional amendment allowing tax allocation districts to siphon education dollars from schools to private development projects, and then with yet another amendment that resurrected the state's Charter Schools Commission, which could override local school boards in approving privately operated charters. The OSD would be the cherry on top, enabling state-authorized charters to access local tax dollars that were still solely available to locally controlled schools.

During the earlier hearing, most Democrats and even some Republicans had sided with the teachers, administrators, educators' associations, and parents who spoke out against school takeover. One Republican legislator balked at what he viewed as an affront to small government and local control, calling the OSD a "poke in the eye for public education."[15]

But popular opinion was up against pressure from the governor and the increasingly powerful influence of StudentsFirst, the lobbying group founded by Michelle Rhee that launched its Georgia chapter with an aggressive campaign in support of the State Charter Schools Commission in 2012. Since then, the group had showered Georgia's elected officials with $1.3 million in campaign contributions. Shortly after Deal unveiled the school takeover plan, StudentsFirst arranged an all-expenses-paid trip for Deal and a delegation of his staff, nine legislators, and the state's superintendent of education to visit New Orleans to learn about the Recovery School District, which was the model for the OSD. StudentsFirst also sent legislators to Memphis for a firsthand look at the Achievement School District, one of the early Recovery School District copycats. And before the OSD even debuted, the state director of StudentsFirst had provided input to Deal's policy advisor, Erin Hames, who wrote the school takeover legislation.[16]

As the House Education Committee grappled over amendments to the bill ahead of a vote, Hames was present to field their questions with a gentle resolve. A pert, brunette woman only a few years older than me, Hames had a wholesome air that spoke of her small-town North Georgia upbringing and belied her political power. Contrary to her unassuming image, Hames held considerable sway over education policy behind the scenes. Under Sonny Perdue, she was an instrumental part of the team that applied for and implemented the Race to the Top grant, and she played a big role in the effort to reestablish the Charter Schools Commission. Over the course of the hearing, she blunted the barbed questions that skeptical lawmakers posed about the legislation she had authored, ushering them toward a vote that green-lighted the school takeover plan, 13 to 6.[17]

Two days later, the Speaker of the House called for a full vote on the OSD legislation, igniting a passionate debate on the chamber floor. Christian Coomer, a Republican representative who served as Deal's mouthpiece for the legislation, tried to reframe the OSD for those in his party who saw it as a form of government overreach. This was simply a way, he said, for the state to take power from local school boards "so it can be pushed down to the local school. The parents, the teachers, and the principals in that local school will ultimately hold the power."

Democratic representative Stacey Abrams gave the minority report against the OSD. Among her many objections was the fact that most of the schools on Deal's takeover list were "poverty stricken" and that years of cuts to education had put them in dire straits. She acknowledged that the governor had recently restored a fraction of the billions of dollars that had been slashed from the state's education budget beginning in 2003. "He has stopped the bleeding and is beginning to restore funding," she said. "But twelve years of deficits cannot be solved with two years of non-hemorrhaging."[18]

After hours of debate, the house passed the OSD legislation, sending it to the governor's desk and eventually to voters to decide.

The next week, on April Fool's Day, my life was upended.

My belly had grown so huge, my calves so swollen, that I had trouble walking. On the last day of closing arguments, my lawyer had requested that I be allowed to stay home, and Judge Baxter assented. My dad continued to show up every day and sit in the quiet courtroom while the jury deliberated. So I was home, napping, when the jury delivered a verdict.

From what I heard later, and saw on the news, the jury filed in, and the head juror handed the verdict forms to Baxter, who gave a short speech sincerely thanking them for their service. "Whatever your verdict is, I will defend it until I die," he said.

Then Baxter began to read.

"State versus Sharon Davis-Williams." Davis-Williams and her lawyer stood. Davis-Williams's faced betrayed no emotion, but her chest rose and fell with quick, sharp breaths.

"Count one, conspiracy to violate the Racketeer Influenced and Corrupt Organizations Act. We, the jury, find the defendant guilty." Davis-Williams's face barely changed, but it looked like her heart would beat out of her chest.

With each name that Baxter read, the defendant and lawyer rose. The first charge he read each time was RICO, and on that charge, each verdict was guilty, except for one, Dessa Curb, who was acquitted on all counts.

Every defendant's reaction was different. Michael Pitts furrowed his brow and seemed to mutter to himself. Dana Evans slowly bowed her head. Other defendants stared straight at Baxter, unwavering. Pamela Cleveland flinched with each "guilty," screwing up her face like she smelled something bad. Buckner-Webb looked like she was holding back tears. Donald Bullock did too. His look of shock was so raw, it was painful to see. When Baxter called my name, Annette Greene stood for me alone. And when he said "guilty," she just closed her eyes.

Cleveland, Buckner-Webb, and I were also found guilty on our underlying charges of false statements and writings. Strangely, several defendants were found not guilty on their underlying charges. How could they be guilty of conspiring if they were not guilty of the acts that supposedly comprised the conspiracy? It was one more baffling piece in a dumbfounding puzzle.

Before dismissing the jury, Baxter again congratulated them for what a great job they had done. Finally he said, "I'ma miss y'all!" Baxter smiled and chuckled as the jury left the room. How he could laugh after rendering such a heavy condemnation, I'll never understand.

Sheriff's deputies packed the aisle between defendants and their families, and more deputies stood along the walls. Baxter announced that sentencing would be scheduled for another time. "We are going to have to take everybody into custody today," he said firmly.

The defense lawyers cried out in protest; no one had expected to go to jail.

"Judge, judge," Bob Rubin pleaded. "They have been out on bond. Showed up every time for seven months!"

"From the day I got this case, I pleaded with people to evaluate it seriously," Baxter countered with mounting agitation. "And now the rubber had met the road here, and they are convicted felons as far as I'm concerned!"

"Could we address the issue of appeal bond?" Ben Davis asked. "Would the court consider—"

"You can file a motion for an appeal bond and I will address it at a later time," Baxter said, cutting him off.

"On behalf of Shani Robinson may I address the court?" my attorney called out.

"Well Ms. Robinson can remain on bond because she is having a child, I believe. But everyone else, I'm sorry."

The lawyers continued jostling to be heard: "There's no reason—," "not been sentenced yet—," "Judge—"

"Your honor, none of these defendants have criminal records," Theresa Mann said, managing to raise her voice above the others.

Baxter lost it.

"They have been convicted of serious felonies," he shouted, throwing his hands in the air. "And I don't like to send anybody to jail. It's not something I get a kick out of. But they have made their bed, and they are going to have to lie in it. And it starts today!"

The lawyers continued to protest, and Baxter continued to shout as
he rose from the bench and headed toward his exit. "You can submit an
appeal bond and I will hear it in due course," he called over his shoulder. And then he was gone.

A somber hush fell over the courtroom, punctuated by the sound
of camera shutters clicking and handcuffs snapping open. The women
began taking off their jewelry and handing their belongings to family
members for safekeeping. Lawyers hurriedly spoke quiet words of reas-
surance and instruction to their convicted clients. Deputies fanned out
and, one by one, shackled the black educators of Atlanta Public Schools
before marching them single file through a side door.

                    I I I I I I I I I I I I I

Late in the evening on April 10, Moses and I were watching TV in our
living room when my contractions began.

I was curled up in the same spot where I had watched helplessly as
my colleagues were carted off to jail nine days earlier. At first, I had
stayed glued to the television, following the hyperbolic news coverage
in the wake of our convictions, feeling a mixture of dread about the future and guilt for being home while Cleveland and Webb were behind
bars. But when Moses convinced me to attend a prayer vigil at First
Iconium Baptist Church, I finally felt some relief. The place was packed
with people who supported us and were outraged by the convictions.
Moses had pushed me in a wheelchair down to the altar while hundreds
of people prayed for me. For the first time since trial began, I let my
tears flow freely. That night, my mucus plug broke, signaling that labor
wasn't far off. But a few days had passed with no further signs.

Moses was keeping a close eye on me and going out of his way to take
my mind off of the disaster my life was becoming. Instead of the news,
we were watching a movie, and Moses was rubbing my feet. It started
with a twinge of pain in my abdomen, sharp enough that I grabbed my
stomach and cried, "Whoa!"

Moses jumped to attention and readied us to go to the hospital. By
the time we arrived, I was suffering what felt like menstrual cramps
on steroids. Once we were checked in, a nurse instructed me to walk
around the maternity wing to help bring on labor. Moses walked with

me up and down the halls for hours, comforting me through the pain. "You did this to me!" I teased him between contractions.

Finally I was offered an epidural and I went straight to sleep. When I awoke, my brother and parents had joined Moses in the delivery room, and my doctor was standing over me. "You need to have an emergency C-section," he said. I never expected to have a C-section, but when he told me my baby's heart rate was dropping, I didn't argue. They wheeled me to an operating room and gave me local anesthesia, with a curtain blocking my view of the process. Moses stayed by my side.

All of a sudden, a weight left me, and I felt lighter. Amari's first cry was the sweetest sound I'd ever heard. I burst into tears as Moses broke into a huge, proud smile.

When I made it back to my room, a nurse brought Amari to me. The moment he was in my arms, I experienced a feeling of love unlike anything I'd ever known.

My baby survived the stressful seven-month trial with me and came into the world perfectly healthy. Seven pounds, 13.8 ounces, 19 inches long, with a full head of hair. It was the greatest blessing. It took all my willpower to believe we wouldn't be torn apart.

The next day, Derrick Boazman, a local community leader, and the Reverend Timothy McDonald III hosted a baby shower for me at First Iconium Baptist Church. I was recovering from surgery, but my family was there to receive the outpouring of community support. We received money, diapers, clothes, and other necessities for the baby from people who had never even met me. One woman even drove from a distant county to bring a monogrammed blanket. My fifth-grade teacher, who I had not spoken with since elementary school, heard about the shower and sent an encouraging card. A group of my elementary school friends took up a collection of money, and my college sorority sisters also sent a donation. I heard from the head of the counseling agency I had worked for, who called to find out how I was doing. She told me that the girls I had worked with were devastated to hear about my conviction. Even the *Journal-Constitution* ran a positive story all about my son's birth.

Deep down, I hoped Judge Baxter would be as compassionate on sentencing day. My sentencing was postponed, but my codefendants were to appear in court three days after Amari was born.

Sentencing began with the defense lawyers bringing witnesses to offer "evidence of mitigation," which entailed saying positive things about the defendants and appealing to Baxter for lenience. But the judge had not changed his attitude since the day of the verdict, when he lashed out and sent everyone to jail. Donald Bullock testified on his own behalf, and Baxter listened diligently as he spoke about his military service, his devotion to family and church, and his tireless work as an educator, until Bullock mentioned the impact of the trial on his well-being.

"My livelihood is gone. My licenses are gone. All because I told the truth," Bullock said, his voice trembling. "I know the jury made their decision, but today—"

"All because you told the truth?" Baxter interrupted him furiously. He then gestured to his right shoulder and said, "You know, the devil is sitting here saying, 'Why don't these people take responsibility?'" Gesturing to his left shoulder he continued, "And the devil is over here saying, 'Throw the book at them. They don't take responsibility.'"[19]

With a devil on each of Baxter's shoulders, things were not looking good.

Baxter's focus on "responsibility" proved to be a sticking point. When the testimony finished, Baxter announced that District Attorney Howard was willing to recommend reduced sentences to defendants who agreed to certain conditions.

"I just think the best thing for our community and this whole sordid mess is for Paul Howard to talk to each of you and we enter pleas and we'll all go on about our business and pray for these kids that got cheated," Baxter explained. "I believe that people who accept responsibility, that their sentences ought to be different from those who don't."

But that wasn't all the DA wanted. His conditions required that we not only "accept responsibility" by making a public apology. We would also have to waive our constitutional right to appeal.

Bullock accepted the agreement the next day. He endured the shame of reading an apology after maintaining his innocence for so long, only for Baxter to slap him with five years of probation, six months of weekend jail, a $5,000 fine, and fifteen hundred hours of community service.

No one else took the bait. Buckner-Webb's lawyer explained his client's refusal saying, "We did not think it was appropriate that she have to give up her appellate rights in order to get an appropriate sentence, that she have to stand here and say, 'I apologize to the judge,' in order to get an appropriate sentence."[20]

When the majority of defendants turned down the sentencing agreement, Baxter became vindictive.

First, he announced that he wouldn't grant anyone first-offender status or an appeal bond, which he had promised the day before. First-offender status would allow those who completed their sentences to have the felony charges wiped from their record, and an appeal bond would keep us out of prison while the appeals process, which could last years, played out. This was a major change from what our outlook had been just a day earlier. When Baxter rescinded these provisions, saying drily "That was yesterday and this it today," Buckner-Webb's lawyer raised his voice with indignation and demanded that Baxter recuse himself, saying, "You are going back and forth based on emotion!"

"You sit down or I'm going to put you in jail!" Baxter shouted.[21]

The School Reform Team directors were next to be sentenced. Prosecutor Fani Willis recommended that Baxter mete out five years, three in prison and the rest on probation, to each. So everyone was shocked when Baxter sentenced them each to twenty years, to serve seven in prison, two thousand hours of community service, and a $25,000 fine.

Twenty years.

One of the defendants' family members screamed when Baxter said those words.

Cleveland later told me it was like the air had been sucked out of the room. She decided right then that she couldn't take it any longer. She would accept the sentence agreement and say whatever she had to say. She turned to Buckner-Webb with wide eyes and whispered, "I'm 'bout to roll."

"There were thousands of children who were harmed in this thing," Baxter lamented, flinging one hand skyward as if he were an actor in a Shakespearean tragedy. "This is not a victimless crime that occurred in this city."

This justification for his overly harsh sentences stood in stark contrast to what happened when the prosecution had an opportunity to present victim impact statements. The only victim they managed to produce was one of the GBI investigators. Defense lawyers asked incredulously how exactly the agent was a victim, to which Clint Rucker replied that the GBI had been "stonewalled" by educators during the investigation. Baxter wouldn't allow it, so there were no victims to express how they had been harmed or to advocate for punishment.

Tamara Cotman's lawyer, Ben Davis, argued for a lighter sentence, pointing out that she was found not guilty of influencing witnesses in her speedy trial. Baxter pushed back, claiming that the jury in that trial said they would have convicted her if cheating was the issue.

"They never said that," Davis contended.

"Yeah they did. They said it in the jury room," Baxter insisted.

In the jury room? What in the world was he talking about? The judge was never supposed to go in the jury room. Had he actually been in there, was he repeating secondhand information, or was he just plain making stuff up? Regardless, it was hardly right, with twenty years of peoples' lives hanging in the balance.

Baxter continued to brush aside the concerns of the lawyers representing the School Reform Team directors and moved on to sentencing everyone else. From that point on, he adhered to the state's recommendations, which included prison time for each defendant. Dana Evans got five years, to serve one, and one thousand hours of community service. Angela Williamson, who worked under Evans, somehow got a heavier sentence than her boss: five years, to serve two, fifteen hundred hours of community service, and a $5,000 fine. The rest of the sentences were similar. And Baxter continued to punctuate his delivery with dramatic flourishes.

"All I want from any of these people is just to take some responsibility, but they refuse. They refuse," he moaned.

Each lawyer brought up the issue of first-offender status and the appeal bonds, taking Baxter to task for reneging.

"Well I guess I'm just an Indian giver," Baxter said in response.

At one point Baxter even had the audacity to say that the cheating scandal was "the sickest thing to ever happen in this town," as if slavery, Jim Crow, and the various attacks on black communities ever since paled in comparison.[22]

Finally Baxter arrived at the Dunbar teachers. He gave Diane Buckner-Webb five years, to serve one in prison, and one thousand hours of community service and a $1,000 fine. Pamela Cleveland read an apology and waived her appellate rights in return for five years of probation, one thousand hours of community service, a $1,000 fine, and home confinement from 7 p.m. to 7 a.m. for one year.

When all the sentences were delivered, the defense lawyers returned to the issue of first-offender status and appeal bonds with full force, and finally Baxter caved. My codefendants could stay out of jail for the time being.

〡〡〡〡〡〡〡〡〡〡〡

If I thought the media maelstrom was bad when we were indicted, after sentencing it was even worse. News outlets nationwide, even globally, rehashed Baxter's histrionics for weeks, while the usual suspects, like Mike Bowers (who donated $500 to Paul Howard's re-election campaign the day after we were convicted), went on at prime time to tell the world we had cheated the children and had gotten what we deserved. In one such interview, Anderson Cooper suggested to Bowers that the impact of cheating would "reverberate" throughout children's lives. Bowers agreed, saying, "It reverberates in the prison system, in the children of unwed mothers. . . . It's a tragedy beyond description."[23]

Public figures of all stripes parroted that overwhelming sentiment, from Mayor Kasim Reed, who said that our consequences should be "severe," to Judge Glenda Hatchett, a celebrity court TV judge who told a local talk-show host that "Judge Baxter was very careful procedurally . . . as he tried this case."[24] *How would she know?* I thought. *I never saw her in the courtroom.*

After my codefendants' sentencing, I was diagnosed with posttraumatic stress disorder. The negative comments in the news didn't help my mental state. In contrast, I was so grateful for the support from people like Judges Penny Brown Reynolds and Thelma Wyatt Moore, Bernice King, and Andrew Young, who publicly called for leniency with our sentencing. Rise Up Georgia, a social justice organization, spearheaded a petition calling for leniency and was able to collect over 35,000 signatures.[25]

Another silver lining was that alternative media outlets finally sat up and paid attention, so there was a lot of critical coverage of the travesty too. Programs like *The Daily Show* made Baxter look like a buffoon and expressed outrage at the idea of sentencing educators to lengthy prison terms.[26] *The Daily Show's* host, Jon Stewart, compared the situation to the 2008 subprime mortgage meltdown, which helped send the global economy into a major recession. He pointed out that both events allegedly entailed falsified information, cover-ups, and bonus money, with no Wall Street financiers prosecuted. And many journalists began writing about our plight in the context of No Child Left Behind and other policies that created conditions ripe for widespread cheating, portraying us as scapegoats for systemic problems in education.

Maybe Judge Baxter took notice, because at the end of April he called the three School Reform Team directors back to be resentenced. Instead of twenty years, he knocked their terms down to ten years, three in prison and the rest on probation, and reduced their fines to $10,000. A day before the resentencing, he gave an exclusive interview to the student newspaper at Grady High School, his APS alma mater, in which he attempted a softer image, sitting outside next to his dog. But he couldn't shake his propensity for exaggeration. He actually had the nerve to tell the reporter, "I think I've got a little bit of post-traumatic syndrome."

Again, the media hype surrounding the trial coincided with Nathan Deal's propaganda promoting his school takeover plan. Between the first sentencing and the resentencing, Deal signed the OSD legislation. That same day, Michelle Rhee visited Atlanta's Morehouse College to give a speech advocating for the state takeover of schools in APS's Carver Cluster. Parks Middle School, the most infamous school in the cheating scandal, was part of this group of schools before it closed in 2013. Now Rhee identified one high school, two middle schools, and several elementary schools, including one that was implicated in the scandal, as ideal for takeover.[27]

Interestingly, the Carver schools were in a South Atlanta neighborhood that had been targeted for "revitalization" by a group founded by Bob Lupton, a Christian missionary friend of developer Tom Cousins. Lupton had contributed to the displacement of low-income black residents in Atlanta's East Lake neighborhood when Cousins redeveloped the public housing complex there into a mix of subsidized and market-rate units. Lupton had created a program, dubbed Strategic Neighbors, that recruited middle-class suburbanites to move to the new apartments and offered them rent reduction in exchange for mentoring their impoverished neighbors. The program was based on the paternalistic belief that poverty could be ameliorated by behavioral changes. Now Lupton's group, FCS Urban Ministries, was making a similar effort in South Atlanta. They bought up dozens of houses, some of which they rented to low-income families, while selling others to people they considered good influences for their tenants. As the neighborhood began to see an influx of wealthier, whiter residents, the schools were the obvious next target for a makeover.[28]

That began to take shape when Erin Hames, the policy advisor who wrote the OSD legislation, left her post in the governor's office to start a private consulting firm called ReformED, through which she would advise school districts on how to "turn around" their failing schools in order to avoid state takeover. Hames located her firm in the same office suite as Purpose Built Communities, the nonprofit that Cousins launched to replicate the East Lake model for privatizing public housing and public schools together.

Deal's office announced Hames's departure on August 10, 2015. Hours later, the Atlanta school board voted to award her a no-bid $96,000 contract to advise the district. Hames also accepted a $30,000 contract from the governor, ensuring that her recommendations to APS would be in line with his vision. Voters wouldn't have to pass the state takeover amendment for Deal to control Atlanta's schools. He could now use the threat of school takeover and Hames's consultancy to push through the reforms he wanted.[29]

As Hames's scheme was underway in August, I was preparing for my sentencing day, slated for September 1. In the months after my colleagues were sentenced, I had been recovering both from childbirth and the trial and learning to be a mom. As hard as this was, I had so much to be grateful for. The trial had taken a toll on all of us, but some of my codefendants suffered more than others. One lost her home. Another endured a traumatic separation from her children while she awaited sentencing in jail. Several were in financial ruin. With help from my family, I had managed to maintain a semblance of stability, and my baby was healthy and strong.

The evening before my sentencing, I received an offer from the DA's office. It was the same offer they extended to the other defendants: make a public apology and waive your right to appeal in exchange for a reduced sentence. In my case, that would be five years of probation, a year of house arrest, a fine, and community service.

I was afraid of prison and wanted to avoid it at all costs. But I thought about my three years of teaching at Dunbar. I thought about what it was like to become completely consumed by the impossible project of trying to give my students everything they needed to survive and thrive, everything from academic skills, to common sense, to food and clothing and love. Then I thought about the educators who had done that thankless, unyielding, difficult, invaluable work for the better part of their entire lives, only to have their legacies tarnished with lies about a conspiracy that never was. I thought about this strange demand for an apology, a public shaming, a concession that everybody against us and the public schools we championed had won.

I said no.

I had a constitutional right to an appeal, and I was going to use it to try to get to the truth.

In court the next day, Judge Baxter held this against me.

"You and your client had the keys in your pocket," he told Greene. "I don't know whether people just drank the Kool-Aid or what."[30]

My mom tried to calm him down, reading a heartfelt statement asking the judge not to send me to prison.

"Amari needs his mother by his side. He wants to be nurtured, cuddled, kissed, reassured, encouraged, taught, raised, and loved by her," she said. "Motherhood has the greatest influence in human life." My mom even presented a letter from Amari's pediatrician emphasizing the importance of breastfeeding for his health. Prosecutor Fani Willis callously responded that the appeal would likely take so long that "the first year of nursing for this child will not be affected."

Baxter agreed with her and lashed out again, expressing anger that I had attended the prayer vigil at First Iconium Baptist Church after the convictions. "I said, certainly, her presence in court is not needed if she is pregnant," he complained. "And then I go home and see her on TV, you know, at this big rally, everybody dancing around."

His characterization was so belittling, I couldn't believe it. At that time, I was days away from having a baby, and I had just seen my co-defendants hauled off to jail. I was a nervous wreck! Church was the only place I knew to go. But to Baxter, I was just playing hooky.

Finally, Baxter did what I had feared for so long. He condemned me to prison.

One year locked in a cage and four on probation, living under the threat of returning to that cage for any small infraction. That was what the future held for me now.

"It looks like you have an unbelievable, strong family system that will care for this child in your absence," he said, each word a sting. "But I have given you every chance and you have turned it down."

I was granted an appeal bond, so I would remain free as long as my case was pending. As Greene set to work getting the bond processed, I sat there, numbly listening to Baxter's next order of business.

Poor old Armstead Salters was being held in contempt of court. He was the former principal of Gideons Elementary who had recanted on the witness stand, saying that no one had ever pressured him to cheat and implying that investigators had coerced him to make that claim. Now he stood before Judge Baxter and read a letter of apology, looking as meek as he had during trial. His voice was barely above a whisper, he had trouble hearing, and his suit seemed to swallow him whole. He was nearly seventy-seven years old.

His pastor and other members of his church testified that he had completed over one thousand hours of community service to fulfill his plea agreement. Even the prosecution didn't want to subject the old man to further punishment. Clint Rucker recommended to Baxter that they leave it be, saying that, even though Salters had lied, "it's over."

"It is not over," Baxter snapped. "He got out from under and then he got up and completely lied on the witness stand under oath, and it made me sick. So I don't think it's over."

With that, he revoked Salters's first-offender status and sentenced him to eight weeks of weekend jail.

When I got home that evening, Moses had just finished bottle-feeding Amari the milk I had pumped before leaving for court. I took my four-month-old son in my arms and carried him to his cheerfully decorated bedroom. There were animal stickers placed around the wall, two-by-two just like in Noah's ark. The crib was beautifully arranged with stuffed animals and a mobile. The closet was perfectly organized. The blankets were neatly folded. I admired how everything was in place and in order, even though the world outside of this room was a mess. I sat in the glider and rocked Amari for a long time.

"We're always going to be together, okay?" I whispered.

He looked at me with a huge grin on his face like he wasn't concerned at all.

"God's got it," I told him.

As we rocked, the feeling of devastation that had gripped me since receiving my sentence began to melt away. In fact, I felt unexpectedly relieved. The day I had long dreaded had come and gone and I was still here; the world hadn't ended.

I watched Amari's eyes travel around the room with curiosity, soaking up every color, texture, reflection, and shadow as his powerful little brain worked to make sense of all the information he was taking in. Before long, he would crawl and then walk and talk. I would begin teaching him to read before he started school, as my mother had done with me. I was going to be there every step of the way somehow. I just knew it. I had to be.

I guess there's one thing Judge Baxter was right about, I thought. *It's not over.*

EPILOGUE

IN NOVEMBER 2016, the constitutional amendment to create a state Opportunity School District that would take over struggling schools and give them to private charter operators was rejected by 60 percent of Georgia voters.

This victory was the result of a statewide grassroots effort that brought together parents, teachers, administrators, students, clergy, and social justice groups across racial identities and party lines to get out the message to their communities: no school takeover.

As usual, corporate education reform money came flooding into the state, and StudentsFirst (which was renamed 50CAN) campaigned hard for the measure. But as the anti-OSD campaign successfully mobilized volunteers to reach thousands of voters, the National Education Association took notice and contributed $2 million so the group could hire field directors and buy advertising. For once there was a level playing field, and Georgia voters had the information necessary to make an informed choice.

The many people who put extensive time and energy into defeating the OSD and saving Georgia schools showed the power that regular people can wield when we organize.

I I I I I I I I I I I I

Atlanta Public Schools superintendent Meria Carstarphen believed the OSD was inevitable. Throughout the state, local boards of education passed resolutions denouncing the governor's plan, but in APS, Erin

Hames worked with a team of consultants paid for by several pro-charter charities, including one of Tom Cousins's family foundations, to come up with a "turnaround strategy" to get the district's struggling schools taken off the takeover list. When the consultants recommended handing over schools to private operators, Carstarphen and the school board awarded a contract to Purpose Built Schools—a new spinoff of Cousins's Purpose Built Communities, headed by Greg Giornelli—to take over Thomasville Heights Elementary, one of the schools in the Carver Cluster, which Michelle Rhee had named as a target for takeover.[1]

The Cousins family essentially bought influence over the school board and reaped the rewards: control of a school in a neighborhood primed for redevelopment. The public housing near the school had come down in 2010. And the Carver Cluster was in an area that included South Atlanta, where a group founded by Cousins's friend and collaborator Bob Lupton was buying up houses and bringing middle-class people to the area to supposedly model good behavior for low-income residents. Within a few years, Purpose Built Schools would expand to take over the high school there as well.

At the same time, the connections between privately operated schools, the real estate market, and the cheating scandal were becoming even clearer. A 2015 study showed that Atlanta charter schools with neighborhood attendance zones boosted property values by an average of 10 percent. Another study showed that during the two-year period when cheating was being exposed in the news and investigated by the state, there was a spike in the number of students from the schools affected by cheating who switched to charter schools.[2]

I I I I I I I I I I I I I

When the school board approved the contract with Purpose Built Schools, it also voted to close and merge several schools, including Venetian Hills, where investigator Richard Hyde started his probe into the cheating scandal. The privatization, school closings, and subsequent layoffs drew outrage. During a tense school board meeting, state senator Vincent Fort, whose district covered parts of Atlanta, gave a scathing public comment. "The same people that are so-called reformers

are the ones that created the cheating scandal, they're the same ones
that tried to cover it up, and now they're the same ones that created the
turnaround strategy," he said.[3]

⎜ ⎜ ⎜ ⎜ ⎜ ⎜ ⎜ ⎜ ⎜ ⎜ ⎜ ⎜ ⎜

APS settled with Invest Atlanta over the BeltLine dispute, agreeing to
accept nearly $64 million less than what was owed to the students of At-
lanta and effectively subsidizing further gentrification. By the summer
of 2017, Invest Atlanta had doled out more than $1.2 billion of school,
city, and county tax dollars to developers, largely for high-end housing,
retail, and office space, and of course the BeltLine. At that point, Ryan
Gravel, who conceived of the BeltLine, had resigned from the board of
the nonprofit tasked with developing it. He was disillusioned because
promises of producing affordable housing hadn't materialized, while
property values along the corridor were skyrocketing.[4]

⎜ ⎜ ⎜ ⎜ ⎜ ⎜ ⎜ ⎜ ⎜ ⎜ ⎜ ⎜ ⎜

Nationwide, the corporate education reform movement is strengthen-
ing, thanks to the other outcome of the November 2016 election. Voters elected a president whose disdain for government, belief that big
business will solve everything, general incompetence, and intense racism and xenophobia threaten to entrench poverty, mass incarceration,
and racialized state violence in marginalized communities.

His education secretary, Betsy DeVos, is a billionaire member of the
Republican donor class who never attended or sent her children to public schools. DeVos and her husband founded the American Federation
for Children, a dark-money group that lobbies for ALEC legislation,
contributes to political candidates who support the corporate education
reform agenda, and funds campaigns for charter expansion, vouchers,
and other privatization measures.[5]

⎜ ⎜ ⎜ ⎜ ⎜ ⎜ ⎜ ⎜ ⎜ ⎜ ⎜ ⎜ ⎜

As someone who benefited from attending a school outside my neighborhood, thanks to a busing program aimed at desegregating schools,
I understand the argument for school choice and charters. The truth is

that parents, like my own, just want their children to get a good education by any means necessary—whether it's through a traditional public school or a charter, private, or religious school. And not all charter schools are bad. In the Atlanta area, there are several black-led, grass-roots, African-centered charter schools that have done a phenomenal job educating students. The problem lies not in any flaw inherent to charters but in the intentional dismantling of public schools to increase demand for charter schools so that private interests can profit.

This is the case not just in Atlanta but in many areas where the corporate education reform movement has taken hold. In Washington, DC, Michelle Rhee and her successor, Kaya Henderson, closed dozens of traditional public schools while charter schools expanded; now nearly half of public school students in DC attend a charter school. The school closures mostly happened in black neighborhoods, many of which are undergoing gentrification. Scholar and community activist Kalfani Turé has argued that these neighborhoods were deliberately made destitute by decades of disinvestment so that now developers can profit from their makeover, much like what has happened in Atlanta.

Even though it's an uphill battle, communities across the country are pushing back on corporate education reform and gentrification, with some triumphs. In 2012, the Chicago Teachers Union staged its first strike in twenty-five years to demand better pay and benefits, while protesting the district's emphasis on student test scores and the proliferation of charter schools. The momentous strike galvanized public school advocates nationwide. That year, community groups in Chattanooga successfully shut down plans for Purpose Built Communities to turn public housing into a mixed-income development with a charter school. More recently, Philadelphia parents, teachers, and activists reclaimed their public school system from a state commission that had closed dozens of schools while green-lighting charters. And a new wave of teacher strikes that began in West Virginia in 2018 spread to other states, where fed-up educators—backed by parents and community members—are demanding better conditions and getting results. These are just a few examples, like Georgia's anti-OSD struggle, that show how when we fight, we win.

| | | | | | | | | | | | |

The Atlanta Public Schools cheating scandal has faded from the limelight, and those responsible for blowing it out of proportion have
moved on with their lives. Sonny Perdue was appointed US secretary
of agriculture. Special investigators Mike Bowers and Bob Wilson continue to run private practices and sometimes investigate big cases. Paul
Howard ran unopposed and was reelected Fulton County district attorney. Judge Jerry Baxter retired, though he agreed to remain on our case.
He occasionally makes public appearances to denounce the educators
who stood trial. The *Journal-Constitution* continues to publish articles
implying that teachers cheated in order to receive bonus money and
raises. In November 2017, Keisha Lance Bottoms was elected mayor of
Atlanta, replacing Kasim Reed, who had reached his term limit. A few
months later, federal prosecutors included Reed in an Atlanta City Hall
corruption subpoena. In a separate incident, Reed ironically became the
object of outrage when the *Journal-Constitution* revealed he had doled
out more than $800,000 in year-end bonuses and gifts to select staff be-
fore leaving office. As of this writing, Fani Willis is running for Fulton
County Superior Court judge.

| | | | | | | | | | | | |

It is still not clear what the real impact has been for children whose tests
were manipulated. The last students who may have been affected will
graduate high school in 2021. APS launched a program in 2016 providing services for an eligible group of about three thousand students.
The program includes services such as tutoring and help with college
admissions exams, but after three semesters, a study of its remedial effects was inconclusive.

The *Journal-Constitution* interviewed a student in the program who
was already doing well in school and who said the biggest help was having access to test preparation books she otherwise couldn't afford. She
also said that the cheating scandal hadn't taken an academic toll on her,
but that she had experienced an emotional impact "when it blew up" in
the news. APS has so far spent $7.5 million on the program, an amount

that pales in comparison to the resources that ultimately went into the cheating investigation and trial.[6]

                                    | | | | | | | | | | | | |

In May 2017, the Georgia Supreme Court found that Fulton County had been improperly compiling its jury pool for years. While the ruling was part of a murder case, this was the same issue that defense attorney Bob Rubin had brought to Judge Baxter's attention during the APS trial, arguing that black people were underrepresented by 11 percent compared to the population of eligible voters in Fulton County. Baxter had dismissed the issue, but the new court ruling affirmed that a private company hired by Fulton's courts had wrongly removed tens of thousands of names from the eligible jurors list, while adding others who should not have been included. Though the ruling directed Fulton County courts to comply with the law governing jury composition, it did nothing to redress the countless cases, like ours, that were adversely impacted.

                                    | | | | | | | | | | | | |

My appeal is still pending, along with those of my codefendants. Our lives have been forever altered by the tribulations we endured throughout the state's bungled and vindictive response to cheating in Atlanta Public Schools. We support one another as best we can while we work to recover from the damage to our relationships, careers, finances, and health.

I have been focused on raising Amari, my greatest joy, who teaches me as much as I teach him every day. I've lent a hand to efforts like the anti-OSD campaign, my local Black Lives Matter chapter, and other opportunities to challenge injustice. And I've found a path to speaking out, so that the record will finally reflect the truth of what happened in Atlanta during the era of No Child Left Behind.

The Atlanta Public Schools cheating trial was a distraction from the root problems that have harmed black communities since slavery. Underlying all of the political and economic developments that set the stage for the trial—school desegregation and the resulting turn toward privatization, federally sanctioned housing discrimination, urban renewal, the drug war, racialized mass incarceration, displacement, and gentrification—is the legacy of forced, unpaid black labor generating white wealth. An elite class of white people acquired the vast majority of land, resources, money, and power in this country by exploiting indigenous people and enslaved Africans. Today, white families hold roughly 90 percent of the national wealth, while black families, in stark contrast, hold only 2.6 percent. And the black wealth that does exist is concentrated among a small percentage of black people.

Black descendants of slaves have never received reparations, and our attempts to better our conditions have been thwarted by brutal violence, apartheid, political suppression, and policies that perpetuate systemic inequalities. To use the words of investigator Richard Hyde in a new context: it has been "nothing but pervasive and rank thuggery!"

Of course, he was referring to the educators of Atlanta Public Schools when he said those words. As if vindication for black children would come by criminalizing their black teachers, when teachers have historically played a critical role in black liberation—from clandestine schools during slavery, to the Freedom Schools of the civil rights era, to public school teachers today.

What would life be like for black children if we had political candidates who were serious about redistributing wealth and resources to the people they were stolen from? If we had a governance system that afforded us control over the decisions that impact our lives? Can you imagine if we defined public safety not by the number of prisons or police but by whether everyone had a home, sustenance, and community? And what if the quality of education wasn't determined by a test but by the ability of our kids to engage curiously, creatively, and meaningfully with the world around them? Ending the long war on black communities will benefit society as a whole, but there's not a single regulation or reform that will do it. It will take a radical rethinking of the systems that structure society in order for us to change course. And we must change course. Otherwise we'll see more of the same for years to come.

ACKNOWLEDGMENTS

TO MY WONDERFUL SON, AMARI, thank you for accompanying me through one of the most challenging times in my life. You inspired me in more ways than you can ever imagine. I am so honored to be your mommy.

To my loving husband, Moses O. Tejuoso, thank you for staying by my side and supporting me with unconditional love. I am so blessed to have you as my partner and best friend.

I would like to express my sincere gratitude to my parents, Beverly and Jessie Robinson, and my brother, Jamal Robinson, and all the other family members and friends who supported me over the years. Your unwavering love will always be appreciated.

To my godsisters, Patrice Williams and Arlissa Williams Jennings, and my cousin, Dorothy Walker, thank you for your assistance in the creation of this book. Your work and dedication will always be appreciated.

I would like to thank Derrick Boazman, the Reverend Timothy McDonald III, and the entire congregation of First Iconium Baptist Church. Your kindheartedness and compassion toward my family and me will never be forgotten. Thank you for your spiritual nourishment during our time of deep turmoil.

—SHANI ROBINSON, April 2018

MANY PEOPLE AND ORGANIZATIONS contributed in various ways to this book, and I am grateful to them all. I especially want to thank Project South, Sarah Abdelaziz, Scott Satterwhite, my colleagues at *Scalawag*, the Rush Center, Park Avenue Baptist Church, Liliana Hudgens, Nik Nerburn, Allie McCullen, and my family—especially my grandma, a teacher, Carmilla Mae Fraser Marbaugh (1915–2018).

A big thank-you to all of my teachers in Atlanta Public Schools, especially those who shared books with me and told me to keep writing.

—ANNA SIMONTON, April 2018

I I I I I I I I I I I I

WE BOTH WISH TO THANK OUR AGENT, Jill Marr at the Dijkstra Literary Agency, and our editor, Rachael Marks at Beacon Press, for valuing this story and taking a chance on us. We also thank Cecily McMillan for helping us get this story into the right hands.

NOTES

CHAPTER ONE: HOOK, LINE, AND SINKER

1. Wendy Kopp, *One Day, All Children . . . : The Unlikely Triumph of Teach for America and What I Learned Along the Way* (New York: PublicAffairs, 2001), 8.

2. Jim Horn and Denise Wilburn, *The Mismeasure of Education* (Charlotte, NC: Information Age Publishing, 2013), 40.

3. Milton Friedman, "The Role of Government in Education," in *Economics and the Public Interest*, ed. Robert A. Solo (New Brunswick, NJ: Rutgers University Press, 1955), 123–44.

4. Peter D. Hutchinson, Kelly Nyks, and Jared P. Scott, dir., *Requiem for the American Dream* (New York: Zeitgeist Films, 2016), DVD.

5. Michel J. Crozier, Samuel P. Huntington, and Joji Watanuki, *The Crisis of Democracy: Report on the Governability of Democracies to the Trilateral Commission* (New York: New York University Press, 1975), https://archive.org/stream /TheCrisisOfDemocracy-TrilateralCommission-1975/crisis_of_democracy _djvu.txt; "The Lewis Powell Memo: A Corporate Blueprint to Dominate Democracy," transcription of memo written in 1971 to the US Chamber of Commerce, Greenpeace, http://www.greenpeace.org/usa/democracy/the-lewis-powell -memo-a-corporate-blueprint-to-dominate-democracy, accessed Aug. 10, 2018.

6. David P. Gardner et al., *A Nation at Risk: The Imperative for Educational Reform; an Open Letter to the American People, a Report to the Nation and the Secretary of Education* (Washington, DC: Dept. of Education, 1983), available at https://eric.ed.gov/?id=ED226006.

7. Jal Mehta, "Escaping the Shadow: *A Nation at Risk* and Its Far-Reaching Influence," *American Educator* 30, no. 2 (Summer 2015): 20–44, http://www.aft .org/sites/default/files/ae_summer2015mehta.pdf.

8. Ibid.; Edward B. Fiske, "Concerns Raised on School Quality," *New York Times*, June 6, 1989.

9. David M. Kotz, *The Rise and Fall of Neoliberal Capitalism* (Cambridge, MA: Harvard University Press, 2015), 67–70.

10. Business Roundtable, *The Business Roundtable Participation Guide: A Primer for Business on Education* (New York: National Alliance of Business, 1990), iii.

11. Ibid., v.

12. Ibid., 103.

13. Ibid.

14. Michel Marriott, "For Fledgling Teacher Corps, Hard Lessons," *New York Times*, Dec. 5, 1990.

15. Rebekah Wilce, "Did ALEC Found SPN? 1991 Report Suggests So, Exposes SPN Agenda," PRWatch.org, Dec. 12, 2013. See also Rebekah Wilce, *Exposed: The State Policy Network, the Powerful Right-Wing Network Helping to Hijack State Politics and Government* (Madison, WI: Center for Media and Democracy, 2013).

16. Robert J. Vickers, "Plan Offers Poor Students a Choice: Public Policy Group Will Help Pay Tuition at 28 Private Schools," *Atlanta Journal-Constitution*, Aug. 10, 1992.

17. Carlos Campos, "Legal Group's Action Stirs Concern; Is It Constitutional Watchdog or Right's 'Attack Dog'?," *Atlanta Journal-Constitution*, July 11, 1999; Jeff Berry, "Glavin Pulls a Boner," *Creative Loafing*, Oct. 14, 2000.

18. Marriott, "For Fledgling Teacher Corps, Hard Lessons"; Rochelle Carter, "Schools Chief Has Her Share of Foes," *Atlanta Journal-Constitution*, Feb. 28, 1999.

19. Laura Kelley, Leslie Boozer, and Drew Echelson, "Beverly Hall, Atlanta Public Schools: From the Living Room to the Boardroom," in *Every Child, Every Classroom, Every Day: School Leaders Who Are Making Equity a Reality*, ed. Robert S. Peterkin, Deborah Jewell-Sherman, Laura Kelley, and Leslie Boozer (San Francisco: Jossey-Bass, 2011), 179–96.

20. Kathleen Teltsch, "Paying Tribute to Six in Public Jobs Well Done," *New York Times*, Dec. 7, 1993.

21. Melody Peterson, "Lunches Imported from Brooklyn Add Insult to Injury," *New York Times*, Sept. 18, 1996.

22. Carter, "Schools Chief Has Her Share of Foes."

23. Jennifer French-Parker, "Atlanta Seeks 'CEO' to Run School System," *Atlanta Journal-Constitution*, Oct. 22, 1998.

24. Quoted in Kevin M. Kruse, *White Flight: Atlanta and the Making of Modern Conservatism* (Princeton, NJ: Princeton University Press, 2005), 149.

25. Rochelle Carter, "Reading, Writing, Revitalizing: Schools Become Key Target of Reform as Migration Reshapes City's Neighborhoods," *Atlanta Journal-Constitution*, May 29, 2000.

26. Rochelle Carter, "Raising the Grade: A Reason for Hope," *Atlanta Journal-Constitution*, Nov. 7, 1999.

27. Rochelle Carter, "School Chief Gets $33,660 Bonus; Half Her Goals Achieved," *Atlanta Journal-Constitution*, Aug. 9, 2000.

28. Cynthia Tucker, "Charter School Will Add to East Lake's Draw," *Atlanta Journal-Constitution*, Oct. 17, 1999; Harvey K. Newman, *The Atlanta Housing Authority's Olympic Legacy Program: Public Housing Projects to Mixed Income Communities* (Atlanta: Research Atlanta, 2002), 16–17, https://web.archive.org/web/20100630195022/http://aysps.gsu.edu/publications/researchatlanta/AHA%20Olympic%20Legacy%20Prog.pdf.

29. Kenneth J. Saltman, *The Edison Schools: Corporate Schooling and the Assault on Public Education* (New York: Routledge, 2005), 71–91.

30. *Transforming East Lake: Systematic Intentionality in Atlanta* (Washington, DC: America's Promise Alliance, 2015), 8, https://www.americaspromise
.org/sites/default/files/EastLake%20FINAL.pdf; "Edison Schools Announces
Opening of Charter School in Atlanta; Partnership with the East Lake Community Foundation," PR Newswire, Apr. 24, 2000, http://www.prnewswire
.com/news-releases/edison-schools-announces-opening-of-charter-school-in
-atlanta-partnership-with-the-east-lake-community-foundation-72783972.html.

31. *Evaluation of the Public Charter School Program: Year One Evaluation Report* (Washington, DC: Planning and Evaluation Services, US Department of
Education, 2000), iii, https://www2.ed.gov/rschstat/eval/choice/pcsp-year1
/year1report.pdf; Guilbert C. Hentschke, Scot Oschman, and Lisa Snell, "Education Management Organizations: Growing a For-Profit Education Industry
with Choice, Competition, and Innovation," Policy Brief 21, Reason Public
Policy Institute, c. 2002, http://reason.org/files/86f373eefe12bf11ff614e1305
ff3362.pdf.

32. "President Stresses Volunteerism at Atlanta High School," remarks by
President George W. Bush, Booker T. Washington High School, Atlanta, Jan.
31, 2002, https://georgewbush-whitehouse.archives.gov/news/releases/2002/01
/20020131-7.html.

33. "Education Briefs: Urban Teaching Force Due This Fall," *Atlanta
Journal-Constitution*, July 20, 2000; "Bush Touts Boost for Homeland Security," CNN.com, Feb. 6, 2002, http://edition.cnn.com/2002/ALLPOLITICS
/02/05/budget.hearings/index.html; Joe Klein, "Who Killed Teach for America?," *Time*, Aug. 17, 2003.

34. Walt Haney, "The Myth of the Texas Miracle in Education," *Education Policy Analysis Archives* (Arizona State University) 8, no. 41 (2000): 10–13,
http://epaa.asu.edu/ojs/article/view/432/828.

35. John Mintz, "George W. Bush: The Record in Texas," *Washington Post*,
Apr. 21, 2000; Shaila Dewan, "The Fix Is In," *Houston Press*, Feb. 25, 1999.

36. Andrew Rudalevige, "The Politics of No Child Left Behind," *Education
Next* 3, no. 4 (Fall 2003), http://educationnext.org/the-politics-of-no-child-left
-behind.

37. Haney, "The Myth of the Texas Miracle in Education," 19–22.

38. "Teacher Pay Plan Needs Only Money," *Atlanta Journal-Constitution*,
Jan. 14, 1993; James Salzer, "School Planning Pays Off; Georgia Teachers
Reap Benefits," *Florida Times-Union*, Nov. 15, 1997; Doug Cumming, "State
May Pass on Exams; Pressure, Cheating Cause Review of 5-Hour ITBS," *Atlanta Journal-Constitution*, Mar. 18, 1999; Paul Donsky, "Sudden Rise in Test
Scores Stirs Concern; Suspicion Grows as Atlanta Schools Fall Off Failing
List," *Atlanta Journal-Constitution*, Sept. 30, 2001.

39. Diane Ravitch, *The Death and Life of the Great American School System:
How Testing and Choice Are Undermining Education* (New York: Basic Books,
2010), 93–111.

40. Ibid.

41. Rebecca Leung, "The Texas Miracle," CBSNews.com, Jan. 6, 2004,
http://www.cbsnews.com/news/the-texas-miracle.

CHAPTER TWO: FINDING MY WAY

1. "Dunbar Elementary School," The Opportunity Gap, ProPublica, https:// projects.propublica.org/schools/schools/130012000054, accessed June 4, 2018.

2. Charles Rutheiser, *Imagineering Atlanta: The Politics of Place in the City of Dreams* (New York: Verso, 1996), 17.

3. "History," Mechanicsville, http://mechanicsvilleatl.org/history, accessed May 31, 2017.

4. Anna Simonton, "Black Communities Destroyed by Publicly Funded Stadium Swindles Are Fighting Back in a New Era of Redevelopment," Alternet.org, Aug. 28, 2015, http://www.alternet.org/economy/black-communities -destroyed-publicly-funded-stadium-swindles-are-fighting-back-new-era.

5. *Vine City Redevelopment Plan* (Atlanta: Vine City Civic Association, 2004), 2, http://www.atlantaga.gov/modules/showdocument.aspx?documentid =3074, accessed May 23, 2017.

6. Doristine Samuel (lifelong Mechanicsville resident), interview by Anna Simonton, Aug. 6, 2015, Atlanta.

7. Heywood T. Sanders, *Convention Center Follies: Politics, Power, and Public Investment in American Cities* (Philadelphia: University of Pennsylvania Press, 2014), 268.

8. Larry Keating, *Atlanta: Race, Class, and Urban Expansion* (Philadelphia: Temple University Press, 2001), 199. See also, generally, Floyd Hunter, *Community Power Structure* (Chapel Hill: University of North Carolina Press, 1953).

9. Harold H. Martin, *William Berry Hartsfield, Mayor of Atlanta* (Athens: University of Georgia Press, 1978), 41–42.

10. Harold H. Martin, *Atlanta and Environs: A Chronicle of Its People and Events, 1940s–1970s*, vol. 3 (Athens: University of Georgia Press, 1987), 497; Keating, *Atlanta*, 91; "History," Central Atlanta Progress, Atlanta Downtown Improvement District website, http://www.atlantadowntown.com/about/history, accessed May 31, 2017; Georgia Department of Transportation, Office of Environment/Transportation, *Historic Context of the Interstate Highway System in Georgia*, Project Task Order 94 (Langhorne, PA: Lichtenstein Consulting Engineers, 2007), 4–6, http://www.dot.ga.gov/AboutGeorgia/CentennialHome /Documents/Historical%20Documents/HistoricalContextof%20Georgia Interstates.pdf.

11. Keating, *Atlanta*, 88.

12. Ibid., 92–93.

13. US Census, 1970, "Total Population of Tracts F44, F45, F46 and F56, 1940, and Tracts 44, 45, 46, and 56," http://www.socialexplorer.com, accessed May 31, 2017.

14. US Census, 2000, "Total Population of Tracts 44, 46, and 56, 2000," http://www.socialexplorer.com, accessed May 31, 2017.

15. Irene Valerie Holliman, "From 'Crackertown' to 'The ATL': Race, Urban Renewal, and the Re-Making of Downtown Atlanta, 1945–2000," PhD diss., University of Georgia, 2010, 203.

16. Simonton, "Black Communities Destroyed by Publicly Funded Stadium Swindles Are Fighting Back in a New Era of Redevelopment."

17. Tom Crawford, "Democrats Hit Perdue Over School Funding Cuts," *Georgia Report*, Jan. 16, 2008, http://gareport.com/story/2008/01/16/democrats -hit-perdue-over-school-funding-cuts.

18. Heather Vogell and John Perry, "CRCT Scores Surge: Miracle or Masquerade? Exam Results Raise Red Flag," *Atlanta Journal-Constitution*, Dec. 14, 2008.

19. Richard Nixon, "Address Accepting the Presidential Nomination at the Republican National Convention in Miami Beach, Florida," Aug. 8, 1968, American Presidency Project, University of California, Santa Barbara, http:// www.presidency.ucsb.edu/ws/?pid=25968, accessed June 3, 2017.

20. Dan Baum, "Legalize It All," *Harper's*, Apr. 2016, https://harpers.org /archive/2016/04/legalize-it-all/.

21. "A Brief History of the Drug War," Drug Policy Alliance, http://www .drugpolicy.org/facts/new-solutions-drug-policy/brief-history-drug-war-0, accessed June 3, 2017.

22. Michelle Alexander, *The New Jim Crow: Mass Incarceration in the Age of Colorblindness* (New York: New Press, 2011), 49–50.

23. Keating, *Atlanta*, 32–39.

24. Deborah J. Vagins and Jesselyn McCurdy, *Cracks in the System: 20 Years of the Unjust Federal Crack Cocaine Law* (New York: American Civil Liberties Union, 2006), https://www.aclu.org/other/cracks-system-twenty-years-unjust -federal-crack-cocaine-law?redirect=criminal-law-reform/cracks-system-twenty -years-unjust-federal-crack-cocaine-law.

25. Alexander, *The New Jim Crow*, 53.

26. Ibid., 56.

27. David A. Harris, *Driving While Black: Racial Profiling on Our Nation's Highways* (New York: American Civil Liberties Union, 1999), https://www.aclu .org/report/driving-while-black-racial-profiling-our-nations-highways.

28. Victoria Loe Hicks, "Red Dog Squad Was a Product of a Very Different Era," *Atlanta Journal-Constitution*, Feb. 7, 2011.

29. Rodney Carmichael, "Why Goodie Mob's 'Soul Food' Is the Greatest Atlanta Rap Album of All Time," *Creative Loafing*, Dec. 10, 2015, http://www .creativeloafing.com/news/article/13085825/why-goodie-mobs-soul-food-is -the-greatest-atlanta-rap-album-of-all-time.

30. Joshua Aiken, "Georgia's Prison and Jail Incarceration Rates," in Aiken, *Era of Mass Expansion: Why State Officials Should Fight Jail Growth* (Northampton, MA: Prison Policy Initiative, 2017), https://www.prisonpolicy .org/graphs/GA_Prison_Jail_Rate_1978-2015.html.

31. Jane Hansen, "Crime and Punishment in Georgia: An Analysis," *Atlanta Journal-Constitution*, Sept. 8, 1996.

32. Laughlin McDonald, *A Voting Rights Odyssey: Black Enfranchisement in Georgia* (New York: Cambridge University Press, 2003), 168–73.

33. Jane O. Hansen, "Mike Bowers, Soldier of Law," *Atlanta Journal-Constitution*, July 21, 1986.

34. Sam Hopkins, "Bowers Suggests Making Possession of Small Amount of Pot a Felony," *Atlanta Journal-Constitution*, Nov. 1, 1986; Allen Frederick,

"Harris Eases Stand on Making Teachers Report Suspected Drug Abuse," *Atlanta Journal-Constitution*, Jan. 13, 1987.

35. Alexander, *The New Jim Crow*, 56; David Kohn, "Three Strikes: Penal Overkill in California?," *60 Minutes*, Oct. 28, 2002, http://www.cbsnews.com /news/three-strikes-28–10–2002.

36. Bill Rankin, "Without More Prisons, Adding Officers Will Be a 'Waste of Time,' Bowers Says," *Atlanta Journal-Constitution*, Aug. 12, 1993.

37. Alexander, *The New Jim Crow*, 56.

38. Georgia Department of Corrections, "'Truth in Sentencing' in Georgia," May 14, 2008, http://www.dcor.state.ga.us/sites/all/files/pdf/Research /Standing/Truth_in_sentencing.pdf.

39. Tom Crawford, "The Business of Incarceration," *Georgia Trend*, May 2010, http://www.georgiatrend.com/May-2010/The-Business-Of-Incarceration.

40. Nzong Xiong, "Private Prisons: A Question of Savings," *New York Times*, July 13, 1997.

41. "Private Prisons," Georgia Department of Corrections, http://www .dcor.state.ga.us/Divisions/Facilities/PrivatePrisons, accessed June 4, 2017; "Contract Prisons," Federal Bureau of Prisons, https://www.bop.gov/about /facilities/contract_facilities.jsp, accessed May 22, 2018; "Robert A. Deyton Detention Facility," GEO Group, https://www.geogroup.com/FacilityDetail /FacilityID/79, accessed May 22, 2018; Jeremy Redmon, "Georgia Lawmakers Back $1 a Day Pay in Immigration Detention Centers," *Atlanta Journal-Constitution*, Mar. 16, 2018.

42. *Criminal: How Lock-Up Quotas and "Low-Crime Taxes" Guarantee Profits for Private Prison Corporations* (Washington, DC: In the Public Interest, 2013), http://www.njjn.org/uploads/digital-library/Criminal-Lockup-Quota,-In-the -Public-Interest,-9.13.pdf.

43. Mike Elk and Bob Sloan, "The Hidden History of ALEC and Prison Labor," *Nation*, Aug. 1, 2011, https://www.thenation.com/article/hidden-history -alec-and-prison-labor.

44. Geoffrey Segal and Kelly McCutchen, "Competition Saves Money, Private Prisons Would Help Georgia Cut Costs," *Reason*, Oct. 8, 2004, https:// reason.org/commentary/competition-saves-money.

45. Laura E. Glaze and Laura M. Maruschak, *Parents in Prison and Their Minor Children*, Special Report, NCJ 222984 (Washington, DC: Bureau of Justice Statistics, 2008), revised Mar. 30, 2010, https://www.bjs.gov/content/pub /pdf/pptmc.pdf.

46. Ross D. Parke and K. Alison Clarke-Stewart, *Effects of Parental Incarceration on Young Children* (Washington, DC: US Department of Health and Human Services, 2001), https://aspe.hhs.gov/basic-report/effects-parental -incarceration-young-children.

47. "Youth Incarceration in the United States," infographic, Annie E. Casey Foundation, Feb. 26, 2013, http://www.aecf.org/resources/youth-incarceration -in-the-united-states.

48. Mark Silk, "State Sued Again over Youth Jail Conditions," *Atlanta Journal-Constitution*, Mar. 28, 1996.

49. "Attorney General Michael J. Bowers, November 1996," Georgia Public Policy Foundation, YouTube video, 28:34, posted July 1, 2013, https://www.youtube.com/watch?v=sMhBzGrYevE.

50. Quoted in Elaine Brown, "Superpredator or Outcast," chap. 7 in Brown, *The Condemnation of Little B: New Age Racism in America* (Boston: Beacon Press, 2002).

51. Brown, "Superpredator or Outcast," 267.

52. Brown, "Superpredator or Outcast," generally.

53. Carlos Campos and Jay Croft, "Crowded Jails; Fulton Facing Tough Issues as Numbers Soar," *Atlanta Journal-Constitution*, May 14, 1997.

54. Sarah Geraghty and Melanie Velez, "Bringing Transparency and Accountability to Criminal Justice Institutions in the South," *Stanford Law and Policy Review* 22, no. 2 (June 2011): 465–68.

CHAPTER THREE: THE POT CALLING THE KETTLE BLACK

1. Nancy Badertscher and Kristina Torres, "State Probe Reveals Cheating on CRCT," *Atlanta Journal-Constitution*, June 12, 2009; Kristina Torres and Nancy Badertscher, "Principals Arrested in Cheating Scandal," *Atlanta Journal-Constitution*, June 20, 2009; Heather Vogell, "Principals Bear Weight of Test Score Results," *Atlanta Journal-Constitution*, July 19, 2009; Kristina Torres, "Official: School Didn't Cheat," *Atlanta Journal-Constitution*, Aug. 22, 2009.

2. Nancy Badertscher, "Board Drops Retest Results," *Atlanta Journal-Constitution*, July 9, 2009.

3. Kristina Torres, "After 10 Years, Atlanta School Chief as Devoted as Ever," *Atlanta Journal-Constitution*, Aug. 19, 2009.

4. "Atlanta Public Schools Report Large Gains on National Assessment," posted by Dan Whisenhunt, Reporter Newspapers, Dec. 7, 2011, http://www.reporternewspapers.net/2011/12/07/atlanta-public-schools-report-large-gains-on-national-assessment.

5. "Statement of Governor Sonny Perdue Regarding State Board of Education Accepting the Recommendations of the Governor's Office of Student Achievement," July 9, 2009, http://sonnyperdue.georgia.gov/00/press/detail/0%2c2668%2c78006749_144947052_145624123%2c00.html; Kristina Torres and Nancy Badertscher, "Governor Calls Out City's Schools Chief," *Atlanta Journal-Constitution*, July 11, 2009.

6. Penn Payne, *Report of Independent Investigation into Allegations of Tampering with Summer, 2008 CRCT Mathematics Retest at Deerwood Academy*, (2009), http://d3gcj4nzojrapq.cloudfront.net/wp-content/uploads/2009/08/APS-cheating-full-report.pdf.

7. Heather Vogell, "Atlanta Schools Soft on Cheats?," *Atlanta Journal-Constitution*, Aug. 30, 2009; Heather Vogell and John Perry, "Drastic Test Swings Valid?," *Atlanta Journal-Constitution*, Oct. 18, 2009.

8. Joyce Leviton, "A Grieving Mother Spurs the Hunt for the Child-Killer Who Is Terrorizing Atlanta," *People*, Nov. 10, 1980, http://people.com/archive/a-grieving-mother-spurs-the-hunt-for-the-child-killer-who-is-terrorizing-atlanta-vol-14-no-19.

9. Ginger Strand, *Killer on the Road: Violence and the American Interstate* (Austin: University of Texas Press, 2012), 97.

10. Bernard Headley, *The Atlanta Youth Murders and the Politics of Race* (Carbondale: Southern Illinois University Press, 1998), 47–52; "Atlanta Remembers: How Muhammad Ali Tried to Help Solve the Atlanta Child Murders," 11Alive.com, June 7, 2016, https://www.11alive.com/article/news/local/atlanta-remembers-how-muhammad-ali-tried-to-help-solve-the-atlanta-child-murders/85-235817918.

11. Headley, *The Atlanta Youth Murders and the Politics of Race*, chap. 1.

12. Robert Keating and Barry Michael Cooper, "A Question of Justice," *Spin*, Sept. 1986.

13. M. A. Farber, "Key Fiber Evidence in Atlanta Case Could Be Focus of Long Legal Battle," *New York Times*, July 1, 1981; Art Harris, "Atlanta Jury Convicts Williams of Two Murders," *Washington Post*, Feb. 28, 1982.

14. Strand, *Killer on the Road*, 118.

15. Headley, *The Atlanta Youth Murders and the Politics of Race*.

16. Strand, *Killer on the Road*, 117.

17. "This Day in Georgia History, November 29, 1935, FDR in Atlanta for Techwood Homes Dedication," Georgia Info, http://georgiainfo.galileo.usg.edu/thisday/gahistory/11/29/fdr-in-atlanta-for-techwood-homes-dedication, accessed July 11, 2017.

18. Edward G. Goetz, *New Deal Ruins: Race, Economic Justice, and Public Housing Policy* (Ithaca, NY: Cornell University Press, 2013), 100. The large amount of public housing constructed in Atlanta was due in part to the rampant pace of neighborhood destruction through slum clearance and urban renewal programs. Federal law required a one-for-one replacement of demolished homes, but even the relatively high number of public housing units did not meet the requirement, and many displaced residents never received replacement housing.

19. Ibid., 28–38.

20. Richard Rothstein, "Public Housing: Government-Sponsored Segregation," *American Prospect*, Oct. 11, 2012, http://prospect.org/article/public-housing-government-sponsored-segregation.

21. Goetz, *New Deal Ruins*, 40–41.

22. Rachel Black and Aleta Sprague, "The 'Welfare Queen' Is a Lie," *Atlantic*, Sept. 28, 2016, https://www.theatlantic.com/business/archive/2016/09/welfare-queen-myth/501470.

23. Goetz, *New Deal Ruins*, 10; Gary Orfield and Carole Ashkinaze, *The Closing Door: Conservative Policy and Black Opportunity* (Chicago: University of Chicago Press, 1991), 83–88.

24. Orfield and Ashkinaze, *The Closing Door*, 89.

25. Steven V. Roberts, "Reagan on Homelessness: Many Choose to Live in the Streets," *New York Times*, Dec. 23, 1988.

26. Art Harris, "Atlanta, Pride of the New South," *Washington Post*, July 17, 1988.

27. Ibid.; Orfield and Ashkinaze, *The Closing Door*, 89; Keating, *Atlanta*, 205.

28. John Perry, "How Test Scores Were Analyzed," *Atlanta Journal-Constitution*, Feb. 13, 2010.

29. Heather Vogell and John Perry, "CRCT Scandal Stuns the State," *Atlanta Journal-Constitution*, Feb. 11, 2010.

30. Kristina Torres, "Law on Honest Testing Sought," *Atlanta Journal-Constitution*, Dec. 13, 2009; Kristina Torres, "Cheating Details Revealed," *Atlanta Journal-Constitution*, Feb. 12, 2010.

31. "Race to the Top Fund," US Department of Education, last modified June 6, 2016, https://www2.ed.gov/programs/racetothetop/index.html; Sam Dillon, "Dangling Money, Obama Pushes Education Shift," *New York Times*, Aug. 16, 2009.

32. John Myers and Sarah Karp, "Duncan's Track Record," *Chicago Reporter*, Dec. 15, 2008, http://chicagoreporter.com/duncans-track-record; Grant Pick, "Duncan Puts New Emphasis on 'Business of Education,'" *Chicago Reporter*, Aug. 22, 2005, http://chicagoreporter.com/duncan-puts-new-emphasis-business-education; Nick Anderson, "Education Secretary Duncan Calls Hurricane Katrina Good for New Orleans Schools," *Washington Post*, Jan. 30, 2010.

33. Corey Mitchell, "'Death of My Career': What Happened to New Orleans' Veteran Black Teachers," *Education Week*, Aug. 19, 2015, https://neworleans.edweek.org/veteran-black-female-teachers-fired.

34. M. Alex Johnson, "U.S. Schools in 'Category 5' Budget Crisis," MSNBC.com, updated Mar. 18, 2010, http://www.nbcnews.com/id/35883971/ns/us_news-education/t/us-schools-category-budget-crisis/.

35. "Georgia's Race to the Top Application," Governor's Office of Student Achievement, submitted June 1, 2010, 51, https://gosa.georgia.gov/sites/gosa.georgia.gov/files/related_files/site_page/Georgia-RTT-Application.pdf.

36. Alexander von Hoffman, *House by House, Block by Block: The Rebirth of America's Urban Neighborhoods* (New York: Oxford University Press, 2003), 161–62.

37. Newman, *The Atlanta Housing Authority's Olympic Legacy Program*, 5.

38. Keating, *Atlanta*, 176.

39. Ibid., 176–81.

40. Henry Cisneros, "A New Moment for People and Cities," in *From Despair to Hope: HOPE VI and the New Promise of Public Housing in America's Cities*, ed. Henry Cisneros and Lora Engdahl (Washington, DC: Brookings Institution Press, 2009), 3–14.

41. Peter F. Cannavò, *The Working Landscape: Founding, Preservation, and the Politics of Place* (Cambridge, MA: MIT Press, 2007), 117–22.

42. Fritz Umbach and Alexander Gerould, "Myth #3 Public Housing Breeds Crime," in *Public Housing Myths: Perception, Reality, and Social Policy*, ed. Nicholas Dagen Bloom, Fritz Umbach, and Lawrence Vale (Ithaca, NY: Cornell University Press, 2015), 64–90; Stephen Steinberg, "The Myth of Concentrated Poverty," in *The Integration Debate: Competing Futures for American Cities*, ed. Chester Hartman and Gregory Squires (New York: Routledge, 2010), 213–28.

43. Keating, *Atlanta*, 56–63.

44. Edward Goetz, *Clearing the Way: Deconcentrating the Poor in Urban America*, (Washington, DC: The Urban Institute Press, 2003), 60; Newman, *The Atlanta Housing Authority's Olympic Legacy Program*, 12.

45. John F. Sugg, "From Public Housing to Private Enterprise," *Urban Land*, Apr. 7, 2011, https://urbanland.uli.org/industry-sectors/from-public -housing-to-private-enterprise.

46. Jill Khadduri, Jennifer Turnham, Anne Chase, and Heather Schwartz, *Case Studies Exploring the Potential Relationship Between Schools and Neighborhood Revitalization* (Cambridge, MA: ABT Associates, 2003), 9, http://www.abt associates.com/reports/Schools_and_Neighborhoods.pdf.

47. John F. Sugg, "Atlanta Urban Developer Egbert Perry Is Inducted into REIAC/GSU Hall of Distinction," *National Real Estate Investor*, Dec. 8, 2010, http://www.nreionline.com/finance-amp-investment/atlanta-urban-developer -egbert-perry-inducted-reiacgsu-hall-distinction.

48. Sugg, "From Public Housing to Private Enterprise."

49. This organization was originally called East Lake Community Foundation, but the name was soon changed to East Lake Foundation. We use the latter name throughout for clarity.

50. Adam Goldstein, "A Purposely Built Community: Public Housing Redevelopment and Resident Displacement at East Lake Meadows," *Atlanta Studies*, Emory University Center for Digital Scholarship, Mar. 14, 2017, https://www.atlantastudies.org/a-purposely-built-community-public-housing -redevelopment-and-resident-replacement-at-east-lake-meadows.

51. Von Hoffman, *House by House, Block by Block*, 190–95; Thomas G. Cousins, testimony to the Millennial Housing Commission, Mar. 12, 2011, https://govinfo.library.unt.edu/mhc/hearings/atlanta.html.

52. Add Seymour Jr. and Milo Ippolito, "Meet the Candidates: Shirley Franklin, City Insider, Seeks Road to Resolution," *Atlanta Journal-Constitution*, Oct. 21, 2001; Jeff Dickerson, "No Room for Politics of Poverty at East Lake," *Atlanta Journal-Constitution*, Nov. 17, 1998.

53. Cousins testimony; von Hoffman, *House by House, Block by Block*, 197–99; Khadduri et al., *Case Studies Exploring the Potential Relationship*, 19; Patricia Sellers, "More Than a Game," *Fortune*, Sept. 3, 2001, http://archive .fortune.com/magazines/fortune/fortune_archive/2001/09/03/309275 /index.htm.

54. Hollis R. Towns, "A Revival at East Lake," *Atlanta Journal-Constitution*, Sept. 15, 1997.

55. Cousins testimony.

56. Keating, *Atlanta*, 185.

57. Various sources have cited differing numbers in this range.

58. Aaron Sojourner, Prudence Brown, Robert Chaskin, Ralph Hamilton, Leila Fiester, and Harold Richman, "Moving Forward While Staying in Place: Embedded Funders and Community Change," Chapin Hall Discussion Paper, Chapin Hall Center for Children, Chicago, 2004, https://community-wealth .org/content/moving-forward-while-staying-place-embedded-funders-and -community-change; *A Chance to Succeed: Economic Revitalization of Atlanta's East Lake Community* (Athens: Selig Center for Economic Growth, Terry

College of Business, University of Georgia, 2008), 19, http://www.terry.uga
.edu/media/documents/selig/east_lake_study.pdf.

59. Paul Donsky, "Seat 8 Candidates Present Contrast in Political Views,"
Atlanta Journal-Constitution, Nov. 22, 2001.

60. Urban Realty Partners, "Our Projects," http://www.urbanrealtypartners
.net/urp-projects, accessed July 4, 2017.

61. Deirdre Oakley, Erin Ruel, and G. Elton Wilson, *A Choice with No Options: Atlanta Public Housing Residents' Lived Experiences in the Face of Relocation*
(Atlanta: Georgia State University, n.d.), 5, http://www2.gsu.edu/~wwwexa
/news/download/gsu_public_housing_report1.pdf.

62. *The Final Report of the National Commission on Severely Distressed Public
Housing* (Washington, DC: National Commission on Severely Distressed Public Housing, 1992), https://portal.hud.gov/hudportal/documents/huddoc?id
=DOC_9836.pdf.

63. Janel Davis, "Families Look to Relocate as End Nears for Projects,"
Atlanta Journal-Constitution, Sept. 13, 2010.

64. Alan Judd and Heather Vogell, "Probe Itself Faces Scrutiny;
Many on Atlanta Panel Have Ties to District or Superintendent," *Atlanta
Journal-Constitution*, July 11, 2010; Alan Judd, "Memo Outlined Strategy for
Hall," *Atlanta Journal-Constitution*, Aug. 18, 2010.

65. Kristina Torres and Heather Vogell, "Perdue Orders School Cheating
Investigation," *Atlanta Journal-Constitution*, Aug. 19, 2010; Kristina Torres and
Alan Judd, "109 Educators Cited," *Atlanta Journal-Constitution*, Aug. 3, 2010;
Ernie Suggs, "The High Cost of Test Cheating," *Atlanta Journal-Constitution*,
Nov. 22, 2011; Justin Heckert, "The Big Break," *Atlanta Magazine*, Apr. 1, 2012,
http://www.atlantamagazine.com/great-reads/public-school-cheating-scandal.

66. Nancy Badertscher and Cameron McWhirter, "$400 Million for Education; Georgia, 26 Districts to Share Federal Money," *Atlanta Journal-
Constitution*, Aug. 25, 2010.

CHAPTER FOUR: PUSHING THE ENVELOPE

1. Bryan Long, "Gov. Nathan Deal and the Longest Corruption Scandal in
Georgia History," *Flagpole*, Oct. 22, 2014, http://flagpole.com/news/comment
/2014/10/22/gov-nathan-deal-and-the-longest-corruption-scandal-in-georgia
-history.

2. Dana Goldstein, "Obama's Education Reform Agenda Under Fire,"
Daily Beast, Oct. 15, 2010, https://www.thedailybeast.com/obamas-education
-reform-agenda-under-fire; Nicholas Lemann, "How Michelle Rhee Misled
Education Reform," NewRepublic.com, May 20, 2013, https://newrepublic
.com/article/113096/how-michelle-rhee-misled-education-reform.

3. Aaron Gould Sheinin, "Jury Rules in Favor of Ex-Ethics Chief; Awards
$700,000 Judgement," *Atlanta-Journal Constitution*, April 4, 2014; Claire Suggs,
*The Schoolhouse Squeeze 2014: State Cuts, Lost Property Values Still Pinch School
Districts* (Atlanta: Georgia Budget and Policy Institute, 2014), https://gbpi.org
/wp-content/uploads/2014/09/Schoolhouse-Squeeze-Final-Report-2014.pdf.

4. Michael J. Bowers, Robert E. Wilson, and Richard L. Hyde, "Atlanta
Public Schools Cheating Investigation Report" (not an official title), 163.

5. Ibid., 164–67.

6. Ibid., 9, 162.

7. Ibid., 355–82.

8. Ibid., 2.

9. Ibid., 350–55.

10. "Deal Releases Findings of Atlanta School Probe," Georgia Office of the Governor, press release, July 5, 2011, https://gov.georgia.gov/press -releases/2011-07-05/deal-releases-findings-atlanta-school-probe.

11. "Statement from Atlanta Mayor Kasim Reed on the State of Georgia's CRCT Test Scores Investigation," City of Atlanta, Office of the Mayor, press release, July 5, 2011, https://www.atlantaga.gov/Home/Components/News /News/6/672?seldept=1&arch=1&npage=51.

12. Bill Rankin, "District Attorneys Weigh Indictments," *Atlanta Journal-Constitution*, July 9, 2011.

13. Jason Koebler, "Educators Implicated in Atlanta Cheating Scandal," *U.S. News and World Report*, July 7, 2011, https://www.usnews.com/education /blogs/high-school-notes/2011/07/07/educators-implicated-in-atlanta-cheating -scandal; Dana Goldstein, "How High-Stakes Testing Led to the Atlanta Cheating Scandal," *Slate*, July 21, 2011, http://www.slate.com/articles/double _x/doublex/2011/07/how_highstakes_testing_led_to_the_atlanta_cheating _scandal.html.

14. Benjamin Herold and Dale Mezzacappa, "2009 Report Identified Doz-ens of PA Schools for Possible Cheating," *Philadelphia Public Schools Notebook*, July 8, 2011, http://thenotebook.org/articles/2011/07/08/2009-report-identified -dozens-of-pa-schools-for-possible-cheating.

15. WSB-TV, "Monica Pearson Tracks Beverly Hall in Hawaii," YouTube, July 12, 2011, https://www.youtube.com/watch?v=Y5aZATevSO8, accessed May 22, 2018.

16. David Pendered, "How Does the BeltLine Grow," *Atlanta Journal-Constitution*, July 18, 2005.

17. Georgia Redevelopment Powers Law O.C.G.A § 36–44–1 through 36–44–23.

18. "Atlantic BeltLine TAD," Invest Atlanta, https://www.investatlanta.com /development/tax-allocation-districts/atlantic-station, accessed Aug. 9, 2017; David Pendered, "Atlantic Station Got Lots of Help; Powerful Friends Pulled Strings," *Atlanta Journal-Constitution*, Apr. 27, 2003; Carolyn Bourdeaux and John Matthews, *Georgia's Redevelopment Powers Law: A Policy Guide to the Evalu-ation and Use of Tax Allocation Districts* (Atlanta: Research Atlanta, 2004), 53–54, http://www.hcpna.org/main-site/wp-content/uploads/2015/01/Redevelopment -Powers-Law-Guide.pdf.

19. Dan Immergluck, *The Beltline and Rising Home Prices: Residential Ap-preciation Near the Beltline Tax Allocation District and Policy Recommendations to Minimize Displacement* (Atlanta: Georgia Stand-Up, 2007), 2–5, https:// saportareport.com/wp-content/uploads/2017/05/immergluck-2007.pdf.

20. Bourdeaux and Matthews, *Georgia's Redevelopment Powers Law*, 50–60; Invest Atlanta, "Approved TAD Projects," Dec. 1, 2013, and "Approved TAD Projects Since 2015," Aug. 7, 2017, unpublished documents in possession of

authors; David Pendered, "Atlanta's Chief of Development Sees Teamwork; Agency Has Had No President Since November," *Atlanta Journal-Constitution*, Aug. 21, 2003.

21. Invest Atlanta, "Approved TAD Projects"; Atlanta Board of Education Legislative Meeting Minutes, Dec. 8, 2003.

22. Invest Atlanta, "Approved TAD Projects"; Tony Wilbert, "DuPree Back as Cousins Executive," *Atlanta Journal-Constitution*, Feb. 19, 2003.

23. Maria Saporta, "Existing Web of Rail Lines Key to Crafting Better Transit System," *Atlanta-Journal Constitution*, Apr. 1, 2002.

24. Stacy Shelton, "Blank Check for BeltLine; Falcons Chief Gives Millions," *Atlanta-Journal Constitution*, Jan. 28, 2005; David Pendered, "Council Urged to Approve BeltLine, Backers Say Project Can't Afford Delay in Tax District Creation," *Atlanta-Journal Constitution*, Nov. 7, 2005.

25. Pendered, "How Does the BeltLine Grow"; Ty Tagami, "Borders Scoffs at Label; Council Chief Says She's No Elitist, Represents All Atlanta," *Atlanta-Journal Constitution*, Aug. 17, 2004.

26. Immergluck, *The Beltline and Rising Home Prices*, iv.

27. J. Scott Trubey, "Creditor's Pursuing Wayne Mason, Family's Wealth," *Atlanta Journal-Constitution*, Aug. 21, 2015.

28. David Pendered, "Commission Trio Won't Buckle to Beltline Pressure," *Atlanta Journal-Constitution*, Dec. 15, 2005; Paul Donsky, "Ruling Jolts Beltline, Other Projects," *Atlanta Journal-Constitution*, Feb. 12, 2008.

29. Paul Donsky, "Beltline Work Begins," *Atlanta Journal-Constitution*, Oct. 20, 2007.

30. Woodham v. City of Atlanta et al., 283 Ga. 95 (657 S.E.2d 528) (2008).

31. Donsky, "Ruling Jolts Beltline, Other Projects."

32. "Counties/Municipalities; Local Boards of Education; Authorize to Use Tax Funds for Redevelopment Purposes/Programs," SR 996, Georgia General Assembly, Senate, 2007–2008 Regular Session.

33. Campaign financial disclosure reports of Georgians for Community Redevelopment Inc., 2008, Georgia Ethics Commission; "Georgia Education Taxes for Redevelopment, Amendment 2 (2008)," Ballotpedia, https://ballotpedia.org /Georgia_Education_Taxes_for_Redevelopment,_Amendment_2_(2008), accessed Aug. 15, 2017.

34. "Dougherty CRCT Investigation Report," Georgia Office of the Governor, Dec. 19, 2011, 1 and 107, document in possession of authors.

35. Jim Wallace, "State Drops Dougherty Co. Schools CRCT Probe," WALB News 10, July 6, 2011, http://www.walb.com/story/15036901/state -drops-dougherty-co-schools-crct-probe; "Bowers: Enough Cheating Evidence to Prosecute," WALB *News 10*, Aug. 25, 2011, http://www.walb.com /story/15334733/bowers-enought-cheating-evidence-to-prosecute.

36. Nancy Badertscher, "Analyst Pressured in Erasure Scandal," *Atlanta Journal-Constitution*, Jan. 19, 2012.

37. Molly Bloom, "Charters' Founder Held on Charges," *Atlanta Journal-Constitution*, Apr. 13, 2016; Molly Bloom, "Inside Largest Charter School Theft Case in Ga.," *Atlanta Journal-Constitution*, June 5, 2016.

38. John Perry, "Cheating Our Children: Suspicious School Test Scores Across the Nation," *Atlanta Journal-Constitution*, Mar. 25, 2012.

39. Bill Rankin, "New Details APS Cheating Scandal; Heavy Hitter to Help DA," *Atlanta Journal-Constitution*, May 12, 2012.

40. Cahill, Gordon, and Reindel LLP, "Supreme Court Rejects Requirement That a RICO Enterprise Must Have a Structure Beyond That Inherent in the Pattern of Racketeering Activity in Which It Engages," memorandum, June 11, 2009, https://www.cahill.com/publications/firm-memoranda/000171.

41. Kevin Poulsen, "Guilty Verdict in First Ever Cybercrime RICO Trial," *Wired*, Dec. 9, 2013, https://www.wired.com/2013/12/rico.

CHAPTER FIVE: THE DARKER THE NIGHT

1. Adell Cothorne v. District of Columbia, No. 1:11-cv-00819, US District Council for the District of Columbia, filed May 2, 2011, http://learningmatters.tv/pdfs/cothorne-v-district-of-columbia.pdf.

2. Jay Matthews, "School Cheating Report Thin and Biased," WashingtonPost.com, Aug. 11, 2012, https://www.washingtonpost.com/blogs/class-struggle/post/dc-schools-cheating-report-thin-and-biased/2012/08/11/569d3f5c-e40d-11e1-a25e-15067bb31849_blog.html?utm_term=.5737788c150e.

3. Stephen D. Anderson, "Closing Memorandum for File 11–000491," US Department of Education Office of Inspector General, Jan. 17, 2013, https://www2.ed.gov/about/offices/list/oig/invtreports/Closing_Memorandum_11-000491.pdf; Jason M. Breslow, "Education Department Finds No Evidence of Widespread Cheating on D.C. Exams," PBS, Jan. 8, 2013, https://www.pbs.org/wgbh/frontline/article/education-department-finds-no-evidence-of-widespread-cheating-on-d-c-exams/.

4. Indictment, State of Georgia v. Beverly Hall, et al., no. 13SC117954, Fulton County Superior Court, filed Mar. 29, 2013.

5. "Cheating Scandal Hits Atlanta Schools," CNN.com, Apr. 2, 2013, http://www.cnn.com/videos/bestoftv/2013/04/02/exp-nr-atlanta-schools-cheating-scandal.cnn/video/playlists/atlanta-school-cheating-scandal/; Bowers, Wilson, and Hyde, "Atlanta Public Schools Cheating Investigation Report," 355.

6. *Chartering in Georgia 2012–2013*, Charter Schools Division Annual Report (Atlanta: Georgia Department of Education, 2013), 12, http://www.gadoe.org/External-Affairs-and-Policy/Charter-Schools/Documents/2012-13%20Charter%20School%20Annual%20Report%20-%202014-01-16.pdf.

7. Aileen Dodd, "Cherokee Rejects Charter Academy," *Atlanta Journal-Constitution*, June 25, 2011.

8. "BOE Strikes Down Charter Proposal," *Cherokee Tribune and Ledger News* (Canton, GA), July 22, 2009.

9. Bruce Baker and Gary Miron, *The Business of Charter Schooling: Understanding the Policies that Charter Operators Use for Financial Benefit* (Boulder, CO: National Education Policy Center, Dec. 2015), http://nepc.colorado.edu/files/rb_baker-miron_charter_revenue_0.pdf.

10. Kent Fischer, "Public School Inc.," *St. Petersburg Times*, Sept. 15, 2002.

11. Gary Miron, Jessica L. Urschel, Mayra A. Yat Aguilar, and Breanna Dailey, *Profiles of For-Profit and Nonprofit Education Management Organizations: Thirteenth Annual Report 2010–2011* (Boulder, CO: National Education Policy Center, Jan. 2012), http://nepc.colorado.edu/publication/EMO-profiles-10-11; "Jonathan Hage," *Florida Trend*, Dec. 26, 2012, http://www.floridatrend.com /article/15060/jonathan-hage.

12. *Putting Students First*, Charter Schools USA, Inc., Investor Presentation, n.d., https://emma.msrb.org/EA480055-EA372423-.pdf, 8 and 20, accessed Jan. 10, 2018.

13. Carolyn Matthews, "State Denies Cherokee Charter School," *Cherokee Tribune and Ledger News*, Dec. 16, 2009.

14. Celia Llopis-Jepsen, "McKenna Long Carves Niche as Charter School Champion," *American Lawyer*, Sept. 21, 2012, https://www.law.com/american lawyer/almID/1202572127678/?slreturn=20180326164652; Matthew Pulver, "Dismantling Public Education," Flagpole.com, Apr. 11, 2012, http://flagpole .com/news/news-features/2012/04/11/dismantling-public-education; *Georgia Charter Schools Association 2009 Annual Report* (Atlanta: GCSA, 2009), 6, http:// gacharters.org/wp-content/uploads/GCSA-2009-Annual-Report-FINAL-2.pdf.

15. Georgia Charter Schools Association profile, CommonGrantApplication.com, https://www.commongrantapplication.com/grantseekers/17130 /Georgia-Charter-Schools-Association.html#gskOrgBackground, accessed Jan. 31, 2018.

16. Internal Revenue Service (2004), Form 990: Return of Organization Exempt from Income Tax: Walton Family Foundation, Inc., retrieved from ProPublica Explorer; IRS (2003), Form 990: Return of Organization Exempt from Income Tax: Georgia Charter Schools Association, retrieved from Pro-Publica Explorer; IRS (2004), Form 990: Return of Organization Exempt from Income Tax: Georgia Charter Schools Association, retrieved from ProPublica Explorer.

17. Valerie Strauss, "The 'Walmartization' of Public Education," *Washington Post*, Mar. 17, 2016.

18. "Become a Sponsor," Georgia Charter Schools Association, cached on Sept. 28, 2012, page discontinued, https://web.archive.org/web/20120928233853 /http://www.gacharters.org:80/membership/become-a-sponsor/, accessed Jan. 31, 2018; "Our Sponsors," Georgia Charter Schools Association, cached Oct. 14, 2012, page discontinued, https://web.archive.org/web/20121014122549/ http://www.gacharters.org:80/membership/sponsors/, accessed Jan. 31, 2018.

19. Jennifer Radcliffe, "Texans Can Charters Schools Not Making Grade," *Houston Chronicle*, Jan. 24, 2010.

20. Gwinnett County School District, et al. v. Kathy Cox, et al., no. 2009CV174907, Superior Court of Fulton County, Georgia, filed Sept. 11, 2009, http://www.cpoga.org/PDF/complaint.pdf.

21. Matthews, "State Denies Cherokee Charter School."

22. Carolyn Matthews, "Board Nixes Charter School Proposal," *Cherokee Tribune and Ledger News*, June 23, 2010.

23. Ibid.

24. Carolyn Matthews, "State OKs Cherokee Charter School," *Cherokee Tribune and Ledger News*, Dec. 21, 2010.

25. Dodd, "Cherokee Rejects Charter Academy."

26. Mike Chapman, "Misquote Clouds Charter's Problem," *Atlanta Journal-Constitution*, Aug. 31, 2011.

27. Sam Dillon, "In Georgia, Court Ruling Could Close Some Schools," *New York Times*, May 17, 2011.

28. James R. Touchton, "A Supreme Decision: The Next Steps for Charter Schools in Georgia," *At Issue* (Georgia Senate Research Office), Nov. 2011, http://www.senate.ga.gov/sro/Documents/AtIssue/atissue_nov11.pdf.

29. State Chartered Special Schools; Revise Funding, HB 797, Georgia General Assembly, House, 2011–2012 Regular Session; Wayne Washington, "Charter School Fight Now in Voters' Hands," *Atlanta Journal-Constitution*, Mar. 20, 2012.

30. Georgia Policy, "Charter School Bill Signing," YouTube, May 3, 2012, https://www.youtube.com/watch?v=xcZHoqVAzbg&list=UU4uOlfbFbDHf2h6wCgOEDxQ&index=2&feature=plcp, accessed Apr. 9, 2018.

31. Shannon McCaffrey and James Salzer, "Billions Behind Charter Issue," *Atlanta Journal-Constitution*, Nov. 4, 2012.

32. Aditi Sen, *Whose Opportunity? Profiting Off of School Turnaround and Takeover in Atlanta* (Atlanta: Rise Up Georgia/Center for Popular Democracy, 2016), 12, https://populardemocracy.org/sites/default/files/Georgia-Schools-Report_WEB.pdf.

33. Americans for Prosperity campaign finance reports, Georgia Government Transparency and Campaign Finance Commission, accessed Nov. 28, 2017.

34. American Federation for Children campaign finance reports, Georgia Government Transparency and Campaign Finance Commission, accessed Nov. 28, 2017.

35. Alan Singer, "Why Is This Charter School Management Company Still in Business?," *Huffington Post*, May 27, 2014, https://www.huffingtonpost.com/alan-singer/why-is-this-charter-schoo_b_5397059.html; Rhea R. Borja, "Bennett Quits K12 Inc. Under Fire," *Education Week*, Oct. 11, 2005, https://www.edweek.org/ew/articles/2005/10/12/07bennett.h25.html; Sen, *Whose Opportunity?*, 12.

36. Sen, *Whose Opportunity?*, 12.

37. Families for Better Public Schools expense reports, Georgia Government Transparency and Campaign Finance Commission, accessed Nov. 28, 2017; Walter C. Jones, "Most Donors for and Against Georgia Charter School Amendment Are out of State," *Florida Times Union*, Oct. 1, 2012.

38. Maureen Downey, "The Charter School Amendment; What Comes Next?," *Atlanta Journal-Constitution*, Nov. 26, 2012.

39. "Georgia Charter Schools, Amendment 1 (2012)," Ballotpedia.com, https://ballotpedia.org/Georgia_Charter_Schools,_Amendment_1_(2012).

40. Greg Toppo, "Memo Warns of Rampant Cheating in D.C. Public Schools," *USA Today*, Apr. 11, 2013.

41. "K–12 Education: States' Test Security Policies and Procedures Varied," US Government Accountability Office briefing to US Secretary of Education Arne Duncan, May 16, 2013, http://www.gao.gov/assets/660/654721.pdf.

CHAPTER SIX: BETWEEN A ROCK AND A HARD PLACE

1. Mark Niesse, "Atlanta Educators Plead Guilty and Prepare for Huge Trial," *Atlanta Journal-Constitution*, May 3, 2103.

2. Bill Rankin and Mark Niesse, "APS Trial Is Next Year; Dozens Plead Not Guilty," *Atlanta Journal-Constitution*, May 4, 2013; Twitter posts compiled by *Atlanta Journal-Constitution*, https://www.ajc.com/news/aps-hearings/, accessed Nov. 14, 2017.

3. Bill Rankin, "Judge Wary in APS Case," *Atlanta Journal-Constitution*, Nov. 26, 2012.

4. "APS Educators Trying to Get Indictments Dismissed," CBS46.com, June 17, 2013, http://www.cbs46.com/story/22609984/hearing-continue-in-atlanta-schools-cheating-case.

5. Bill Rankin and Mark Niesse, "APS Case Appears at Risk," *Atlanta Journal-Constitution*, June 19, 2013.

6. Bill Rankin and Mark Niesse, "How Did APS Case Run into Trouble," *Atlanta Journal-Constitution*, June 19, 2013.

7. Amy Napier Viteri, "Parents Worried About Mold and Raw Sewage at School," WSB-TV Atlanta, Aug. 8, 2013, http://www.wsbtv.com/news/local/parents-worried-about-mold-and-raw-sewage-school/243327994; "This $147 Million School in Atlanta Has Things Yours Never Did," MyAJC.com, date unknown, http://www.myajc.com/news/this-147-million-school-atlanta-has-things-yours-never-did/iWJwvDSsTqepeqOJJw3jDJ/#bzsDkDyESE uLKAXKnqGwZw; "Tyler Perry Donates $100K to Atlanta High School," WSB-TV Atlanta, Sept. 24, 2013, http://www.wsbtv.com/news/local/tyler-perry-donates-100k-atlanta-high-school/242982712.

8. Bill Rankin and Mark Niesse, "In First APS Trial, All Eyes on Cotman," *Atlanta Journal-Constitution*, Sept. 1, 2013.

9. Mark Niesse and Bill Rankin, "Principals Say APS Cheating Defendant Cotman Didn't Tell Principals to 'Go to Hell,'" *Atlanta Journal-Constitution*, Sept. 4, 2013.

10. Mark Niesse and Bill Rankin, "Jury Finds Cotman Not Guilty in First Atlanta Cheating Trial," *Atlanta Journal-Constitution*, Sept. 6, 2013.

11. Mark Niesse, "No Charges Filed in S. Ga. Cheating Case," *Atlanta Journal-Constitution*, Sept. 14, 2013.

12. Bill Rankin, "First Guilty Plea in Test-Cheating Case," *Atlanta Journal-Constitution*, Nov. 21, 2013.

13. Anna Simonton, "How Wall Street Power Brokers Are Designing the Future of Public Education as a Money-Making Machine," AlterNet, Dec. 5, 2013, https://www.alternet.org/education/how-wall-street-power-brokers-are-designing-future-public-education-money-making-machine.

14. Campaign financial disclosure reports of Atlanta Board of Education candidates, 2013, Georgia Ethics Commission.

15. Mark Niesse, "Hope and Challenges Await New Atlanta School Leaders," *Atlanta Journal-Constitution*, Dec. 5, 2013.

16. Mark Niesse, "Future of Atlanta School Board to Be Decided in Runoff," *Atlanta Journal-Constitution*, Nov. 10, 2013.

17. Wayne Washington, "State's Panel Irks Some," *Atlanta Journal-Constitution*, Nov. 2, 2013.

18. Mark Niesse, "Atlanta May Bar New Charters," *Atlanta Journal-Constitution*, Aug. 9, 2013.

19. Darwin Bond Graham, "The Long Hurricane—10 Years Later," Political Research Associates, Aug. 29, 2015, http://www.politicalresearch.org/2015/08/29/the-long-hurricane-10-years-later/#sthash.IbodosPB.CcgwZOfR.dpbs.

20. Ibid.

21. Scott Olson, "Investor Buffet Gets Behind East-Side Revitalization Project," *Indianapolis Business Journal*, Sept. 28, 2011, https://www.ibj.com/articles/29800-investor-buffett-gets-behind-east-side-revitalization-project; James Briggs, "Indianapolis Gets $55 Million for Neighborhood Development," *Indianapolis Star*, Jan. 24, 2017.

22. Addison Wiggin, "Charter School Gravy Train Runs Express to Fat City," *Forbes*, Sept. 10, 2013, https://www.forbes.com/sites/greatspeculations/2013/09/10/charter-school-gravy-train-runs-express-to-fat-city/#1f49cc4f2be8.

23. Juan Gonzalez, "Albany Charter Cash Cow: Big Banks Making a Bundle on New Construction as Schools Bear the Cost," *New York Daily News*, May 6, 2010.

24. "East Lake Foundation Lands New Market Tax Credits for Campus Expansion Project Led by PNC Bank," press release, Low Income Investment Fund, Oct. 15, 2013, http://www.liifund.org/news/post/east-lake-foundation-lands-new-markets-tax-credits-for-campus-expansion-project-led-by-pnc-bank.

25. Bill Torpy, "'D' Is for Darn Good Charter School," *Atlanta Journal-Constitution*, Nov. 16, 2014.

26. Approved TAD Projects 2000–2014, records provided by Invest Atlanta; "Corinthian Colleges," U.S. Senate Committee on Health, Education and Labor, Memo, date unknown, https://www.help.senate.gov/imo/media/for_profit_report/PartII/Corinthian.pdf.

27. Lance Williams, "How Corinthian Colleges, a For-Profit Behemoth, Suddenly Imploded," *RevealNews*, Sept. 20, 2016, https://www.revealnews.org/article/how-corinthian-colleges-a-for-profit-behemoth-suddenly-imploded; Janel Davis, "Atlanta's Four Everest College Locations Included in Company's Sale," *Atlanta Journal-Constitution*, Nov. 21, 2014.

28. "Summary of BeltLine TAD Contract Between APS, City, and ADA," Atlanta Public Schools, PowerPoint presentation, date unknown, https://www.atlantapublicschools.us/cms/lib/GA01000924/Centricity/Domain/1/Summary%20of%20Beltline%20TAD%20Contract%20between%20APS%20.pdf.

29. Simonton, "How Wall Street Power Brokers Are Designing the Future of Public Education."

30. Mark Niesse, "Six Enter Guilty Pleas in APS Test-Cheating Case," *Atlanta Journal-Constitution*, Jan. 6, 2014.

31. Motions Hearings Proceedings, Oct. 18, State of Georgia v. Sharon Davis-Williams et al., Transcript of the Voir Dire Proceedings, Superior Court of Fulton County, 2013.

32. Bill Rankin, "Defendants: Remove Judge from APS Case," *Atlanta Journal-Constitution*, May 7, 2014; Bill Rankin, "Judge Hears Arguments on Removing Judge in APS Test-Cheating Case," *Atlanta Journal-Constitution*, May 20, 2014.

33. Bill Rankin, "Judge to Stay on APS Test-Cheating Case," *Atlanta Journal-Constitution*, June 4, 2014.

34. *Atlanta BeltLine Inc. Annual Report 2012*, 9–10, 29, https://beltline org-wpengine.netdna-ssl.com/wp-content/uploads/2013/04/ABI_2012_Annual -Report.pdf; *Atlanta BeltLine Inc. Annual Report 2013*; https://beltlineorg-wpengine .netdna-ssl.com/wp-content/uploads/2014/03/annual-report-2013-FINAL.pdf; Zillow.com listing for 1147 Metropolitan Pkwy SW, Atlanta, GA 30310, page now discontinued, accessed July 1, 2015.

35. "Atlanta Mayor, Superintendent in Standoff over BeltLine Funds," WSB-TV Atlanta, June 18, 2014, http://www.wsbtv.com/news/local/atlanta -mayor-superintendent-standoff-over-beltlin/138304524.

36. Richard Whittaker, "After Carstarphen, What Then?," *Austin (TX) Chronicle*, Apr. 18, 2014.

37. Ibid.; Molly Bloom, "9 Companies Boost APS Fund," *Atlanta Journal-Constitution*, June 21, 2014; Maureen Downey, "New APS School Chief Meria Carstarphen; School Chief a Catch," *Atlanta Journal-Constitution*, June 23, 2014; Molly Bloom, "What's Changing at APS Under New Superintendent Meria Carstarphen," *Atlanta Journal-Constitution*, July 8, 2014.

38. Nikole Hannah-Jones, "The Continuing Reality of Segregated Schools," *New York Times Magazine*, July 31, 2015, https://www.nytimes.com /2015/07/31/magazine/the-continuing-reality-of-segregated-schools.html.

CHAPTER SEVEN: GETTING COLD

1. Aug. 11, State of Georgia v. Sharon Davis-Williams et al., Transcript of the Voir Dire Proceedings, vol. 1, Superior Court of Fulton County, 2014.

2. Aug. 21, State of Georgia v. Sharon Davis-Williams et al., Transcript of the Voir Dire Proceedings, vol. 2, Superior Court of Fulton County, 2014.

3. Sept. 3, State of Georgia v. Sharon Davis-Williams et al., Transcript of the Voir Dire Proceedings, vol. 4, Superior Court of Fulton County, 2014.

4. Ibid.

5. Ibid.

6. Sept. 8, State of Georgia v. Sharon Davis-Williams et al., Transcript of the Voir Dire Proceedings, vol. 5, Superior Court of Fulton County, 2014.

7. Ibid.

8. Katie Leslie, "Memos: BeltLine Dispute Worsens," *Atlanta Journal-Constitution*, Aug. 21, 2014.

9. Molly Bloom, "APS Committee to Recommend District to Pursue New System Model," *Atlanta Journal-Constitution*, Sept. 27, 2014; Jenny Jarvie, "School Cheating Trial Set to Open; in the Nationally Watched Atlanta

Case, 12 Educators Could Face Decades in Prison," *Los Angeles Times*, Sept. 7, 2014.

10. Greg Bluestein, "Deal Sees Statewide Charter System as an Option," *Atlanta Journal-Constitution*, Sept. 11, 2014.

11. Greg Bluestein, "Debate Over Uncollected Taxes Puts Spotlight on Sale of Deal Firm," *Atlanta-Journal Constitution*, Aug. 30, 2014.

12. Greg Bluestein, "A Surreal Moment: Nathan Deal and Ludacris Together at a Campaign Stop," *Atlanta-Journal Constitution*, Sept. 26, 2014.

13. Sept. 29, Sept. 8, State of Georgia v. Sharon Davis-Williams et al., Transcript of the Voir Dire Proceedings, vol. 4, Superior Court of Fulton County, 2014.

14. Ibid.

15. Ibid.

16. Ibid.

17. Ibid.

18. Ibid.

19. Ibid.

20. Ibid.

21. Oct. 6, Sept. 8, State of Georgia v. Sharon Davis-Williams et al., Transcript of the Voir Dire Proceedings, vol. 18, Superior Court of Fulton County, 2014.

22. Oct. 7, Sept. 8, State of Georgia v. Sharon Davis-Williams et al., Transcript of the Voir Dire Proceedings, vol. 19, Superior Court of Fulton County, 2014.

23. Oct. 9, Sept. 8, State of Georgia v. Sharon Davis-Williams et al., Transcript of the Voir Dire Proceedings, vol. 21, Superior Court of Fulton County, 2014.

24. Oct. 27, Sept. 8, State of Georgia v. Sharon Davis-Williams et al., Transcript of the Voir Dire Proceedings, vol. 28, Superior Court of Fulton County, 2014.

25. Oct. 30, Sept. 8, State of Georgia v. Sharon Davis-Williams et al., Transcript of the Voir Dire Proceedings, vol. 31, Superior Court of Fulton County, 2014.

26. Molly Bloom, "Charters' Founder Held on Charges," *Atlanta Journal-Constitution*, Apr. 13, 2016; Bloom, "Inside Largest Charter School Theft Case in Ga."

27. Nov. 6, State of Georgia v. Sharon Davis-Williams et al., Transcript of the Voir Dire Proceedings, vol. 34, Superior Court of Fulton County, 2014.

28. Nov. 10, State of Georgia v. Sharon Davis-Williams et al., Transcript of the Voir Dire Proceedings, vol. 35, Superior Court of Fulton County, 2014.

29. Ibid.

30. Ibid.

31. Ibid.

32. Nov. 18, State of Georgia v. Sharon Davis-Williams et al., Transcript of the Voir Dire Proceedings, vol. 38, Superior Court of Fulton County, 2014.

33. Torpy, "'D' Is for Darn Good Charter School."

34. Jeff Breedlove, "Gov. Nathan Deal: Celebrates Victory, Vows to Keep Georgia No. 1," *Atlanta Journal-Constitution*, Nov. 5, 2014.

CHAPTER EIGHT: NOT THE BRIGHTEST BULB IN THE BOX

1. Dec. 2, State of Georgia v. Sharon Davis-Williams et al., Transcript of the Voir Dire Proceedings, vol. 42, Superior Court of Fulton County, 2014.

2. Ibid.

3. Dec. 4, State of Georgia v. Sharon Davis-Williams et al., Transcript of the Voir Dire Proceedings, vol. 44, Superior Court of Fulton County, 2014.

4. Dec. 3, State of Georgia v. Sharon Davis-Williams et al., Transcript of the Voir Dire Proceedings, vol. 43, Superior Court of Fulton County, 2014.

5. Ibid.

6. Ibid.

7. Ibid.

8. Dec. 4, State of Georgia v. Sharon Davis-Williams et al., Transcript of the Voir Dire Proceedings, vol. 44, Superior Court of Fulton County, 2014.

9. Dec. 8, State of Georgia v. Sharon Davis-Williams et al., Transcript of the Voir Dire Proceedings, vol. 45, Superior Court of Fulton County, 2014.

10. Dec. 3, State of Georgia v. Sharon Davis-Williams et al., Transcript of the Voir Dire Proceedings, vol. 43, Superior Court of Fulton County, 2014.

11. Ibid.

12. Dec. 8, State of Georgia v. Sharon Davis-Williams et al., Transcript of the Voir Dire Proceedings, vol. 45, Superior Court of Fulton County, 2014.

13. Dec. 9, State of Georgia v. Sharon Davis-Williams et al., Transcript of the Voir Dire Proceedings, vol. 46, Superior Court of Fulton County, 2014.

14. Ibid.

15. Ibid.

16. Ibid.

17. Ibid.

18. Ibid.

19. Dec. 16, State of Georgia v. Sharon Davis-Williams et al., Transcript of the Voir Dire Proceedings, vol. 50, Superior Court of Fulton County, 2014.

20. "Cox Business Welcomes Students Back to School with Enhanced Communications Technology," Cox Business, press release, Aug. 22, 2012, http://newsroom.cox.com/news-releases?item=622; email from Todd C. Smith, Cox Communications Media Relations Director, to Jay Riestenberg, Common Cause Research Analyst, Sept. 30, 2014, http://www.commoncause.org/issues /more-democracy-reforms/corporate-accountability/alec/whistleblower-complaint /supplemental-complaint-2015/Exhibit_45_Cox-Communications.pdf.

21. Jan. 5, State of Georgia v. Sharon Davis-Williams et al., Transcript of the Voir Dire Proceedings, vol. 53, Superior Court of Fulton County, 2015.

22. Jan. 21, State of Georgia v. Sharon Davis-Williams et al., Transcript of the Voir Dire Proceedings, vol. 62, Superior Court of Fulton County, 2015.

23. Jan. 27, State of Georgia v. Sharon Davis-Williams et al., Transcript of the Voir Dire Proceedings, vol. 64, Superior Court of Fulton County, 2015.

24. Feb. 2, State of Georgia v. Sharon Davis-Williams et al., Transcript of the Voir Dire Proceedings, vol. 67, Superior Court of Fulton County, 2015.

25. Feb. 3, State of Georgia v. Sharon Davis-Williams et al., Transcript of the Voir Dire Proceedings, vol. 68, Superior Court of Fulton County, 2015.

26. Feb. 4, State of Georgia v. Sharon Davis-Williams et al., Transcript of the Voir Dire Proceedings, vol. 69, Superior Court of Fulton County, 2015.

27. Feb. 5, State of Georgia v. Sharon Davis-Williams et al., Transcript of the Voir Dire Proceedings, vol. 70, Superior Court of Fulton County, 2015.

28. Feb. 11, State of Georgia v. Sharon Davis-Williams et al., Transcript of the Voir Dire Proceedings, vol. 73, Superior Court of Fulton County, 2015.

29. "Deal Unveils Opportunity School District Legislation," Georgia Office of the Governor, press release, Feb. 11, 2015, https://gov.georgia.gov /press-releases/2015–02–11/deal-unveils-opportunity-school-district -legislation.

30. "Georgia's Proposed Opportunity School District Overview," Georgia Office of the Governor, policy brief, May 18, 2016, https://gov.georgia.gov /sites/gov.georgia.gov/files/related_files/site_page/GA%20OSD%20Overview %20051816.pdf.

31. Anna Simonton, "Gov. Deal Wants State to Take Over, Privatize Struggling Schools; Democrats Offer Alternative," *Atlanta Progressive News*, Feb. 18, 2015, http://atlantaprogressivenews.com/2015/02/18/6288; Christina A. Samuels, "Critics Target Growing Army of Broad Leaders," *Education Week*, Apr. 10, 2018, https://www.edweek.org/ew/articles/2011/06/08/33broad_ep .h30.html.

CHAPTER NINE: SPEAK OF THE DEVIL

1. Feb. 19, State of Georgia v. Sharon Davis-Williams et al., Transcript of the Voir Dire Proceedings, vol. 76, Superior Court of Fulton County, 2015.

2. Mar. 16, State of Georgia v. Sharon Davis-Williams et al., Transcript of the Voir Dire Proceedings, vol. 82, Superior Court of Fulton County, 2015.

3. Ibid.

4. Ibid.

5. Mar. 17, State of Georgia v. Sharon Davis-Williams et al., Transcript of the Voir Dire Proceedings, vol. 83, Superior Court of Fulton County, 2015.

6. Ibid.

7. Ibid.

8. Mar. 18, State of Georgia v. Sharon Davis-Williams et al., Transcript of the Voir Dire Proceedings, vol. 84, Superior Court of Fulton County, 2015.

9. Ibid.

10. Ibid.

11. Mar. 17, State of Georgia v. Sharon Davis-Williams et al., Transcript of the Voir Dire Proceedings, vol. 83, Superior Court of Fulton County, 2015.

12. Mar. 18, State of Georgia v. Sharon Davis-Williams et al., Transcript of the Voir Dire Proceedings, vol. 84, Superior Court of Fulton County, 2015.

13. Ibid.

14. Anna Simonton, "Georgia School Takeover Plan Passes Despite Protests," *Atlanta Progressive News*, Mar. 28, 2015, http://atlantaprogressivenews .com/2015/03/28/georgia-school-takeover-plan-passes-despite-protests; Anna Simonton, "Teachers, Parents Challenge Deal's School Takeover Plan Ahead

of House Committee Vote," *Atlanta Progressive News*, Mar. 22, 2015, http://atlantaprogressivenews.com/2015/03/22/teachers-parents-challenge-deals-school-takeover-plan-ahead-of-house-committee-vote.

15. Anna Simonton and Allie McCullen, "This Governor Wants to Take Over 'Failing' Schools and Turn Them into Charters," *Nation*, Nov. 3, 2015, https://www.thenation.com/article/this-governor-wants-to-take-over-failing-public-schools-and-turn-them-into-charters.

16. Chris Joyner, "Lobbyist Paid for Deal Trip," *Atlanta Journal-Constitution*, Mar. 25, 2015; Simonton and McCullen, "This Governor Wants to Take Over 'Failing' Schools."

17. Joy Purcell, "From Raider Country to the Gold Dome," *Now Habersham* (Clarksville, GA), Oct. 19, 2014, https://nowhabersham.com/hchs-state-capitol; Hearing Before the House Education Committee, Georgia General Assembly, House, SB 133 and SR 287, Mar. 25, 2015.

18. Floor debate, Georgia General Assembly, House, SB 133 and SR 287, Mar. 25, 2015.

19. Apr. 13, State of Georgia v. Sharon Davis-Williams et al., Transcript of the Voir Dire Proceedings, vol. 93, Superior Court of Fulton County, 2015.

20. Apr. 14, State of Georgia v. Sharon Davis-Williams et al., Transcript of the Voir Dire Proceedings, vol. 94, Superior Court of Fulton County, 2015.

21. Ibid.

22. Ibid.

23. Transcript, *Anderson Cooper 360*, April 14, 2015, http://transcripts.cnn.com/TRANSCRIPTS/1504/14/acd.01.html.

24. Post of Fox 5 interview with Glenda Hatchett, posted April 14, 2015, https://www.facebook.com/thejudgehatchett/videos/vb.104874863152/10153022828968153/?type=2&theater; Ty Tagami, "Mayor Reed Says Punishment Fit the Crime in Atlanta Cheating Scandal," *Atlanta Journal-Constitution*, April 23, 2015.

25. Tagami, "Mayor Reed Says Punishment Fit the Crime in Atlanta Cheating Scandal." *Good Day Atlanta*, Fox 5 Atlanta, Apr. 15, 2015.

26. *The Daily Show*, Comedy Central, Apr. 22, 2015.

27. Maureen Downey, "As Deal Signs School Takeover Bill, Signs from Michelle Rhee and Kevin Johnson That APS Cluster May Be Target," *Atlanta Journal-Constitution*, Apr. 21, 2015.

28. Anna Simonton, "Gammon Street Closure Escalates Racial Tensions in Gentrifying South Atlanta," *Atlanta Progressive News*, June 23, 2015, http://atlantaprogressivenews.com/2015/06/23/gammon-street-closure-escalates-racial-tensions-in-gentrifying-south-atlanta.

29. Sen, *Whose Opportunity?*; Anna Simonton, "Sen. Fort Announces Ethics Bill in Response to APS Erin Hames Contract," *Atlanta Progressive News*, Nov. 4, 2015, http://atlantaprogressivenews.com/2015/11/04/sen-fort-announces-ethics-bill-in-response-to-aps-erin-hames-contract.

30. Sept. 1, State of Georgia v. Sharon Davis-Williams et al., Transcript of the Voir Dire Proceedings, vol. 96, Superior Court of Fulton County, 2015.

EPILOGUE

1. Anna Simonton, "Citizens Denounce APS Turnaround Strategy That Favors Developers, Private Interests," *Atlanta Progressive News*, Feb. 9, 2016, http://atlantaprogressivenews.com/2016/02/09/citizens-denounce-aps -turnaround-strategy-that-favors-developers-private-interests.

2. Carlianne Patrick, *Willing to Pay: Charter Schools' Impact on Georgia Property Values* (Atlanta: Georgia State University, Andrew Young School Fiscal Research Center, 2015), http://frc.gsu.edu/files/2015/08/Georgia-Charter -Schools-Property-Values_August2015.pdf; Tim R. Sass, Jarod Apperson, and Carycruz Bueno, *The Long-Run Effects of Teacher Cheating on Student Outcomes: A Report for the Atlanta Public Schools* (Atlanta: Atlanta Public Schools, 2015), https://www.atlantapublicschools.us/crctreport.

3. Clyde Bradley, "Atlanta Public School Board Meeting 2 1 2016," Feb. 2, 2016, YouTube, 4:00, https://www.youtube.com/watch?v=qTSkPDj86EA.

4. Anna Simonton, "Atlanta Schoolchildren Lose $63.6 Million in APS/ BeltLine Deal," *Atlanta Progressive News*, Jan. 30, 2016, http://atlanta progressivenews.com/2016/01/30/atlanta-schoolchildren-lose-63-6-million -in-apsbeltline-deal; Approved TAD Projects 2000–2017, records provided by Invest Atlanta; Maria Saporta, "Ryan Gravel and Nathaniel Smith Resign from BeltLine Partnership Board Over Equity Concerns," *Saporta Report*, Sept. 26, 2016, https://saportareport.com/ryan-gravel-nathaniel-smith-resign-beltline -partnership-board-equity-concerns; Willoughby Mariano, Lindsey Conway, and Anastaciah Ondieki, "How the Atlanta Beltline Broke Its Promise on Affordable Housing," *Atlanta Journal-Constitution*, July 13, 2017.

5. Erica L. Green, "To Understand Betsy DeVos's Educational Views, View Her Education," *New York Times*, June 10, 2017.

6. Vanessa McCray, "APS Tries to Aid Cheating Victims but Impact Is Small," *Atlanta Journal-Constitution*, Feb. 22, 2018.

INDEX